Liebe Hanya

STUDIES IN DANCE HISTORY

A Publication of the Society of Dance History Scholars

Titles in the Series

Liebe Hanya

❧

Mary Wigman's Letters
to Hanya Holm

COMPILED AND EDITED BY
Claudia Gitelman

WITH AN INTRODUCTION BY
Hedwig Müller

LETTERS TRANSLATED BY
Marianne Forster AND Catherine T. Klingler

ADDITIONAL TRANSLATION BY
Shelley Frisch AND Joanna Ratych

THE UNIVERSITY OF WISCONSIN PRESS

The University of Wisconsin Press
1930 Monroe Street
Madison, Wisconsin 53711

www.wisc.edu/wisconsinpress/

3 Henrietta Street
London WC2E 8LU, England

1   3   5   4   2

Printed in the United States of America

Library of Congress Cataloging-in-Publication Data
Wigman, Mary, 1886–1973.
Liebe Hanya: Mary Wigman's letters to Hanya Holm / compiled
and edited by Claudia Gitelman; introduction by Hedwig Mueller;
letters translated by Marianne Forster and Catherine T. Klingler;
additional translation by Shelley Frisch and Joanna Ratych.
p. cm.
Includes bibliographical references and index.
ISBN 0-299-19074-9 (paper: alk. paper)
1. Wigman, Mary, 1886–1973—Correspondence 2. Dancers—Germany—
Biography. 3. Dancers—Germany—Correspondence. 4. Holm, Hanya,
1893–1992—Correspondence. 5. Dancers—United States—Biography.
6. Dancers—United States—Correspondence. I. Title: Mary Wigman's
letters to Hanya Holm. II. Title.
GV1785.W5A32 2003
792.8—dc21

2003005657

Contents

Illustrations

Preface and
Acknowledgments

The personal letters collected in this volume document the lives of two women artists whose careers were rooted in Germany's "golden twenties" and who were agents of transatlantic aesthetic exchange during the five decades that followed. The purpose of the book is to provide primary sources never before available for use in research and learning in dance history and, more broadly, twentieth-century European and American culture. Mary Wigman wrote to Hanya Holm between 1920 and 1971 against a background of economic instability, fascist ascendancy, World War II, German reconstruction, and the cold war, providing a vivid personal account of a century in turmoil.

Mary Wigman (1886–1973), leading figure in the concert art form known in prefascist Germany as Ausdruckstanz, or dance of expression, was engaged with the times and places that confronted her throughout a Promethean career. Under the tutelage of the educator and dance theorist Rudolf Laban, she abandoned the conventions of bodily harmony identified with art dancers such as Isadora Duncan and instead used distortion and dynamic extremes to awaken audiences to irrevocabilities of life. Dances that she created from 1914 to 1942, when the Nazis forced her to stop performing, alive in photographs and contemporary descriptions, are recognized in the twenty-first century as radically modern. Wigman stimulated the development of modern dance in the United States with three concert tours in the early 1930s, the legion of American dancers who studied with her in Germany, and through her disciple and colleague Hanya Holm, who came to New York in 1931 to establish a school authorized to teach the Wigman method.

Wigman's relationship to Nazi ideology is a subject of historical and moral controversy. Some historians find evidence of fascist aesthetics in her dances and writings. Although Wigman neither commented on the political situation of the time nor revealed sympathy with the ideology of a master race, her writings and actions imply a strong connection to a collective tradition of German cultural consciousness. Wigman was the most celebrated modern dancer in Germany when Adolf Hitler came to power in 1933. She refused invitations to emigrate and complied with directives of the German Cultural Ministry, which included purging her school of Jews. She performed in the opening ceremony of the 1936 Berlin Olympics. Later, harassment from the Nazi regime forced her to leave her school in Dresden and flee to Leipzig, where she worked under medieval conditions during World War II and its aftermath. Then, finding herself exploited by the Soviet-dominated East German government, she relocated to West Berlin, where she once again attracted students from around the world. In the last period of her life Wigman became a prominent choreographer and director of opera and large-scale productions such as Igor Stravinsky's *Le Sacre du Printemps*.

In 1920 Hanya Holm (1893–1992) stepped into the heady atmosphere surrounding Wigman in Dresden, a city where gifted youth were making new beginnings in all the arts. Holm, who was born in Worms and grew up in Mainz, had defied her family by marrying outside her Roman Catholic faith and then by agreeing to a divorce; she was caring for an infant son. Fortified with keen intelligence, the kind of nerve that Wigman admired, and a teaching certificate from the Dalcroze Institute, she became Wigman's chief assistant teacher, often managing the school when Wigman was away on tour.

By 1928 Holm was the lover of an intelligent, worldly industrialist. She introduced Hanns Benkert to Wigman and an awkward love triangle developed, with Benkert finally admitting to Holm that he loved both women but that "Mary has become everything to me." His messy break with Holm occurred in 1930 as Wigman prepared her first tour of the United States. Her success led to plans for a branch school in New York City. Who better to lead the school than Holm? Holm had organizational skills and she was an excellent teacher—and the directorship of a school, independence, and distance appealed to her.

Holm successfully adapted the subjectivity of Wigman's philosophy of expressive individualism to the more objective, results-oriented dance culture in the United States. In the next several years she became known as one of the "Big Four" of American modern dance, along with Martha Graham, Doris Humphrey, and Charles Weidman. In 1936 Holm cut her business ties to Wigman and began an independent professional and personal life. She brought her son, by then a teenager, out of Germany, and applied for U.S. citizenship. In 1948 Holm turned her attention to musical theater and in the next fifteen years achieved popular acclaim and financial success as a Broadway choreographer of such hit musicals as *Kiss Me, Kate*; *My Fair Lady*; and *Camelot*. Her decision to work in commercial theater led some in the concert dance community to suspect her of betrayal of elite cultural values.

Mary Wigman's letters to Hanya Holm do not answer all the questions raised by the women's professional choices, but they provide new evidence that should be considered in the critical analysis of their work and lives. Written in German and translated for the first time, the letters provide English-language readers with Wigman's unguarded commentary on her work and personal affairs. Numbering 146, the letters are arranged chronologically in groups that reflect major periods of Wigman's life and are annotated with material that contributes to an understanding of the domestic and social contexts within which Wigman and Holm worked on two continents.

Hedwig Müller, Wigman's biographer, introduces the book with a discussion of the historical, political, and theoretical factors that led to the formation and conduct of Wigman's Dresden school, where the lifelong friendship of Wigman and Holm began. Supplementary material in three appendixes elucidates aspects of their relationship—the love triangle that tested their friendship, their business partnership, the disparity between conditions in the victorious United States and vanquished Germany after World War II, and the cold war politics that prevented Wigman from coming to the United States as a guest teacher.

Many wise and generous people contributed to this volume. I am grateful to the Holm family for entrusting the letters to me, and I am honored that Madeleine Nichols, curator of the Jerome Robbins

Dance Division of The New York Public Library for the Performing Arts, allowed me to work with them before turning them over to the library, which the Holm family has chosen as their permanent repository. I thank Marlies Heinemann and the Mary Wigman Society for endorsing our project and permitting the publication of Mary Wigman's letters.

I am deeply grateful to translators Marianne Forster and Catherine T. Klingler, who met the challenge of Wigman's ornate gothic script and worked diligently to uncover her voice. As a researcher, Forster contributed invaluably to the volume. In many discussions she shared with me her considerable knowledge of twentieth-century European modern dance and passed on information accessible only in documents and historical writing in German. Her close reading of Hedwig Müller's biography of Wigman, which has not been translated into English, supplied important detail to the annotation of the letters. I thank Joanna Ratych for translating supplemental material and for her conversations with me about German culture. She translated passages of Wigman's biography when I sought further understanding of events in Wigman's complex life. I also thank Amy Oberst and Ruth Kriehn for incidental translations. Dorothy Madden, Marcia B. Siegel, and George Jackson read an early version of my manuscript and with their generous commentaries helped me to recognize the broad context of the Wigman-Holm relationship. Jackson returned to help prepare the book for publication.

This project had two angels whom I mention with admiration and gratitude: Madeleine Nichols, who began negotiations for rights to the letters and their translations, and who sustained me in periods of high anxiety; and Lynn Garafola, who championed publication of the letters early on and made a number of suggestions for their presentation. I would like to be able to thank the late Louise Kloepper for the many questions that she answered and for documents and photographs that she entrusted to me, and the late Jan Karski, who provided letters and memorabilia belonging to his wife, Pola Nirenska. I am grateful to Frank-Manuel Peter for his permission to publish photographs in the collection of Deutsches Tanzarchiv Köln, and to others who made photographs available for this publication. The staff of the Dance Division at the New York Public Library supported my research with ever-gracious professionalism. I also received help at the San Francisco Performing Arts Library and Museum, and from Kevin LaVine at the Library of Congress, Annette Fern at the Harvard Theater Collection, and Stephan Dörschel at Stiftung Archiv der Academie der Künste in Berlin. I am grateful for the guidance and encouragement lent me by Barbara Palfy and for the moral support and wise counsel of Lisa, Hillary, and Alix Gitelman. The care and attention of the editorial staff at the University of Wisconsin Press far exceeded the routine. That the Press and the editorial board of the Society of Dance History Scholars embraced this project so enthusiastically will always bring me pride, and has earned my unending gratitude.

Editorial Note

The story of assembling the letters in this volume began on March 3, 1993. Hanya Holm had died four months earlier, and a committee of former students and colleagues determined that her memorial should be a celebration of what would have been her one-hundredth birthday. We knew that Holm had hoped to live to one hundred and that her greatest wish had been to have great-grandchildren. At the celebration her oldest granddaughter, Karen Trautlein, told the gathering at St. Mark's Church in Manhattan that she and her husband were expecting their first child.

After birthday cake and a toast Karen and her sisters asked me to guide them in placing their grandmother's effects. In the following months I arranged a home for a large store of costumes at Florida State University, where I knew Tricia Young would catalog and preserve them, as she had a group of Denishawn costumes. The dance department at Rutgers University, where I was on faculty, accepted Holm's famed collection of percussion instruments. I convinced Karen that Holm's papers should reside with the Jerome Robbins Dance Division, The New York Public Library for the Performing Arts.

In June 1993 I drove to Wilkes-Barre, Pennsylvania, where the family had stored Holm's possessions, to help sort the material. When Karen showed me a folder of letters, I recognized immediately that they had been written by Mary Wigman. My heart skipped a beat as I contemplated their significance. Holm's family and Madeleine

Nichols, curator of the Dance Division, trusted me to hold the letters while I ascertained their content and condition.

Not a German reader, I showed the letters to Marianne Forster, a journal editor and director of The Dance Experience, a center for dance activities in Basel, Switzerland. Forster's reading of a few letters convinced us both that they were a vibrant record of Wigman's life and valuable documentation of her relationship with Holm. Forster agreed to translate the letters for publication in English. She visited the Mary Wigman Archive at the Academy of Arts in Berlin and gathered pertinent information from Wigman's diaries and other German-language sources to help me annotate the letters.

Late in 1993 the Holm family telephoned to tell me that they had found sixty-five additional letters from Wigman to Holm (there had been eighty-one in the first set) and letters signed by "Hanns," whom I knew was Johann Georg Benkert, Holm's lover in the late 1920s and then Wigman's lover from 1930 to 1941. In the spring of 1994 I contacted the Department of German at Rutgers University to find a second translator. As luck would have it, the department had a graduate student looking for a translation project. I showed her and her adviser a few letters—"Much more interesting than translating BMW manuals," one of them quipped. Master's candidate Catherine Klingler made typed transcripts of Wigman's handwritten letters, and her adviser, Joanna Ratych, director of the Program in German Translation, checked them thoroughly against the originals. Ratych supervised Klingler's translations, which her thesis committee also scrutinized. Both Forster and Klingler translated the letters written from February 1954 through March 1960, providing me with the unusual opportunity to choose from among their inevitable variations in word choice and syntax.

One group of letters that Holm received from Wigman seemed ready for the historian. Found upstairs in Holm's desk, they lay unfolded in chronological order. Where Wigman had not supplied a date, Holm had penciled one in. The second cache turned up in Holm's basement. She had put the letters back in their envelopes, bundled them without strict concern for chronology, and cast them into a box with other correspondence and Christmas cards. To give a seamless picture of an extraordinary relationship, I have interlaced the two sets for this publication. A Roman numeral after the date of each letter signifies the set in which it was found—(I) for upstairs set, (II) for basement set. I included a few contracts and letters of agreement because Holm saved them with the letters.

To honor the intimacy and spontaneity of the personal letter, the translators and I agreed to a literal style of translation rather than a literary one. We retained some irregular punctuation and sentence fragments. In rare cases a word or phrase was lost because of the fragility of the documents; we have used [illegible] to denote lost material. Wigman occasionally used an English word or phrase; this material has been set in small capital letters. Although Wigman used underline for emphasis and for book titles, the book uses italics. A reference list at the end of the book provides complete information on sources cited in introductory material and notes following letters. Material not credited to a specific published source, interview, or personal communication comes from encyclopedias, biographical indexes, or documents of record such as programs, school brochures, and publicity materials. Wherever possible, I verified with a second source the background material that I gleaned from history texts. The designation "Forster," when it appears without a specific reference means information provided by Marianne Forster from similar German language sources.

After she supervised Klingler's translations, Ratych confessed that she was "hooked" on Wigman and she translated Hanns Benkert's letters so that I could summarize them. The first appendix contains these summaries. Appendix 2 consists of two letters Wigman wrote to Louise Kloepper in 1932 and 1933 (translated by Klingler) and one letter Holm wrote to Kloepper from Germany in 1934 (translated by Forster). Appendix 3 contains five of the many letters that Wigman wrote in English to Pola Nirenska. Amy Oberst translated the occasional German phrases in these letters.

Wigman was an ardent correspondent, generous in her personal relations. Many letters from her to the United States exist in private collections and libraries.* Few of these predate the war, however, and none document as mature and multifaceted a relationship as was hers with Holm.

---

* The Jerome Robbins Dance Division, The New York Public Library for the Performing Arts holds several collections of letters from Mary Wigman in addition to those published in this volume. Letters to Walter Sorell, dating from 1946, are in German and concern his translation of Wigman's book, *The Language*

of Dance (Middletown, Conn.: Wesleyan University Press, 1966) and his book *Hanya Holm: The Biography of an Artist* (Middletown, Conn.: Wesleyan University Press, 1969). Letters in English to Margaret Erlanger are post–World War II; those folders also contain two letters that Wigman wrote to Howard Potter while she was vacationing in 1932. Letters to Margaret Gage, also in English, run from 1947 to 1973. With them are twenty-four letters in German from Dr. Herbert Binswanger, who wrote to Gage in the last years of Wigman's life. The Dance Division also holds fifty-nine letters in English to Katharine A. Wolfe, who corresponded with Wigman from 1947 to 1960 about a book of dance history Wolfe hoped to publish. Letters and postcards to Louise Kloepper, written between 1932 and 1935, are in German. A folder of twenty-seven letters and notes in English from Wigman to her student Shirlee Dodge, written between 1947 and 1973, also contains a letter written by Anni Hess (Hesschen) after Wigman's death. Folders of miscellaneous correspondence contain sixteen items, some in English and some in German. A letter to Howard Potter, postcards and two scrapbooks commemorating the Wigman tours that he managed are in uncataloged boxes of Hanya Holm photographs in the Dance Division. Archives of the American Dance Festival in Durham, North Carolina, contain several letters from Wigman in the early 1950s. Jacob's Pillow in Lee, Massachusetts, holds one letter from Wigman to Ted Shawn. Special Collections of the Golda Meir Library at the University of Wisconsin–Milwaukee, holds five letters in English to Ruth Kriehn, written from 1947 to 1971. Letters to Pola Nirenska, some in German and some in English, are in the Dance Division. Three letter cards predate the war, and fifty-one letters span the years 1946 to 1958. The Library of Congress holds another three letters to Nirenska, 1935–48, and one to Franziska Boas written July 14, 1934. Sorell, in his edited and translated writings of Mary Wigman, *The Mary Wigman Book* (Middletown, Conn.: Wesleyan University Press, 1975) includes some of Wigman's letters to former students and patrons in the United States. Pamela and Edmund McIlhenney, in *Dodge Days: Dance and Other Adventures of Shirlee Dodge* (Avery Island, La.: Pamela McIlhenney, 2000) include several notes written to Shirlee Dodge. One letter from Wigman to Hanya Holm appearing in this volume and paragraphs from four others were previously published in *Dance Chronicle,* Vol. 20, No. 1 (1997).

Introduction

A Matter of Loyalty—
Hanya Holm and Mary Wigman

HEDWIG MÜLLER

"Hanya was as tiny, alert, and intellectual as ever—but she has also grown 'wise,'" Mary Wigman wrote to her best friend and cousin, Martha Reuther, in April 1951 after Hanya Holm had been visiting Wigman in Berlin for a week (Wigman 1951). When I met Holm for the first time more than thirty years later, she was just as Wigman had described her.

The Wigman Centennial of the Society of Dance History Scholars brought me to New York in February 1986, and I had the delightful opportunity to visit Holm in her apartment. She was sitting, wrapped in a blanket, in her large easy chair, her long white hair tied back in a thin braid that hung straight down. She had recently suffered a stroke and was still recovering. Holm told me that just after the stroke she had forgotten every word of English and spoke only in German, which mildly dismayed the people around her. After several days she was once again able to communicate normally in English. She clearly enjoyed relating this story, and it astonished her to learn how deeply our mother tongue is embedded in our memories. When we are faced with a crisis, she found, the language of our childhood reemerges in our consciousness. Holm spoke slowly. Her German was good, still marked by a regional accent.

During this meeting I quickly became aware of how solidly Holm embodied two identities and how significant her German heritage was to her. In her 1951 letter to Reuther, Wigman had described Holm as follows: "She had truly become a little woman of Frankfurt, and her Americanisms are really just perched on the surface." I think that Wigman may have misjudged her most loyal collaborator in this regard. Holm's American identity was not merely sitting on the surface; it lay deep inside her. Her life in the United States shaped her artistry. The philosophy of dance that she had learned from Wigman at the Dresden school was an aspect of her German identity. Holm supplied precise and thorough answers to all the questions that I asked her about Wigman and their collaboration. Her responses were invariably concise and clear on one point: Mary Wigman was a great artist.

The relationship between the two women had a special quality. Neither personal crises nor World War II compromised their friendship. They were able to maintain a staunch alliance for more than half a century. During my visit it was apparent to me that Holm's loyalty remained intact even after Wigman's death. Not a single critical remark about Wigman crossed Holm's lips, whether she was discussing personal, artistic, or political matters. Their mutual devotion to dance was their bond.

Holm spent ten years at the Mary Wigman School in Dresden. Those ten years laid the foundation for her artistic convictions and her friendship with Wigman. During those years Wigman built a school that brought modern German dance to the international stage. Holm played a significant role in establishing the school and disseminating Wigman's concept of dance.

The school's location in Dresden was pure coincidence. Wigman had had her greatest success there on her first tour, which had brought her back to Germany in 1919 after six years in Switzerland. She was accompanied on the tour by her Swiss pupil Berthe Bartholomé Trümpy, who was in charge of the technical scenic aspects and the acoustic accompaniment of the dances with gongs and other percussion instruments. Trümpy was passionately devoted to Wigman. When the board of the Dresden Opera offered Wigman the directorship of the opera ballet in 1920, Trümpy moved to Dresden with Wigman. The Dresden Opera ultimately retracted its offer, but Wigman opted to stay in Dresden. Her residence visa for Switzerland was running out, and the Swiss authorities had informed her that they would not be extending it. She decided to open a school in Dresden with Trümpy for two reasons: she was driven by her missionary zeal to convey her vision of the new art of dance, and she needed to make a living.

Wigman's evenings of solo performances soon brought her renown, and young women came to her asking whether they might study with her. Thus began the school, which had a home but lacked a pedagogical orientation. Trümpy took charge of the daily instruction and gave lessons to amateurs, and Wigman instructed those who intended to pursue a professional career in dance. When Holm arrived as a student, she essentially followed Wigman's own quest for the essence of dance. Like Wigman, Holm had completed her training in the Rhythmische Bildungsanstalt (Rhythmic Educational Institution) in Hellerau and received her diploma as a teacher of rhythmic exercise, or eurythmics. Wigman had graduated seven years earlier and had realized, as had Holm, that she could not see her own artistic future in the teaching methods of Émile Jaques-Dalcroze. Also, Wigman, had found somebody who could point the way to her calling. Rudolf von Laban was the teacher who awakened the hidden artistic forces in Wigman and led her to dance; now Wigman herself was making a dancer out of Holm. Wigman's relationship to Laban had resulted in bitter competition at times, but Wigman and Holm developed a relationship marked by intense collaboration and friendship. In the 1930s an element of artistic competition entered into their relationship, but it did nothing to alter their profound attachment.

As a new pupil, Holm experienced the open creative outlook that the Wigman School fostered in those initial years. We should bear in mind that the political situation in Germany after the end of World War I was chaotic. The prevailing order of the German Empire had broken down, and the traditional values of the nineteenth century's strict moral and ethical precepts for society were no longer valid. The Weimer Republic was established, and the politically aware sector of the German populace tried from one day to the next to adjust to democracy, a form of government whose rules few understood, let alone mastered. Everyone was trying to cobble together some sort of personal future from the ruins of society. Artists and intellectuals embraced a spirit of optimism. They threw overboard anything that was old and probed all sorts of new avenues. There were no limits or barriers. All paths to art were wide open. Wigman's school was a place to embark on a search for oneself.

In July 1920 Trümpy bought a house for Wigman on what was then Schiller Street, later renamed Bautzen Street. On September 1, 1920, the first official year of the Wigman School began with an enrollment of eight pupils, and by the summer of 1922 the first evening of dance was presented. Holm was among the pupils who performed their own choreography that evening. Wigman taught in a large empty space adjacent to her private living room and bedroom. It was not until 1922 that a former stable was converted into a dance studio. Holm was already in the advanced class, which Wigman taught regularly.

In the first two years of the school Wigman established the foundations for further development of a curriculum that was based on her convictions about dance. Looking back to those beginnings in Dresden, Wigman mused, "The pedagogical work was set because the people were there. And when it came to theory: nothing! And thematics: nothing! We were as free as the birds in the air and simply did and tried out everything possible. In the end it became evident that it all really did have meaning and make sense. But basically not until later" (1982:39). The Wigman School drew its energy from the personality of its director. The pupils who came to Wigman were fascinated by the woman they had seen on stage and enthusiastic about the way she danced. Holm was so captivated by Wigman's extraordinary stage presence that she was prepared to surmount all the difficulties of daily life as a single mother to train with Wigman. This high degree of motivation was characteristic of Wigman's pupils. They were brimming with eagerness to confront new and unknown realms and to work with Wigman unreservedly. Acceptance to the school meant being accepted into a group that was committed to a common goal and a mission: free dance. Joining this mission was a life-altering decision. The young women had a strong desire for emancipation. Some had decided to pursue the art of dance in opposition to their parents, and most had to provide their own living expenses and school tuition. Their determination to assert their independence lent a special atmosphere to the school. The focus of their quest for autonomy was an exploration of their bodies and themselves. In an essay Wigman described the young women's desire for movement as follows: "I believe that all young females today experience a strong healthy pleasure in pure movement. I also believe that all these young women are entitled to a healthy dose of egotism, which begins by exploring itself before turning to the world around it. Seek yourself, feel yourself, experience yourself!" (1929:14).

Of primary concern to Wigman's pupils was movement and the perception of their own personalities in the movement. Their bodies

revealed the thinking of the dancers. This open attitude, direct phys-
icality, and naturalness of expression were new to the world of dance
and reflected the prevailing message of the new dance: authenticity,
use of oneself as a basis for dance, and establishment of an honest
outlook about oneself through choreographic form.

An open attitude toward the body, which is required for dance
training, made dance a vehicle of awareness of psychic and emotional
disposition. Dance was literally a matter of the students' existence.
Wigman's approach explicitly asked dancers to take themselves seriously and to come to terms with their own needs. Consequently, the
focus on existential human feeling, experiences, and emotions—the
content of the dances of Wigman and her pupils—was an act of emancipation and the basis of expressive dance. In the early 1920s Wigman
herself was still trying to find herself, and to an extent she experienced this process along with her students: "Because throughout the
previous period of study, during which, in the last analysis, we were
learning, we were so closely knit together that, as a result of it, the
creative and artistic work became a matter of fact" (quoted in Sorell
1969:19). Wigman instituted a master class for her best students and
accepted those dancers with whom she wished to collaborate artistically and develop her group choreography. Among her unpublished
notes is an outline from 1923 of a lesson plan for this master class.
It was the first recorded lesson plan of the Wigman School, and
Wigman intended that it be used to ensure that future male and female
dancers received systematic training. The plan comprises seven points,
and it demonstrates the dominance of the creative portions of the
training over pure work for the body.

The work of the master class, as Wigman outlined it, consisted of
the following: "1. correction of individual work in front of the class;
2. exercises in directing; 3. composition theory; 4. technique (once or
twice per week with Bartholomé, pure gymnastics, speed, strength,
etc.); 5. percussive rhythm, applied; 6. drills and rehearsals; 7. theory,
presentations by individual pupils on previously announced themes;
8. presentation by M.W. with free discussion; 9. readings of essays on
dance, music, theater, or possibly the fine arts" (undated a). It is important to note what a strong emphasis Wigman placed on theory in
dance training.

With the most talented students of the master class—Holm was
one of them from the start—Wigman founded her first dance group.

Now Holm experienced, as daily practice, the process of choreographing in direct collaboration with Wigman. The seed was sown for Holm
as both choreographer and pedagogue. Wigman was often away on
solo tours and unable to train the group herself or rehearse the group
dances. The dancers in the group took on these tasks themselves,
but, as Wigman often described the situation, she was able to leave
the group in good hands because she could rely on Holm to take over
the training and to promote disciplined work. Wigman could pay the
dancers in her group only a small wage, and therefore they were simul-
taneously engaged as teachers in the school. In this way they were
able to earn a living and devote themselves to the work of the dance
group full time. Thus Holm, as a member of the dance group, auto-
matically became a pedagogue without ever studying pedagogy. As a
member of the teaching staff at the Wigman School, she also helped
structure the lesson plans and thereby contributed to the development
of the artistic goals of the school as a whole.

At the teacher conferences the faculty discussed and debated the
written instructional programs that Wigman drafted for the school
curriculum. The earliest source is Wigman's sketch of the three stages
of the development of a dancer. The teaching material needed to be
tailored to the student's level of development at each stage. We can
assume that Holm was trained in the spirit of this pedagogical para-
digm and supported it as a teacher at the school. Wigman described
the decisive aspect of the first stage in the development of a dance as
follows: "Instinctive groping; emphasis on expression without regard
to content or form; expression for its own sake. Randomness, chaos,
and rapture emanating from an awareness of one's body, which is felt,
experienced, loved, and exaggerated; an unconscious total experience"
(undated b). Dancers initially experienced only themselves and their
own bodies. In this phase Wigman was not concerned with making
any technical demands on the body. The student needed instead to
experience the unity of body and personality and give outer corporeal
expression to what was inside, with no significance other than expression itself. The method of dance for this phase was improvisation.
Content and form could not be mandated; they had to be sought in
free movement.

The great fascination of the Wigman School derived from this
presentation of dance, and it is certainly one reason that so many
students—notably, Hanya Holm, Gret Palucca, Vera Skoronel, and

Yvonne Georgi, as well as the male dancer Harald Kreutzberg—developed into outstanding independent artists in the school's early years.

After the first stage of a dancer's development, dominated by random experimentation, Wigman regarded the second stage as one of growing awareness of shape and form. She wrote, "A sense of orientation awakens. The next step is confrontations, which seek to clarify the instinctual process of movement. Expression, content, function, form, etc., begin to diverge. Everything typical asserts itself against everything that is personal and individualistic, and vice versa. . . . Characteristic of this stage of development is a lack of unity, wavering between expression for the sake of expression and form for the sake of form. The body is no longer mere corpus and not yet an instrument, and becomes an arena of interior and exterior struggles. Divergence is experienced."

A quest for orientation is the key to this phase of the individual dancer's development. The experience of self broadens out to reflection on what the dancer has experienced. This is the crossroads that separates those who possess the requisite talent for the artistic profession from those who fail to display any gift for creative work beyond pure experimentation with movement. Here, once again, improvisation is an important means of recognizing and fostering individual creativity. The dancer must attain a state of autonomy. Naturally, conflict also plays a role in this phase. Conflict is inevitable when, on the one hand, dancers must know their own mind, and, on the other, the extraordinary person of Mary Wigman dominates. Wigman was omnipresent as a role model and teacher in the dancers' daily routines and fantasies. This conflict applies especially to the later dancers in the dance group, who worked as independent creators yet were also expected to bring Wigman's ideas to the stage.

Conflict is resolved in the third stage of a dancer's development. Wigman wrote, "Clarification begins to take place. Expression and movement as dance experience condense into an emotionally gratifying form. Dance is expressed as *language*. Mastery of the means and mastery of the material become manifest. Indicating the limits of the prototype while deliberately expanding beyond those limits. . . . Harmonization of the dancer's personality."

These were the artistic skills that Holm gained at the Wigman School. On the basis of this approach, Wigman and Holm maintained a common language that united them for the rest of their lives.

In addition to her artistic inspiration and pedagogical talent, Holm had a very pragmatic way of dealing with school problems, which predestined her as a member of the board of directors and, to a certain extent, to become Wigman's spokesperson. Here she learned all aspects of a school's organization and administration, from financial and legal questions to diplomacy in dealing with untalented but well-to-do students. All her experiences from her ten years at the Wigman School molded Holm into an artist whom Wigman could entrust with the difficult task of attracting U.S. students to German modern dance. With the experiences of ten years of close collaboration with Mary Wigman, Holm left Germany.

Wigman's letters to her most loyal artistic associate for fifty years shed light on Holm's achievements on behalf of Wigman's dance and methods as well as on Holm's emancipation from her mentor.

Wigman was a lifelong, passionate letter writer. In many thousands of letters she maintained contact with her closest friends, especially with Reuther, her closest and lifelong confidant, and with the large flock of students from every corner of the globe. Unfortunately, no complete collection of letters is extant, because Wigman did not keep the letters that were addressed to her. We therefore have only the letters that she wrote, which their recipients usually preserved carefully, as keepsakes.

The loss of Holm's letters to Wigman is extremely unfortunate, considering the interesting questions that Holm no doubt addressed in them. The contents of Wigman's letters are quite diverse and range from the private to strictly professional communication. They provide information about people whom both women knew either from the Dresden school or the Mary Wigman Dance Group, generally other dancers whose development and whereabouts the letters trace over decades. And they clarify one of the important reasons behind Holm's willingness to leave the Dresden school, namely, her estrangement from her lover, Hanns Benkert, who had turned to Wigman.

A perpetual subject of debate is whether private matters are relevant to a broader public. The triangle of Holm-Benkert-Wigman was certainly significant for the artistic development of Holm, because it propelled her into a new life that led her to independent choreographic work and eventually to her making her mark on the history of American dance. Beyond the private sphere, Wigman's letters to Holm contain information that illuminates the finances of the Wigman School in New York and Holm's major role in the development of the school, which was eventually renamed for her. In addition, the letters offer us some highly interesting insights into the artistic questions that the two women discussed. Readers can form their own opinions concerning the relationship of these two women, as every interpretation is highly subjective. That is the appeal of working with primary material, and this volume adds dimension to that appeal.

Translation by Shelley Frisch

Mary Wigman's Letters
to Hanya Holm

1920–1930

DRESDEN

A complex and remarkably durable relationship emerges in five documents spanning ten years. With her first letter Wigman responds to a request for instruction from Frau Kuntze (later, Hanya Holm). Her second letter inscribes a growing friendship and the women's employer-employee status. Then Wigman offers a trusted friend the codirectorship of her school; Holm accepts gladly. A fifth letter lets us read the rich emotional interior available to Wigman's pen. The impulse behind her caressing words of confidence and affection in the letter postmarked January 16, 1930, is complicated, however, by the fact that Wigman and Holm's lover, Hanns Benkert, had met by that time and discovered a mutual attraction.

❧

MARY WIGMAN
Dresden-Neustadt
Schillerstrasse 17

September 27, 1920 (II)

Dear Frau Kuntze![1]

I apologize that your inquiry remained unanswered for so long, but I was ill and only recently was I able to get back on my feet.

I have a group of private students who have devoted themselves to dance as a profession, and I can only take on serious students such as these, as I have received an enormous number of inquiries.

I do not know what you have in mind. If you are interested in dance and gymnastics as a general means of development and furthering physical education, I would encourage you to work with my current assistant, who participates in the instruction of all my students and also provides courses and individual instruction in dance and dance gymnastics.[2]

The fee for individual lessons with me is 50 Marks, for class lessons 20 Marks.

With my assistant: individual lessons 20 Marks, class lessons (up to 6 persons) 10 Marks, up to 20 persons 5 Marks.[3]

If you would like more details I invite you to simply inquire, by telephone if necessary (10488).

I will be happy to provide any further information.

Sincerely yours,
Mary Wigman

1. Johanna Kuntze (née Eckert) married the painter-sculptor Reinhold Kuntze in 1917. They divorced in February 1921. She had custody of their son, Klaus Valentin Kuntze, who was three months old when Wigman wrote this letter. Holm's biographer states that Holm sought instruction after she saw Wigman perform and "was gripped by the wish to find out whether one could acquire the knowledge and skill which led to Wigman's art" (Sorell 1969:15).

2. Wigman's assistant was Berthe Trümpy (her original name was Berthe Bartholomé-Trumpis), who lived from 1895 to 1983. A Swiss student who had accompanied Wigman on her first tour in 1919, Trümpy subsidized the founding of the Mary Wigman School in Dresden. Trümpy left the school and dance group in 1924 to give concerts on her own and found a school in Berlin.

3. Later, Wigman required professional students to take a monthly private lesson with a teacher of their choosing to work on their individual interests and needs (Thimey 2000:58–59).

∿

Mary Wigman • Dresden-Neustadt • Bautzner Strasse 107

Uttwil[1]

undated[2] (I)

Dearest Hanya,[3]

Thank you for the letter! Hopefully you are having nice weather at the seashore and are getting some relaxation. As far as the knee is concerned, I can comfort you. The period I did not work, all kinds of dumb things happened, and when I began to exercise again I thought things would go wrong. But careful training is the best antidote! At any rate you must not stop exercising daily with weights. [Name illegible] told me very urgently: don't stop moving and, especially, move with weights.

I personally would give you a day off without hesitation, but I want to avoid offending the other teachers. After all, everybody could come and ask for it.[4] Knowing that on September first nothing, or hardly anything, is to be done, all ought to be assembled [illegible]. Therefore I am asking you to organize yourself so you can be in Dresden by September first. To travel through three nights is bad, but, then, you could leave a day early. In case Dr. Kohler should be in Freiburg the thirty-first of August, there would not be another possibility, and you would have to go back a little later. In the interest of the work and the general attitude, I am asking you again to be here in time, all right?

Thank you for the address of the architect. I will make inquiries!

How I would have enjoyed being with you in Paris! But perhaps I would have been too worn out to get anything out of it. Now it is

Mary Wigman in the late 1920s. Photograph by Charlotte Rudolph. © Charlotte Rudolph/ARS, New York 2003. Courtesy Jerome Robbins Dance Division, The New York Public Library for the Performing Arts, Astor, Lenox and Tilden Foundations.

peaceful here. Finally, I can work again. For quite a while it was impossible. The nerves were on strike.

I am also sad because vacation is already half over! Addìo, love! Greetings to the others. To you all my love and my heart. The Schlegels all send their regards.[5]

See you soon!

Your

Mary

1. Uttwil is a Swiss village on the Lake of Constance. Wigman spent summers there in the 1920s, resting and preparing dances for her fall tours.

2. Dating of this letter is problematic. Holm penciled July 20, 1938, at the top of the letter and placed it in that order in the folder in her desk. However, Holm was not in Europe in 1938, as the letter suggests. The letter must have been written between 1922, when Holm began teaching in the Dresden school, and 1929, when she became codirector.

3. Sorell (1969:22–23) suggests that Johanna Kuntze changed her first name because international students had difficulty pronouncing "Johanna." Informal notes in the Hanya Holm Collection, Jerome Robbins Dance Division, The New York Public Library, show that earlier she sometimes used the name "Hanja" or "Hannya." She chose "Holm," a stage name that she adopted when the first Wigman group was formed in 1923, for its alliteration. The word *holm*, Sorell explains, has Nordic and Anglo-Saxon roots with various references to the natural world (23).

4. By 1926 Wigman needed a large staff to teach as many as 360 professional and amateur students in the Dresden school (Jeschke and Vetterman 2000:59).

5. Wigman stayed at the Schlegels' house when she was in Uttwil. In 1924 Ernst Schlegel was instrumental in founding a Society of Friends of the Mary Wigman Dance Group, guaranteeing an endowment of several thousand marks for three years. Schlegel became Wigman's business adviser and a member of her school's board of directors. However, the two had a falling out and Schlegel left in 1929 (Forster).

∽

WIGMAN   SCHOOL   DRESDEN

Bautzner Strasse 107

April 29, 1929 (II)

Hanya Holm,
Bautzner Strasse 117,
Dresden-N.

The undersigned request Hanya Holm to assume Will Goetze's position in the official co-directorship of the Wigman School, effective September 1, 1929.

The Directors of the Wigman School, Dresden:
Mary Wigman
Elisabeth Wigman[1]
Will Goetze[2]

1. Mary's sister, Elisabeth, younger by seven years, had not been trained as a dancer, but after joining Wigman's household she developed into a good teacher of children and beginners.
2. Wigman worked with the composer William Goetze from 1923 to 1929. He joined her staff as music instructor in 1924. With Goetze, Wigman developed the practice of having music improvised as she developed a dance. Goetze would set a composition for piano and/or percussion from musical ideas that he and Wigman selected.

∽

Dresden-N.
Bautzner Strasse 117
May 2, 1929 (II)

To the
Directors of the Wigman School, Dresden,
Bautzner Strasse 107,
Dresden-N.

In reference to your letter of April 29th, I hereby thank you deeply for your confidence in me and gladly declare that, effective September 1, 1929 I will accept the position of co-directorship of the Wigman School, Dresden.

Most sincerely
[unsigned carbon copy]

∽

Mary Wigman • Dresden-Neustadt • Bautzner Strasse 107

[Postmarked Hamburg,
January 16, 1930] (II)

My dearest Hanya,

It often happens that I get the completely spontaneous urge to write to you, and in most cases this rising wish sinks in exhaustion or in the ever-changing work environment of touring.

Mary Wigman in *Hexentanz II*, 1926. Photograph by Charlotte Rudolph.
© Charlotte Rudolph/ARS, New York 2003. Courtesy Jerome Robbins
Dance Division, The New York Public Library for the Performing Arts,
Astor, Lenox and Tilden Foundations.

This morning there was another such moment and this time I did not want to let it pass by.

I was rehearsing in the Curiohaus.[1] My mother appeared, and when the rehearsal was over I asked her about Dresden. At first she did not want to discuss the matter, so as not to upset me, but then she told me that Elisabeth was ill, and Tina as well.[2]

Then with full clarity something happened in me that has happened so often lately: I surprised myself by not becoming uneasy or doubtful about the situation for even one moment, because the name "Hanya" rang through me confidently and clearly. And you see, Hanya, this was so wonderful in its naturalness and simplicity that it did not only make me happy; rather, it gave me a very sincere urge to be able to express and to say to you what boundless confidence you have raised in me, not with many words, but through a state of being that is called loyalty to the work, complete devotion, responsibility and conscience.

The *knowledge* of your achievement is always there and always awake in me. But a person is not always able to acknowledge selfless devotion in words. Rather, it expresses itself in daily togetherness, through a look, through the tone of voice, often in silence and often in action.

Unrelenting everyday life creates assumptions that may be completely different with other people. So I asked myself quite suddenly this morning in light of my own feelings: Does Hanya *know* of my confidence, of my love for her, the way I know it?

Dearest, be still a moment and listen to me: I know who you are, I know what you do, I know of your love for me and of your devotion to my work, which is also partially yours. And I take you in my arms with all my thoughts and express what moves me strongly and sincerely: I thank you, Hanya.

There are not very many people to whom I would assign the term "friend." But you are among these few and are very close to me, very trusted and endlessly dear to my heart.

My dear, true and fearless comrade, take these lines as they come to you, without ruse, without reservation, out of genuine human relationship, and out of the unshakable confidence that flows from me to you.

Ever your
Mary

1. Curiohaus was one of the main performance spaces for dancers in Hamburg in the 1920s. In 1930 the Hamburg branch of the Wigman School, under the direction of Gretl Curth and Hans Huber, opened there. Wigman had had her first big success as a solo dancer at Curiohaus in 1919 (Stöckemann 1989:15 via Forster). In 1949 she recalled the event: "Hamburg was the miracle . . . a storm, an ovation, the public frantic with enthusiasm" (Wigman 1949).

2. Tina Flade was the youngest member of Wigman's first performing group. She later pursued a career in the United States.

1930–1931

NEW YORK, DRESDEN

Among the letters that Hanya Holm brought with her to New York when she arrived in September 1931 was one that she had received from Mary Wigman after the debut concert of her first U.S. tour (December 1930 to March 1931). There followed contracts and agreements between the women as Holm organized a New York branch of the Wigman School with the backing of the impresario Sol Hurok. A note that Wigman handed to Fé Alf, just before the dancer left to join Holm in New York as her assistant, reveals that Wigman had already heard from Holm, and we read Holm's uneasiness.

∾

The St. Moritz
On the Park
New York

December 29, 1930 (I)

Dearest Hanya,

Many heartfelt greetings, and many warm thoughts and wishes. The first dance concert is already behind me. It was a huge, complete success yesterday.

I want to tell you about it but it will not be possible — too much to tell and too much to do. I have seen nothing of this crazy city. Only reporters, photographers, dancers, managers, and so on.

I am living on the eighth floor of a skyscraper hotel and I can rehearse on the thirty-seventh floor when the room is free. To drive two blocks by car during rush hour you need eighteen minutes. (Like from Lieschen's bar to Wasserschlösschen.)

Each room has radio, [illegible], 3 of them, bath, and so on. Everything mechanical functions very well. The people not so well. For example, someone persuaded me to have dinner today. Usually one eats at 7:00 and now it is 9:00! Another person made an appointment at the hairdresser for me, but didn't tell me which one, and could not be reached. It's laughable! And that's the way it is with almost all appointments.

Wallmann[1] talks even more than ever!

But the dance concert was wonderful.[2] The reviews could not be better.[3] Tomorrow is the second performance, then Friday will be the third, and Sunday the fourth. It's a lot of work!

Even though people are very kind, I feel homesick, really homesick. I feel like a prisoner. This morning I was dragged off to the photographer. At two o'clock a fast breakfast, at three an interview, at four another, at five the third. Since six o'clock I have been waiting for an unreliable person and I can't get in touch with her by phone in this Babylon. And I am so hungry. The food is awful here. Some wonderful things, but in such strange mixtures that it does not matter what you order!

The reception of the Dancers' League was very beautiful and interesting.[4] Everybody was here: Argentina, Kreutzberg, Yvonne, Ruth St. Denis, Doris Humphrey, Martha Graham, all those names.[5] Wiener and Aschermann are charming; Hasting is staying with them and he is spoiled quite nicely.[6] He already speaks English very well. The two, Menz and Hasting, went on a New York stroll today and I wasn't allowed.[7] I am quite jealous. Oh dear, sometimes it is really hard to be a celebrity.

How are things in Dresden? I have not had a letter from Germany and I'm really hungry for it. How are you and Kläuschen?[8] Have you celebrated Christmas? We didn't!!

Strange city — beautiful? I don't think so. One really would like to see the countryside but it seems so far away. Stone, nothing else, no tree, no bush, all rocks and houses. At the moment I'm very tired, still quite exhausted from yesterday.

The first two concerts were sold out for weeks in advance and everybody was bursting with expectation. I, myself, was nervous as never before. And yet it went perfectly. And then something happened that rarely happens here. The audience shouted and screamed. Afterwards there was a reception on the stage, hundreds of people full of enthusiasm.

My dear, I think of you a lot and often, sending you all my most beautiful wishes for the New Year,

I am from my heart,

your

Mary

1. Margarethe Gretchen Wallmann (name also given as Margaret or Margherita) was born in Vienna in 1904 and became a child prodigy in classical ballet. After seeing Wigman perform, she studied with her and danced in the first Wigman group. When a hip injury forced Wallmann to give up performing, she established a school in Berlin that Wigman authorized to be her only official school in that city. Ted Shawn invited Wallmann to teach at the New York Denishawn School in the late 1920s, and he traveled to Europe to dance in her *Orpheus* at the Munich Dance Congress in 1930. Her success with that work was a springboard to a career of heading opera ballet companies and directing operas. She worked at the Salzburg Festival and in Vienna, Milan, London, and Paris. She staged opera at the Teatro Colón from 1938 to 1948 and then produced opera in Italy and New York. She died in Monte Carlo in 1992.

2. In her U.S. debut performances Wigman filled the Chanin Theater on West 46th Street three times a week for a month. Having presented Anna Pavlova and Isadora Duncan, Sol Hurok now offered an artist who equaled them in personal magnetism and disciplined achievement but whose work Hurok himself did not appreciate. He found her overly intellectual, "like a course in the philosophy of Nietzsche and Schopenhauer" (quoted in H. Robinson 1994:150).

3. A vast amount of press had preceded Wigman's arrival in the United States. The dance critic Mary F. Watkins compared Wigman to Isadora Duncan: "The American artist struck the shackles of convention and artificiality from the dance, her German successor has relieved it of its prettiness, sweetness and light, with the result that in her person is cherished the essence of modernism for the profession of today and tomorrow" (*New York Herald Tribune*, December 17, 1930). In his review of Wigman's first concert, the critic John Martin referred to audience expectations as "odds which probably no other dancer had to face within memory." He judged that Wigman "achieved an unequivocal triumph" against these odds (*New York Times*, December 29, 1930). At the end of the first of what would be three U.S. tours, Martin called Wigman's dancing the "most memorable adventure in the history of dancing in America," and he thanked her for "an awakening" (*New York Times*, March 8, 1931).

4. New York's prominent solo dancers and leaders of professional groups formed the Concert Dancers' League, Inc., early in 1930 for the purpose of mutual protection and advancement of the art.

5. Harald Kreutzberg (1902–1968) and Yvonne Georgi (1903–1975), both students of Wigman's in the 1920s, had preceded her in giving concerts of the German modern dance in the United States.

6. Johann Maria David Wiener (1908–1966) had also shown German modern dance in the United States. Born in Vienna, he studied with Laban, Wigman, and Jaques-Dalcroze. In 1928 Wiener arrived in the United States via Asia, where he had studied Chinese dance and established a school in Shanghai. He gave concerts under the name Hans Wiener for a number of years and then changed his name to the less German-sounding Jan Veen. Otto Aschermann met Wiener in China and came to the United States with him. He remained with Weiner for eight years and danced in some of his programs.

7. The musician Hanns Hasting became connected with the Wigman schools in 1928. He composed music for Wigman's four dance cycles, *Shifting Landscape, Sacrifice, The Way,* and *Women's Dances,* as well as for many recital pieces. Hasting toured Europe with Wigman and accompanied her on her three tours of the United States. Meta Menz played the gongs, cymbals, drums, wood blocks, and other percussion instruments that accompanied many dances.

8. Diminutive for Klaus, the name of Holm's son.

∾

Mary Wigman • Dresden-Neustadt • Bautzner Strasse 107

April 10, 1931 (I)

Dearest Hanya,

I have to acknowledge a promise concerning your son. It is to help you with a regular contribution toward Klaus's education, when Klaus, as is the case now, goes to a boarding school.[1] I will put at your disposal a monthly sum of 40 marks, from April 1, 1931, as long as you are not able to take financial care of your son entirely on your own.

The sum of 40 marks for the month of April is enclosed and also enclosed is a receipt for you to sign and send back.

With all good wishes

from my heart,
your
Mary

1. When Holm came to the United States, Klaus remained in Germany at a boarding school.

༄

Mary Wigman • Dresden-Neustadt • Bautzner Strasse 107

May 13, 1931 (I)

Certificate

Hanya Holm began her studies at the Wigman School, Dresden, in spring, 1921. She fully completed the professional course of the Wigman Dresden School.

In 1922 she became an assistant, and from 1924, a main teacher of the professional and amateur classes as well as of the summer courses of the Wigman School, Dresden. She was a member of the Mary Wigman Dance Group from its inception (1923) until it was dissolved (in the summer of 1928) and she distinguished herself in every way.[1]

In recognition of her achievements she was appointed one of the directors of the Wigman Dresden School in the fall of 1929.

In the summer of 1930 Mary Wigman trusted her with the assistant stage direction of "Totenmal" (festival of choric stage works in the 1930 Munich Festival). In addition, she danced in "Totenmal."[2]

She left the Wigman School, Dresden, in the fall of 1931 at the request of Mary Wigman to take over the artistic and pedagogic responsibilities of the newly opened "New York Wigman School of the Dance."

Hanya Holm excels with her artistic and pedagogic talents, and in many years of collaboration she has acquired the full trust and complete recognition of her students and co-workers through her conscientiousness, sense of responsibility, commitment, and devotion towards the idea of her task.

My best wishes accompany her.

Mary Wigman

1. The first Wigman group toured for long periods through Germany and other European countries. Because of strained economic conditions the dancers traveled in unheated third-class compartments, sometimes eating only bread and butter on long journeys (Müller 1986:143). Holm described the primitive conditions of their performance venues in a 1981 television interview, *The Contributions of Hanya Holm to American Modern Dance.*

2. Koegler translates the title *Totenmal* as *The Monument of Death* (1974:19); Howe translates it as *Memorial to the Dead* (1996:107); and Manning as *Call*

of the Dead (1993:351). Historically controversial, it is called "proto-fascist" by Manning, (1993:131) and "an anti-war pageant" by Sorell (1969:27). It was a joint project of Wigman, the writer Albert Talhoff, and sound and lighting designers. Technical problems with the performance hall and engineering caused a cancellation of its scheduled premiere, and it received but one performance. John Martin, who was in the audience, felt that the text, sound, and light did not serve Wigman well. He wrote that her own performance was "beautiful and moving, for she is a rare personality and fills great spaces of the somber hall with the consciousness that here is a living, dynamic presence" (*New York Times,* July 20, 1930).

∾

Mary Wigman • Dresden-Neustadt • Bautzner Strasse 107

Kölpinsee[1]

undated (II)
[context implies late summer, 1931]

Dearest Hanya,

The picture looks like sun and vacation, doesn't it? But the same thing happened to us in our exile as happened to you. Rain, storms, cold. Too bad! The stove burns day in, day out. But what good does it do to complain? I have promised myself to endure, although there are times I would gladly leave, when the wind blows every morning and melancholy gray lies over the landscape.

Even going for drives is no fun in this weather; I do not have the courage to venture out onto the life-threatening sand-roads, which turn into mud puddles in the rain. The mud sprays over the roof, and no amount of steering can hold the car on the road. The only place we can drive is back and forth on the Chaussee.[2]

Nevertheless, the days race by; I don't know how. I am going to great pains to relax nerves and body, and I go for walks in the woods since we cannot go on the beach due to the wetness. So I am basically in good shape.

Hopefully your knee has become well again. These treacherous things![3]

Is Hasting back? If so, he should immediately write to Hurok, and remind him of your contracts! As well as the money for your trip!

A discreet question: Do you find it necessary that in Schwinghammer's contract there is a clause which forbids him work other than that in the school or assigned by you? This question brought to my attention by Hasting because of the "fee requests" from the examinees for compositions, etc.[4]

The thought that you are leaving us already is amazing, Hanuschka![5] But how nice that we will see each other again soon over there. That will help make the departure easier for you, too, won't it? And besides, you have a wonderful, interesting job ahead of you, for which, God knows, it is worth working.

Until then, my dear! And in the meantime the warmest greetings

from your
Mary

1. Kölpinsee is a Baltic Sea resort town.
2. Wigman appreciated good automobiles and liked driving.
3. Upon entering a cold studio one early morning in Dresden, Holm had thrown herself into a back-arching jump. Her knees locked, and she fell onto them, causing an injury that plagued her throughout her career (Kloepper 1976).
4. This passage provides evidence that the New York Wigman School was modeled on Wigman's German schools in expecting dancers working toward a certificate to pass examinations. Students were required to present original dances, which they would have had to rehearse with an accompanist, in this case, Victor Schwinghammer, who came with Holm from Germany. Students would have paid him for his time. Wigman and Holm had expected that New York students would travel to Dresden for their final months of training, take their exams there, and, if worthy, receive their certificates from Wigman herself, but this plan was dropped when the National Socialists came to power in January 1933 (Dudley 1996).
5. An invented diminutive of Hanya that Wigman sometimes spelled Hanyuschka.

❧

Mary Wigman • Dresden-Neustadt • Bautzner Strasse 107

Agreement
  Between

Mary Wigman as giver of the name of the Wigman School New York and Hanya Holm as principal teacher, responsible for the artistic and pedagogic work.

M.W. guarantees H. Holm 10% of the proceeds that will accrue to Mary Wigman (according to the contract with Mr. Hurok). These 10% will be calculated at the end of the school year, considering the total sum received. The amount will be personally paid by M.W. to H. Holm after payment to M.W. of her share of the profits.

H. Holm, for her part, promises to apply all her strength to the advancement of the New York Wigman School, to conduct the work according to Mary Wigman's ideas and those of the Central Institute in Dresden, and to see that the M.W. philosophy of dance is implemented faithfully within and outside the New York Wigman School in every possible way. She takes on the supervision in our stead of the work of her co-workers who will assist in this endeavor.

Dresden, September 12, 1931 (I)
Mary Wigman
Hanya Holm

Staff of the New York Wigman School clowning at a Christmas party in New York City, 1931. From left: Hanns Hasting, wearing Sol Hurok's hat; Gretl Curth, balancing a piece of fruit on her head; Fé Alf; Hanya Holm; Mary Wigman; and Sol Hurok, wearing Wigman's scarf. Gift of Louise Kloepper. Courtesy Jerome Robbins Dance Division, The New York Public Library for the Performing Arts, Astor, Lenox and Tilden Foundations.

⌒◡

Mary Wigman • Dresden-Neustadt • Bautzner Strasse 107

undated (II)
[context implies October 1931]

Dearest Hanya,

Fee's departure is so rushed that I cannot give her a lengthy greeting for you.[1] Breathe deeply, Hanuschka; that helps with tempo and nervousness. In 3 weeks you will be laughing over the "beginning of the USA tour!"

Your letter just came this morning. How well I understand the uneasiness! Do not let anything get to you. Things are not as bad as they seem! Actually it is quite lovely!

Here: Work craziness — last-minute rush! Nov. 1 matinee at the Schauspielhaus Dresden. Nov. 4 Hamburg. Nov. 11 Cherbourg. Nov. 15th or 16th New York! Hurrah.

Loving, tender greetings and a kiss as well!

Your

Mary

1. Fé Alf (née Felicitas Ahlff) lived from 1910 to 1996. Wigman consistently wrote her name with a double *e*, but during a long career in the United States the dancer was known as Fé. Alf broke with Holm after one year and opened her own studio, where she taught into the 1950s. She was in sympathy with politically radical New York artists in the 1930s and performed in concerts of the Workers Dance League and the New Dance League (Graff 1997:177).

1932

THE UNITED STATES

The success of Wigman's first appearances in the United States during the winter of 1930–31 dictated a second tour. Hurok booked her into theaters in the Midwest and West after performances in the East. Some audiences were uncomprehending, but it would be difficult to exaggerate Wigman's general success. Reports of frenzied appreciation and bulging theaters were common. Critics referred to her dances as amazing and beautiful and, approvingly, as horrifying and elemental.

The tour took her on a zigzag path through the Midwest and on to a West Coast debut at the Tivoli Theater in San Francisco, California. Then she danced in theaters from Seattle, Washington, in the north, to San Diego, California, in the south, sometimes doubling back for repeat performances. She continued through the Southwest and then went north to dance in Missouri, Wisconsin, Illinois, and Ohio. During her tour Wigman wrote to Holm in New York as she piloted the Wigman School through its first season. It was a difficult year for Holm, yet by June she had decided to stick with it, and she returned to Germany to seek the necessary papers and make arrangements for the continuing care of her son.

~

Congress Hotel & Annex
Chicago

January 16, 1932 (I)

Dearest Hanya,

Please see to it that a prospectus of the New York School is
sent to the following address: Miss Zervas, 312 Ninth St. North,
Moorhead, Minnesota.

Where is a decent report from the school? The school has been
open for three and a half months and not a *single* report about the
work, the students, the teachers, has arrived.

Dresden is complaining about this. Please sit down at once and
produce one. All right? And then regularly each month!

Are you keeping your fingers crossed today? Since being in New
York I have not danced "Das Opfer" again.[1] So far the performances
have been beautiful, but the strain is brutish because of the huge
distances.

Detroit, Cincinnati, will again be murderous in terms of energy.
A night trip between two performances on the 18th and the 19th:
train, hotel, theater, that's it! Yet, we are in good spirits. In Los
Angeles there is snow now. This ardently desired climate could be
winter instead of summer, and this within fourteen days! Just
imagine.

Last night Sol Hurok surprised us and we had a nice dinner with
him. He talked about the school in a positive way.[2] I liked that
because from his words I gathered that there is stronger contact
and an IMPROVEMENT on all sides. So, GO ON, DEAR!!

What's the matter with Fee? She sent me a desperate letter. I
guess you had talked to her about the work because she said
something like "Hanya, Mary, and Gretl are tying my hands and
feet."[3] Maybe you haven't found the right tone in talking with her,
Hanuschka, or the wrong moment. This can happen, and is not
tragic. I am just letting you know so you can also show people the
positive side of their work and support them after they have heard
the negative.[4]

It would be sad if something would go wrong here. Fee is a
valuable exemplar of our work, maybe a little too young to be sober
in all things. At any rate, I wrote her a long letter and tried to

clarify her situation. When she understands the meaning and spirit of my letter, everything will be all right.

How are you, Hanuschka? Is the work a little easier now? Are you getting used to the situation? Have you good news from Kläuschen? Send a line, ALL RIGHT?

For today, the most beautiful regards for you

With a kiss
from your
Mary

Students of the New York Wigman School of the Dance on the roof of Steinway Hall, New York City, 1932. Courtesy Jerome Robbins Dance Division, The New York Public Library for the Performing Arts, Astor, Lenox and Tilden Foundations.

1. The dance cycle *Sacrifice* formed the core of Wigman's programs. She had premiered it on November 1, 1931, shortly before departing for the United States. A Boston audience received it coolly, but the dance and music critic H. T. Parker praised it, asking, "Who else in the dance works upon such lofty planes; in such exalted imagination; to cosmic ideas and emotions gives such intimations of projection?" He concluded his review: "Beside Stravinsky's "Sacre" set Wigman's "Opfer" (*Boston Evening Transcript*, December 4, 1931). New York audiences shouted their pleasure. Martin called *Opfer* "a magnificent achievement." He described each of its six sections, "Song of the Sword," "Dance for the Sun," "Death Call," "Dance for the Earth," "Lament," and "Dance into Death," lingering over the fourth: "It is grotesque . . . a personification of all things that grow out of the earth or that move close to it" (*New York Times*, December 11, 1931).

2. Hurok had installed the only school in the United States authorized to teach the Mary Wigman method in Steinway Hall at 113 West 57th Street in Manhattan. Wigman herself was supervisor, Holm was chief teacher; Alf, associate teacher; Hasting, musical director; and Schwinghammer, accompanist. Hurok's commitment was for one year, so Wigman and Holm knew that his backing was temporary. Throughout Wigman's tour she was seeking another backer for the school (Kloepper 1996b).

3. "Gretl" was Gretl Schwiengh, secretary of the school.

4. Students say that disagreements between Holm and Alf were never apparent, but they register no surprise that conflict arose. They portray Alf as a strong, confident woman who would not agree to work in the shadow of Holm (Stein 1996; Dudley 1996).

❧

Hotel Benson
Portland, Oregon

February 1, 1932 (I)

Dear Trio,

Out of the southern spring warmth into the northern winter
snow.
The following song is to be sung with melancholy and feeling.

From the hot desert
Into the cold winter snow,
Beautiful California
My heart is hurting.

Sad is the heart
And so tired, oh the gut.
Only when dancing on the stage
Are inside and outside warm.

And so travel, travel, travel,
We through this huge country.
We have no time, and everything
Remains unknown to us.

Interviews, receptions,
Dinners, luncheons, teas, by God!
In general that is
Really our biggest misery.

Don't be discouraged!
Keep your head up, hurrah!
After all there are six of us.[1]
Now here comes America.

Oh! To Schwinghammer a thousand thanks for the photos. Aren't
they delightful? I am so pleased with them.
To all three of you most cordial regards!

Your
Mary

1. To Holm, Alf, and Schwinghammer in New York, Wigman adds herself and her two accompanists, Hasting and Gretl Curth, who had taken Menz's place as percussionist.

∾

Hotel Benson
Portland, Oregon
undated (I)

Dearest Hanya, cordial regards.

The elastic band is to be worn for putting makeup on, etc. Practical!
Dead tired. Constantly sleeping cars. Again, snow.
How are you, the school?

One thousand dear regards!
Mary

∾

CASCADE
Southern Pacific Railroad

February 8, 1932 (I)

During a 50-hour train trip from Spokane to Santa Barbara. *CASCADE* is the name of our train.

Dearest Hanya,

Thanks for your letter. I wonder if another of your letters has been lost. I did receive the one with the New York School report. This travel life is so terribly trying that not even letter writing is easy. One is numb. After the performance, to bed at one-thirty at night, out of bed at six in the morning, and then two days and two nights on the train. In the morning, arrival dead tired, finished, then reporters, and so forth, and in the evening, a performance.
Yet we are traveling through the most wonderful country. We see the sun rise and set, desert, rocky snowy mountains, glaciers, lakes, the ocean, palms, orange groves.
It drives you mad not to be able to smell the air.
I'll be glad if I survive this.
About the English summer school: I received a letter from the lady, Lobel, but can hardly read it, it's so scribbled.[1] A pity that they do not want Leslie.[2] Still — if the thing would pay off I

would favor the idea of sending someone from Germany. If Elisabeth does not take it on herself, I'd propose Trude Engelhart, after asking her first, of course.[3]

As to the Wallmann case — the trial is going on in Dresden. Wallmann is pressing for a settlement because her lawyer wants to resign as he has not yet received a penny from her. Trude has been fired, and W. is said to be treating her very badly.[4] So it seems to me that to get Trude a task for the summer would be a good idea, one that pushes her a little with work. Last year was hell for her! At any rate, I have telegraphed Dresden concerning this, and also sent a telegram to Lobel saying that a final decision can only be made after getting an answer from Germany. Naturally, I have nothing against Fee and the idea of her taking it over. But the above reasons are sound, I think!

Margaret Gage wrote to me very enthusiastically about the demonstration, Hanuschka![5] You were going to send me your lecture!? I have not received it. Perhaps it's lost?

I am going to ask Mr. Goode to send Hasting an exact accounting of the school.[6] Goode writes to me very optimistically about the school, and from your letter I learn that the work is a considerable success. I would like to point out to the office that the cut in salaries is no longer necessary, but I can only do it when I see black on white, when I can prove with figures that the school is able to carry through with the salaries that were originally agreed to, plus meet the expenses and pay off the investment. So please see to it that we are sent a careful accounting, all right?

Have you received my letter with the elastic band?

I am so glad that you are going to Bennett and to Vassar. The people there, Kennedys, M. Gage, and at Vassar Miss Flanagan, are charming.[7]

I would love to tell you about Seattle: Cornish School is exemplary, I tell you![8] American in every detail. But very seriously, a beautiful work environment!

Lore Deja: a chapter in itself![9] Thin, pale, melancholic, working well with a group. A beginner, naturally. Difficult, a very difficult situation, but positive. Lore has almost forgotten how to speak German. She hasn't heard one German word since she was here. It was not easy for her and when I left she broke down completely. — [illegible sentence]

The summer course, New York, also depends on your permit to stay. Please, make an effort. I mean if you want to take on the course yourself all measures have to be taken so that you will have no difficulties!!!! This is not so easy. It has to be done very thoroughly from the OFFICE. Otherwise I would propose Louise Kloepper. She doesn't have a lot to do and I am not happy about that. She is too close to the Cornish School and she cannot succeed as a private teacher against it alone.[10]

I can't go on. The train is rocking along the Sacramento River Canyon. Early today we were a few thousand meters high. The ears roar, the head is numb.

Addio, dear Hanya,

All my love!

Mary

1. Sali Lobel was a British teacher and organizer of the First International Summer School of Dance in Buxton, England, July 25 to August 20, 1932.

2. Leslie Burrowes, the first British woman to train with Wigman, established a studio in England in 1933 and was the best-known promoter of German dance in England. She married Leon Goossens of the prominent musical family.

3. Gertrude Engelhart (1892–1989) danced in the first Wigman group and was an assistant teacher at the Dresden and Berlin Wigman schools. In 1936 she immigrated to Sweden, where she continued to teach, joining the staff of Birgit Culberg's Swedish Dance Theatre in 1946.

4. Licenses to teach and certifications were jealously guarded in Germany at this time, and the dispute was probably about an alleged violation of one of these (Kloepper 1996b).

5. In the 1920s Margaret Gage had studied with Florence Fleming Noyse, the Duncan girls, and with Elizabeth Selden at the Bennett School of Liberal and Applied Arts in Millbrook, New York. Gage then taught at Bennett and choreographed and performed in the annual Greek Drama Festival. She became enthralled with Wigman upon seeing her perform and meeting her on her first tour of the United States. Gage and Gage's mother bought the New York Wigman School from the Hurok organization in 1932, "so that Hanya Holm's important work could continue" (Gage 1979). Gage helped Holm financially in other ways, especially in bringing her son from Germany in 1936, and she gave Wigman financial support from the end of World War II until her death in 1973.

6. Gerald Goode headed the publicity department for the Sol Hurok organization. He had seen Wigman concerts in Germany in 1930 and became a fan. He managed her publicity for Hurok and continued to work for the impresario for fifteen years, contributing to many negotiations and publicity campaigns.

7. The English playwright and classical scholar Charles Rann Kennedy and his wife, the actress Edith Wynne Matthison, staged Greek drama at the Bennett School. The playwright, educator, and administrator Hallie Flanagan ran a

successful experimental theater program at Vassar College in Poughkeepsie, New York. In 1935 President Franklin D. Roosevelt appointed her director of the Federal Theatre Project of the Works Projects Administration; she ably administered the theater project until its demise in 1939. She then returned to Vassar and later taught at Smith College in Massachusetts.

8. The Cornish School of Applied Arts, founded by Nellie Centennial Cornish in Seattle in 1914, was a major center for training in music, drama, and painting. Ballet was added to its curriculum in 1916 and modern dance in 1921.

9. Lore Deja, who had trained with Wigman in Germany, began teaching at the Cornish School in 1931. West Coast journalists noted her use of elements of German modern dance, such as masks and percussion accompaniment (*Theatre Arts*, July 1931, p. 531, and April 1932, p. 267).

10. When Kloepper (1910–1996) returned to the United States after two years of study with Wigman and Holm in Germany, she tried to run her own school in Tacoma, Washington. Upon Wigman's suggestion she taught the summer session at the New York Wigman School in 1932 and then became Holm's chief assistant. Kloepper was known for the beauty of her dancing, her conscientious teaching, and a gentle, self-effacing manner. In 1942 she left Holm and began studies with Margaret H'Doubler at the University of Wisconsin, Madison, then stayed on at the university, where she eventually achieved professorial rank and became head of the Dance Program.

∽

Santa Barbara Biltmore

February 10, 1932 (I)

Dearest Hanya!

We are sending a parcel with unnecessary dead weight to your address. Please keep it for me, won't you? Last night we had number 31 in a very small but charming theater. I was able to dance so especially well that even I was amazed. Then we had a four-hour delay (because of flooding) and we arrived here at 10:30 in the morning wracked. It rained in streams.

Potter is in bed with bad influenza.[1] That's why we are not leaving today, but tomorrow at the crack of dawn to Los Angeles for a huge convention of the Dance Teachers of America. For our tight schedule and work we are now being rewarded. The sun shines, I have had breakfast outside on the balcony, the ocean is roaring, the eucalyptus trees are whispering, the palm trees look wonderful against the blue sky, and toward the garage there is a long alley with high flowering mimosa trees. This Pacific location and the hotel are a dream. Not in Italy, not in the south of France, can I remember such a ravishing place. One day to breathe! It was desperately needed. I was at the end — the nerves couldn't take any more. Above all, the organism goes on strike with this sort of life, days and nights immobilized on the train, then to the stage, and on. It is terrible. Terrible also, is the constant change of climate. No one can endure this.

Dear, a fast kiss and a thousand dear regards

from your
Mary

1. Howard Potter was Wigman's road manager and treasurer for the Hurok organization. He had begged Hurok for the job after he saw Wigman perform in Newark, New Jersey, and was both repelled and attracted. He and Wigman remained correspondents for many years.

∾

Los Angeles Biltmore

February 29, 1932 (I)

Crazy days Hanuschka!

Sometimes I think I cannot survive this. But until now it has always worked out. Heavy flu epidemic in the company. Potter was so wretched that I was seriously concerned. Now he seems to be a little better. Gretl and Hasting are fighting, fighting the flu. Everybody is coughing. I don't want to talk about myself. I got over a sore throat and inflammation of the bladder in silence without complaining one word and I hope I have overcome it.

The fast changes of climate are awful! From ice to tropical climate in the theaters.

Thank you for your dear letter. We received a detailed telegram from Dresden about the summer course in England. The letters of Miss L (I have *not* met her personally!) are so vague and so boastful without telling anything about the subject or the organization, that I really think we should abandon the idea. At any rate, I have telegraphed her that the teachers are needed to teach in Dresden and New York, and therefore participation in England is really not possible. I thought that when I am performing in London we can still sit down and talk and if necessary we can still send someone else.

Dear, I am three-quarters dead! Last night in San Diego we
arrived midday, danced in the evening, and this morning had to
leave early. We had a beautiful drive by car along the ocean and
mile-wide orange groves. At 2:30 we arrived in Los Angeles without
lunch, immediately changed, and at 3:30 sharp, back into the car to
Hollywood for publicity. The studios had to be seen. Disgusting
profession, the filming. We saw a few takes and of course I had to
pose with Novarro.[1] Oh hum! (Naja!)

The performances were wonderful here.

Murderous, the whole thing. The tour is not being put together
responsibly. I mean that at no point was it considered that the
so-called artist is a human being who has a body. And in the
special case when the human being is a dancer, and the body is
its one and only, it makes it much worse. You know, the nights
sleeping on the train don't bring a quiet sleep. The constant sitting
in the compartment or in the cars makes every function lame. The
guts are on strike. The irregularity of life (to eat at night at 12:30)
is devastating. In addition: one can *never* sleep in. After the
performance (when I am in bed at 2:00 or 3:00) out of bed at
6:00 or even earlier. But still there are moments when you forget
all of this. Like the first night in San Francisco or the first in Los
Angeles. Both *so beautiful*! And stolen moments like a view of
Los Angeles from a hill, a car drive through, over, and around San
Francisco with the German consul general. Unforgettable!

Dear, goodnight.

Keep your chin up, and also remember to relax, so the swelling
in your glands will go down, all right?

Many, many regards to Fee and to Schwinghammer.

You yourself I kiss very cordially,
your
Mary

The accounting from Goode has not yet arrived!

1. The romantic leading man Ramón Novarro was making the film *Mata Hari*
when Wigman visited (Forster).

꙳

[Picture postcard showing a field of blue flowers and titled "'Blue Bonnets,' The State Flower of Texas"]

undated[1] (I)

This is how the country is supposed to look in the spring! Instead: the rain pours into the gutters. And instead of COW-BOYS, SHOE-BOYS. The whole hotel is full of Shoe-Fritzes. THEY COME FROM ALL OVER THE COUNTRY!

Children, three days of holiday rain, cold, stupidity, no peace and quiet, radio, drunken sluts, and so on. Brrr!!!

Today when we have to work, the sun is shining and it is almost southern. Enough to make one sick!

Anyway, many dear regards to you three!

Your

Mary

1. Holm saved this postcard between letters of 1936, but it was probably written in 1932 from Houston, where it rained. See next letter.

꙳

The Galvez
Galveston, Texas

March 4, 1932 (I)

Dear Faculty,

One and a half days to breathe. Therefore the Wigman COMPANY got on the STREETCAR in Houston, pale and shot, and rode to the Gulf of Mexico where breakers are accompanying these lines. It's really summer and each action is accompanied by little sparkling drops of sweat that the sun and the humid heat bring out of the pores. But this is nothing. You should have seen me during the performance in Houston. Outdoors there was a thunderstorm, and maybe because she was announced as HIGH PRIESTESS OF THE DANCE, M. W. was allied with nature, so indoors it rained as much as the dark skies outside.[1] Water collected in the navel and had to be drained after each dance. Makeup floated, and out of the flying curls, when she did "Monotonie," sparkling drops whirled through the air; the whole an absolutely humid thing.[2] With all of this, the dancing, naturally, went like butter.

It is almost frightening to be away from the street noise and the city hotels and to hear the roaring of the breakers. We are at a resort in the United States style, but out of season, and therefore cheap and shabby.

Thank you for the school report, which has given me a special pleasure this time. The pertinent part is short and clear and gives a good overview. And then I welcome the appendix that will be especially instructive for the Germans because it shows something of the background of the American dancers. Beautiful work!!

Meanwhile, has the summer course question been cleared up? I mean the story with the permit? Has Hanya talked with the OFFICE and headquarters about the financial solution? This must be done in time. And you must not expect us to do it. We can do damn little from far away. Not even the regulation of our own tour finances can be completely clarified. Besides, this life on tour is so desperately trying that you need all your energy to endure it and one is happy to get through each day. By the way, we have received financial statements about the school. The accounting cannot be completely checked because receipts that should belong to it, naturally, could not be sent. (It will be checkable only after our return.) But the general picture is pretty bad: it is a deficit. To be honest, under these circumstances I really cannot propose a raise in salaries. I am proposing to you, if it hasn't happened yet, to arrange a business conference. Depending on the "political" state, either Hanya alone or all of you, so you are able to get a clearer picture of the situation.

What I miss a little bit is, once in a while, when there is news from you, a more positive *yes* about the work in New York. Work is probably *always* effort and exhaustion, I think, but does it always have to be accompanied by groans? I would like to receive an energy-loaded letter, with the *joy* of work jumping out of it. Until now it has been only complaints, annoyances, dissatisfaction, etc.

Zum Donnerwetter![3] There you are, protected and secure in a fascinating country with a task that is in general positive and, god knows, rewarding. Why are you not beaming? Because you have debts at home and responsibilities? In the end, this is your private problem. It *must* not concern me.

Why, for example, is Fee angry at Mr. Hoerisch and about the attitude of the Dresden school toward the English summer school?[4] Hanya's own communication to me is pretty much negative. When Fee has such a burning interest in this course and would like to go to England, why doesn't she write it clearly? After all there is a difference if someone takes this on as her own responsibility or if a school as an institution does it. Then a contract of basic conditions would be necessary. The vague phrases of Miss Lobel are surely not quite enough, and are forcing the organization to be somewhat careful.

Also, let's not quite forget, New York as well as Dresden must carry through their summer courses because they are necessary for the schools' existence and not a luxury. A third official course in England would mean damage to the New York as well as the Dresden side!

It is not always possible to do justice to the interests of each individual. In such cases *the larger picture* has to be foremost. In the case of England, the interests of the schools in New York and Dresden seem to be most important.[5]

As we will be in London in the beginning of May, we will try to inform ourselves on the spot about the story and if it is worth it we can still attend to it.[6]

And now my dears, the end. After all I am here to take a rest and I am supposed to go out into the air!

My most beautiful greetings from all my heart and wishes to all three of you!

Your

Mary

1. Referring to Wigman as "High priestess of the dance" was a publicity ploy of Hurok's that he credited with securing Wigman's abundant press coverage and large audiences.

2. *Monotonie* was a whirling dance that Wigman often presented in her solo concerts; it was from the 1928 group work *Celebration* (Die Feier).

3. Zum Donnerwetter, literally "thunderweather," is a mild curse used with an admonition. One English translation would be "for God's sake!"

4. Werner Hoerisch was business manager for the Wigman schools.

5. Eventually, Lobel did schedule Burrowes to teach the Wigman method at the First Annual International Summer School. Lobel may have objected to Burrowes because she was English, not German. The festival was an ambitious one; Lobel engaged teachers of many nationalities and dance genres and scheduled performances and lectures. In June 1932 *Dancing Times* reported that enrollments for the course were "coming in slowly but steadily" (p. 265), but in September the journal lamented that the course had "not, unfortunately, met with the success it deserved" (p. 567). There was no course the following year.

6. Wigman gave three matinee performances in London at the Globe Theatre on May 10, 13, and 17, 1932.

PROGRAM

TANZCYKLUS "OPFER"
   (Dance Cycle, "Sacrifice") (New)
   1. Schwertlied (Song of the Sword)
   2. Tanz fuer die Sonne (Dance for the Sun)
   3. Todesruf (Death Call)
   4. Tanz fuer die Erde (Dance for the Earth)
   5. Klage (Lament)
   6. Tanz in den Tod (Dance Into Death)

INTERMISSION—FIFTEEN MINUTES

AUS DEM TANZCKYLUS "SCHWINGENDE LANDSCHAFT"
   (From the Dance Cycle, "Shifting Landscape")
   7. Sommerlicher Tanz (Summer's Dance) (By special request)

AUS DER SUITE NACH SPANISCHEN LIEDERN UND RHYTHMEN
   (From the suite based on Spanish Songs and Rhythms)
   8. Allegro Arioso

*   *   *

   9. A la Polonaise (New)
   10. Rondo (New)

Music for Numbers 1 to 6, 7, 9 and 10 by HANNS HASTING
Musical Accompaniment . . . . HANNS HASTING
Percussion Instruments . . . . . GRETL CURTH

Costumes by Elis Griebel, Dresden

(Steinway Piano furnished by Jenkins Music Company)

WIGMAN SCHOOL OF THE DANCE
New York City—113 West 57th Street
Dresden, Germany—107 Bautzner Strasse (Central Institute)
Direction: Mary Wigman, Elizabeth Wigman, Hanya Holm
Courses for Amateurs, Beginners, Professionals

Exclusive Management—Hurok Musical Bureau—New York City

Kellogg-Baxter Printing Company
301 Admiral Blvd., Kansas City, Mo.

Program of Mary Wigman concert, Kansas City, Missouri, March 15, 1932.
Gift of Louise Kloepper. Courtesy Jerome Robbins Dance Division, The
New York Public Library for the Performing Arts, Astor, Lenox and Tilden
Foundations.

∽

At the end of her tour and before embarking for Europe, Wigman spent two weeks in New York and taught classes for the regularly enrolled students of the New York Wigman School. She apparently continued to mediate the dispute between Holm and Alf, calling it an "ugly mess" in her diary (Forster).

Congress Hotel
and Annex
Chicago

March 20, 1932 (I)

Dearest Hanya,

I know your birthday is in March. I think the solemn moment was the third, wasn't it? My birthday booklet is in Dresden on my desk, alas. Don't be angry if I am late with congratulations. The times were too hard to be able to have any thoughts besides the most necessary for the day. I was going to get you something exotic. Impossible. As the situation was, there was never a moment for anything like shopping. And here it's not much fun because in New York there are more beautiful things. Therefore, the enclosed check with my most heartfelt wishes and entreaties to get something for yourself that you like. I wish New York were closer and I could spend Easter there with you. But the excursion is too far and too expensive for me, as the tour will go on in these Midwest regions.

With a late but no less heartfelt birthday kiss,

I am your
Mary

1932–1935

DRESDEN

Letters rich in detail carry us through a period during which Holm established herself as a leader in American dance and that continues to cast up conflicting judgments of Wigman. The crux of their situations occurred in 1936, when the New York Wigman School of Dance became the Hanya Holm Studio, and the Nazis appropriated the modern dance movement that Wigman had led.

Holm received just two letters from Wigman between her second tour of the United States, in 1931–32, and her third tour, in the winter of 1932–33, for Holm was in Germany during the summer of 1932. In a brief note to Howard Potter dated November 8, 1932, Wigman wrote, "No one knows what shall happen to our country. Madness and helplessness everywhere" (among Holm's personal photographs, Jerome Robbins Dance Division, The New York Public Library). The author Horst Koegler records 1932 as a year in which political deterioration in Germany accelerated: "Strikes, mass-unemployment, bankruptcies, assassinations became everyday occurrences" (1974:27). Adolf Hitler's promises of a return to order and decency offered hope to a terrified middle class. The financial situation of dance professionals was desperate.

No letters from Wigman during her third U.S. tour survive. Undoubtedly, she had her hands full with a newly formed group. Audiences in the United States were disappointed with her group choreography, and Wigman performed solos in some concerts. The Wigman mystique survived; in a deeply felt review in the *Oakland Tribune* on January 18, 1933, Ronald Scofield wrote, "The audience did more than marvel, they shouted and cheered with enthusiasm that is seldom evoked by anything except a superb performance of grand opera."

When Wigman returned from her third U.S tour, Hitler was chancellor of Germany. She was anxiously aware of drastic political change, to which she referred as a "revolution" in her diary entry of March 10, 1933. An April entry recounts that her school was searched and she was interrogated by the government on suspicion of Communist sympathy (Forster). Non-Aryan artists, musicians, and writers were being denied employment or were forced to resign their positions. Many artists emigrated. Wigman, Gret Palucca, and Berthe Trümpy were among the dancers who stayed in Germany, affiliating their schools with the National Socialist Teachers Organization and the Group for German Culture and complying with directives of the Third Reich. In a letter to Pola Nirenska dated February 18, 1951 (appendix 3), Wigman would remind her correspondent that all artists joined these organizations, that they had to do so to survive.

Holm was invited to teach at the embryonic modern dance institutions in the United States, first at the Perry-Mansfield Camp in Steamboat Springs, Colorado, then at Mills College in Oakland, California, and, in 1934, at the Bennington School of the Dance in Vermont. Her invitation to be one of the artists around whose teaching Bennington organized its summer program secured her position alongside Martha Graham, Doris Humphrey, and Charles Weidman as one of the "Big Four" of American modern dance. Founders of the Bennington School considered Holm a significant force in the New York dance community and wanted to help her dispel anti-German feelings that were beginning to plague her (Schönberg 1996). Sali Ann Kriegsman hints that another motive for inviting Holm was to counter competition from Wigman's teaching in Europe (1981:10). The dancer May O'Donnell also hints at this motivation in an interview by Tobi Tobias (1981:86).

In her first five years in the United States, Holm dedicated herself to presenting the Group of the Mary Wigman School of Dance in lecture-demonstrations, which she titled "Demonstration of the German Dance," and she published an essay, "The German Dance in the American Scene" (1935:79–86). Holm's connection to German dance was becoming a liability, however. One social activist, the Jewish dancer

Mimi Kagan Kim, who later became a member of the Hanya Holm Company, spoke for many when she said, "It just was not possible to study [at Wigman's school] when it was connected to fascist Germany" (Kim 1995). Edna Ocko, the influential dance reviewer for leftist New York newspapers and journals, said, "Nobody accused Hanya of being a Nazi, but her loyalties were divided. She was in a difficult situation" (Ocko 1996).

Holm faced other challenges. German dance training emphasized individual artistic development gained through guided exploration and discovery, but Holm found that dancers in New York were interested in mastering the personal styles of American modern dance masters. Jane Dudley, one of Holm's first students, said, "After a while I realized that Hanya was not making me the dancer I wanted to become" (Dudley 1996). Although Dudley remained grateful for her study with Holm, she enrolled in Martha Graham's school and became a member of Graham's company. Referring to political and pedagogical challenges that Holm faced during her first years in New York, her assistant teacher, Louise Kloepper, said, "Hanya had her back against the wall" (1996a).

∾

Mary Wigman • Dresden-Neustadt • Bautzner Strasse 107

August 19, 1932 (I)
[dated by Holm]

Dear Hanuschka!

Many regards! What does it look like steamship-wise, etc.? I enclose a few photos. Besides Louise Kl's report, which I sent to Hoerisch, there is no news from over there. However, I have received another letter that's a little crazy from Fee Alf. Noble, self-concerned phrases and a vague remark that she may have to teach to make a living.

Meanwhile, a thousand dear regards,

from your
Mary

⌒

Mary Wigman • Dresden-Neustadt • Bautzner Strasse 107

October 2 (II)
[Context implies 1932]

Dearest Hanya,

Every day I think about whether everything is well with you and how you feel in the city of stone. Sometimes I would like to be a little gray mouse, looking on unseen and listening in to what goes on in the school, what kind of people you meet, etc.

My God, time flies so ridiculously fast! Night after night the gongs in the Yellow Studio drone and the xylophone screams, so that a person's nerves fray, the knees wobble, the fat melts.[1] Three new dances composed, but not yet danceable! Just as England abolished the gold standard, I would like to be able to abolish the time standard!

Loving, affectionate greetings for you! Greetings also from Schwinghammer, Goode, Mr. Hurok and everyone else who is around here.

Fee Alf is here. Nice, refreshed, healthy.

Send a line about how you are doing!

Your

Mary

1. When Wigman's school and residence were remodeled in 1927, an additional building was erected in the garden. The building contained two small studios and a large hall, der Gelbe Saal. Much of the remodeling cost was borne by friends from abroad. The city of Dresden, the state of Saxony, and the national government also contributed (Forster). Contributions from Jews later raised suspicions about Wigman in the Nazi regime (Müller 1983:12).

⌒

Mary Wigman • Dresden-Neustadt • Bautzner Strasse 107

July 31, 1933 (I)
[question mark penciled in by Holm]

My dear Hanya!

The activity of the past weeks, through the end of term of the professional school, the conference, summer course, plus all the organizational things that came about through changes in the law and the intervention of the professional organizations, has eaten us all up. In addition, Elisabeth is not yet able to work fully and for fourteen days has been at the Erzgebirge [Mountains] for further recovery.

I have asked Hoerisch to send you the facts about the program of the conference and want to tell you personally a little more so you can get the general picture. We were a pretty diverse group of people and it was in no way easy to get these different people under one roof. Yet, these two weeks of collaboration can be looked at very positively, as the goal was completely fulfilled: making contact again, deepening it, and last but not least, renewing the courage and commitment of everybody.[1]

Leslie Burrowes was wonderful; from the human and the artistic point of view she matured a lot and became stable within herself. Her performance was a true, pure joy; not one sided, but versatile, and in that way, especially, she has grown tremendously.

Grown also, and especially toward the female side, was Ruth Boin, creatively very gifted and a talented performer. This was also a pleasure.

It was painful to see the outcome of Trümpy; as far as I am concerned, she is in a critical state. God knows what will come out of it. With the help of her phenomenal memory, and willpower that extends toward madness, she dances Vera Skoronel's solo dances besides some solo stuff of her own.[2] She has educated herself to an astonishingly detailed technique, but it does not *dance* in her, or out of her. Although she assured me she would not show these things in public, I'm afraid she will try anyway, and the damage that will come out of it for the dance is surely worse than if a little average talent tries out in public, for such a one cannot be held responsible in the same way that Trümpy really has to be responsible. She had actually just promised me that she would hold back in theoretical discussions, but she could not keep her mouth shut and the result was pretty much demoralizing.[3]

In short, she has not changed a bit. Her effect within a community that is not under her dictatorial force is basically catastrophic.

Hilde Loge is intelligent, silent, full of experience. She gave an excellent paper about the community-building power of dance. My own paper has not been copied yet, otherwise I would be sending it with this letter.

Hans Huber is sympathetic, trustworthy, and superior, especially in all the pedagogic and organizational things. It is a real pleasure to work with him!

With her mouth and brain, Hanna Münch is running her place in Chemnitz really well.

What is happening with the refresher course is fantastic. How bitterly necessary is such a review from time to time!

The summer course was quite well attended. Unfortunately, from the financial point of view nothing much may result. Fifty percent foreign students! Isn't that something — an English and a German course. Louise Kloepper arrived very nervous and tired, but is now in better condition and has left for Italy.

Hopefully you have recovered nicely in Bermuda, Hanuschka! I am pleased that you went there and wish I could do the same. And the New York summer course?

And then the camp work begins. Should I be jealous of your being in Colorado?[4]

Something goes through my mind often. (I already told Louise.) Couldn't you, with Tina [Flade], found something like a working collaborative? I don't like to think of that particular person with whom we have collaborated so long being so isolated. A structure must be found that shows cooperation for the world to see and does not include financial ties. Please sit down and find a solution to the matter. Tina's attitude has always been clean and very free, and I wish for all of us that her belonging to us can be expressed somehow.[5]

I was delighted with your last long letter dearest Hanya! Because for the very first time it contains complete, and positive, disclosure of your work over there. I'm asking you for the future to take comments from me very objectively and not make them into a personal reproach. This would be an unnecessary misunderstanding. Louise has told me about the work and I have asked her not only to write reports but also to send very short account-book excerpts that would enable me to get to know the financial situation of the school. By not knowing, I'm often in a painful situation toward Gage. It should simply not be that way. Therefore, I must insist on being informed about the figures.

A few days and — finally — I will be allowed to leave, too. The season was long and hard this year. On weekends there were organizational meetings and conferences in Berlin, so I can say that since September I have worked without interruption. Now it is high time for a drive into the "green," and of course I don't know where to go. Therefore, into the blue unknown in the Mercedes with Hesschen.[6]

Addio, my beloved. My most beautiful greetings and wishes,

your
Mary

1. The conference was Wigman's own gathering of teachers of her method. She had branch schools in Berlin, Hamburg, Erfurt, Frankfurt, Leipzig, Munich, Magdeburg, Freiburg, Riesa, and Chemnitz. Former students directed other private studios that used the Wigman method. The conference discussed how best to adjust teaching methods to new government regulations emphasizing the Germanness of German art (Koegler 1974:34).

2. Vera Skoronel, who went on to a brilliant performing career, was one of Wigman's early students. In 1926 she joined her fellow Swiss, Trümpy, in directing a school in Berlin. Skoronel was only twenty-six when she died in 1932.

3. Trümpy took an uncompromising stance against ballet, insisting that German modern dance alone was appropriate for German culture. Her writing has been called abusively confrontational (Preston-Dunlop and Lahusen 1990:4–5).

4. Holm taught at the Perry-Mansfield Camp, where many modern dance leaders taught in the 1930s. For Holm, it proved to be an important summer, as students followed her to Mills College the following summer and later to Bennington. Colorado friends and students, especially Martha Wilcox, were helpful in arranging for the successful debut of Holm's company in Denver in November 1936 and influenced the early success of her Summer Program of Instruction and Dance Production at Colorado College.

5. Holm and Flade worked out an alliance of sorts, alternating summer teaching at Mills College. Flade became director of the dance program at Mills in 1934 and held the position until 1938.

6. Anni Hess, always known by the diminutive Hesschen, had been Wigman's housekeeper since 1923; Hess had left her position as receptionist and maid-of-all-work in the house/practice of the psychiatrist Dr. Hans Prinzhorn, once Wigman's lover and her close friend until his death in 1933 (Forster). Hesschen remained with Wigman for fifty years.

∽

Berlin
November 28, 1933 (I)

My dear Hanya,

Your letter has just arrived and I want to send you a warm greeting very quickly. I'm very pleased that you have already recovered so well and I'm very convinced — when the last traces of the operation will have disappeared — that you will feel much stronger than in the last couple of years.[1] But you won't be careless, will you, and put something at risk by doing too much too early!?

I am writing as a poor invalid. The broken arm came out of the plaster cast yesterday; it has become a poor little child's arm with completely inorganic thick dead skin fastened to it. There is constant pain and daily massage treatment and careful, tentative movements. You go up the walls because of the pain, and two hours later you are nauseous from the exertion of enduring it. Well, I have no choice but to grind my teeth and I do what I can so I may dance, learn to dance, again. I must not think about the consequences of the accident. It happened after the first dance concert of this season, at the beginning of a tour through Germany (twenty performances) up to Christmas. They could not be made up because right away in January we were supposed to take off again, fourteen performances were already set.[2]

What does it help to complain? One has to go through with it! I try to do that with all my energy and stubbornness.

I haven't been to Dresden yet. I am being treated here by an excellent doctor. Hesschen is here for my special needs because I'm not allowed to move the broken arm yet and I'm pretty much helpless. Everybody sends cordial regards and best wishes for your recovery — Hesschen, Frau Renger, Hanns Benkert.[3]

In the meantime, my letter to Louise will have arrived. How I would love to be with you in your shared apartment![4]

A thousand dear regards to both of you and to you, dear Hanuschka, with most beautiful wishes for a good recovery,

from your
Mary

1. Holm's family believes that she had a hysterectomy in the fall of 1933 (Heidi Holm 1997). Hysterectomies were performed at this time to correct excessive bleeding (Tejani 1996). Holm had had a difficult delivery of Klaus in 1920 and suffered internal injuries, according to family members. One of Wigman's letters to Kloepper (appendix 2) suggests that the procedure was performed in California and that Holm was under the wing of Margaret Gage.

2. Wigman broke her arm after a performance on November 6, 1933, in Hamburg. When she resumed dancing in late January, rehearsals and performances were so painful that she sometimes cried. She endured in order to recruit students and keep her name before the public (Müller 1986:224).

3. Renger was Hanns Benkert's housekeeper.

4. Holm and Kloepper shared an apartment while the New York Wigman School was in Steinway Hall. When the school moved to West Eleventh Street and Waverly Place in the fall of 1935, Holm lived above the studio and Kloepper found her own apartment nearby.

∾

Mary Wigman • Dresden-Neustadt • Bautzner Strasse 107

January 20, 1934 (II)

My dear Hanya,

You will think I am faithless because I have not written for so long. The whole time I was under the sign of the "broken arm" and it was a singular torment. In the truest sense it was a time of pain, because the problem was not just the healing (that does what it has to do all on its own!) but rather the retraining of the broken arm for dance. I cannot describe the toll on my energy, patience, and concentration. Sometimes it seemed outright presumptuous of me to want to teach this helpless limb in 6 weeks for which the healthy arm needed 20 years. Yet it is incredible to observe how nature manages systematically to rebuild so as not to be left ravaged.

In eight days I am to return to the stage for the first time. Can you imagine how, in spite of the joy, it is a little stifling to my courage? That I will manage, I know! But I do not yet know how arm and hand will hold up to the continuous strain of the dance without the tender daily care that they have now. Twice daily Widmänchen comes to massage it and helps me faithfully with all the exercises. Hasting helps just as much with the training. Four times a day a heated bath. All of that will have to fall by the wayside for the upcoming rush, which resembles the USA tour. Often 3 or 4 evenings in different cities without a break. There is neither time nor opportunity for special attention. NEVER MIND! WE'LL GET THROUGH IT!

And you, my dear? Is everything back to normal? The strength back again? How often I wished we could be together, how often I wished you were here, working with us like before!

And yet I hope that all is going well for you over there, that you are happy to be there, and feel well.

Let us hear from you soon!

Greetings to Louise, to the students, also.
A loving kiss and countless happy greetings from

your
Mary

∽

Mary Wigman • Dresden-Neustadt • Bautzner Strasse 107

March 31, 1934 (II)

My dear Hanya,

How wonderful that another letter from you finally came. I have asked myself so many times how things are going for you and am happy to hear that you are healthy and back in form.

It was a little odd that this winter went by without a trip to the USA. After the past few winters we almost took it for granted. Well, instead of that came the broken arm in fall to keep me occupied — lame — for 3 months. It has now recovered, though there is still pain with movement and more than anything else, strength still has not completely returned. Can you imagine the unconfessed fear I had about returning to the stage? I did not know if the arm would stand the extended strain. And from one day to the next it had to go without the careful attention that Widmänchen had bestowed on it twice daily. The baths, exercises, knitting of washcloths, and playing ball — what wasn't done to increase the mobility. But we pulled it off! And well, at that. Twenty-nine evenings in 50 days! American tempo, but in a European environment, that is, no Mr. Potter, no Charlie Regan, no drawing room in a Pullman car, etc.[1] Success fantastic, financially tolerable, even acceptable, considering how things are here! We often ran around with our tongues hanging out, so to speak. But I managed, and that is good to feel and to know. On Easter Saturday it starts again: 7 evenings. Then comes the school with a thousand problems that just cannot be solved right away. And how next year will turn out, heaven only knows.

I was very happy to read in your letter that you are so sincerely and wholly ready for the work in New York. And it is wonderful that you have been offered a position at Mills College.[2] I was invited there myself but had to decline, naturally, since a summer trip simply could not be worked into the schedule.

Will you let me know sometime (in strictest confidence) about the economic situation of the school? Will everything work out without a loan? How is Louise? Please send her, and also the students, my best wishes.

I spent a few wonderful days in Würzburg with Hanns B. and Frau Renger. We drove through Franconia in gorgeous weather and were excited about all the cities, towns and villages, the castles and churches, the landscape of Main, the Spessart [mountain range], and LAST NOT LEAST: Bocksbeutel wine.

Now I have to use the Easter holidays for training. And my muscles twinge quite a bit!

I fear you will come at a time when I am not in Dresden! In any case I must remain here until mid-July, possibly even until the end of July. So August will have to be the month for vacation.

Do not let so much time go by again. As nice as such a long letter is, it is even nicer when they come more often, even if they are shorter. In my thoughts I take you in my arms with love and am

your

Mary

1. Charles Regan, who had worked with David Belasco for twenty years, stage-managed Wigman's concerts in the United States.

2. While Holm taught at Mills College, Nancy McKnight (Hauser) represented her at the first Bennington Summer School of the Dance. Holm arrived for the last week of the Bennington session to supervise a Demonstration of Technique from Modern German Dance by a group of selected students on August 10. Then she went directly to Europe, visiting Wigman in early September. From Europe Holm wrote a detailed business letter to Louise Kloepper (appendix 2) that reveals the difficulties she was having in showing a profit in the New York school.

ᧁ

May 29, 1934 (I)

Dearest Hanya,

It is beautiful that you have written so soon. And I am going to continue the good example and quickly tell you a little bit.

1. The Mary Wigman solo tour ended mid-April — fantastic success and fantastic press. This was good for the entire situation (of the dance) and also necessary for me.

2. The mayor of the city of Essen has actually offered me the directorship of dance of the Folkwang School.[1] I had to say no because I didn't want to leave my school alone, and also because they wanted, and needed, a very fast decision.

3. There were a lot of extra things to be done, Saturday an excellent lecture with (A-one) demonstrations in the Lessing School in Berlin. After the reviews were out, my publisher made me an offer. I will most probably accept. It will be a nice documentation of our method. The theme was natural movement as a base for dance.[2] The theme of the demonstration was the step, always taking off from the natural walk, enhanced through imagination (for example, feeling, direction in space) to become a dance step.

4. On the thirteenth of May there was a matinee at the Volksbühne — it was a memorial for Dr. Schikovski, and the fun was: Yvonne Georgi, Palucca and I danced one after the other.[3] It was a situation like in the old days, the early times of the group. Alice Uhlen and Erika Lindner from "ours" were there as well.

5. Our exams are being prepared. I give you the topics for the written theme:

1) Is maturing of the personality possible within education that emphasizes community, and what inner significance has physical education (education of the body)?

2) Describe the method of the Wigman School in relation to health, education, and from an artistic point of view. (The lecture given for information and public appreciation of Tanz Gymnastik.[4])

3) Discuss pyramid, temple, and cathedral as emblems/symbols of contrasting expressions of life.

4) Describe German dance as a building block for a new national, racial culture.[5]

6. At Easter my house was full of guests. Benkert, his mother, and Frau Renger — two dogs and a car. Benkert and Frau R. send their cordial regards.

7. Our old Mariechen is not with us anymore and instead a new small young Saxon girl. But Mariechen comes by often and enjoys her retirement.

8. A strange situation has just occurred here. The ballet is angry — young dancers often don't pass the theater exams. We talk about a general ballet-friendly attitude of the theaters. In the newspaper

there are fights, a lot of discussion is going on in the wings. In short, it's not nice, but necessary. Now we will see who has something to say!! We're holding out.

9. I have a spring cough and I am wheezing heavily. Recovery weeks in the Engadin are out of the question for this summer. Nobody has money for something like this here anymore. But I promise myself wonders from a little inhalator that I bought.

10. Hesschen says hello, she is happy and looks like eternal life.

11. Elisabeth says hello, too. I think she is in excellent shape. She often looks tremendous and is very lively.

12. The school is in high gear. All studios are occupied. (Examination — solo dances) Your two, Drusilla and Lucretia, are working well.[6] Drusilla is an exceptional talent. A wonderful worker, she has grown a lot as a dancer. Lucretia is pretty, nervous, very charming, and she makes a little less of an impression than does Drusilla; she is not quite as strong.

13. When I did the work for the demonstration my heart was really bleeding that I couldn't keep the five collaborators together to build a group with them. This would have been a group with hands and feet! Because the collaboration of the five (Drusilla, Gretl Curth, Gisela Sonntag, Annamarie Grashey, Ursel Breitig) was exemplary and far above dilettantism. Yella, who saw the thing in Berlin, was quite taken away.[7] It's a misery that the circumstances make such a group impossible!

Dearest Hanuschka I can't go on anymore. Therefore the end. How is Louise? I greet her very, very cordially. In my thoughts I embrace you affectionately.

Your

Mary

1. Wigman was offered the directorship of the Dance Department, Folkwang-schule, Essen, when Sigurd Leeder left with twenty-two students in April 1934 to follow Kurt Jooss into exile in England (Forster). Jooss had fled Germany with his company in 1933 rather than submit to Nazi directives to dismiss Jewish dancers and colleagues.

2. Neither Wigman nor Holm codified a movement vocabulary for use in their teaching and choreography. Dance writers recognized this as a distinguishing feature of Holm's work in the United States (Gitelman 2000:56).

3. Gret Palucca (1910–1993), who used only her last name for professional purposes, was an early student of Wigman's. She developed a virtuosic technique

and came to rival Wigman as a performer. She opened a school in Dresden in 1925 and toured solo and group programs. Although half Jewish, she managed to maintain a career under the fascists, who considered her an ambassador of German optimism because of the high-spirited cheerfulness of her dancing (Koegler 2001:233). Although she was finally banned from performing and saw her school taken over by deputies, she escaped the Holocaust. She taught in East Germany after the war and attracted students until her death.

4. In reminiscences written in the 1960s Wigman explained that Tanz Gymnastik was a natural system of rhythmic exercise that she had developed for amateur students in 1920 (1975:53).

5. Wigman used the word *völkisch,* a term in use from the fifteenth century that means "concerning the people." Nazi rhetoric appropriated it around 1920 to mean racially pure, Aryan, and not Jewish (Forster).

6. Drusilla Schroeder earned the Wigman certificate in 1933 and danced in the Wigman group in 1934 and 1935. She married the accompanist Victor Schwinghammer and remained in Germany (Forster). Lucretia Barzun returned to the United States and danced in the Group of the New York Wigman School, staying on when Holm changed the name of the group to her own in November 1936. Barzun composed music for Holm's 1935 *Primitive Rhythm.*

7. Yella Schirmer had been a classmate of Holm's at the Wigman School, and she performed in the first Wigman group.

∽

Mary Wigman • Dresden-Neustadt • Bautzner Strasse 107

undated[1] (I)

Dearest Hanya,

I have been looking at your canyon postcard quite jealously. It is wonderful for you to see these things.[2] I am curious how you like California and Mills College. Tell me about the work and the people there.

A short report from here:

Drusilla Schroeder and Lucretia Barzun have both passed the exam. Drusilla was really good, achieving the level for professional training. Lucretia was good, achieving the level for preparatory professional training.[3]

Drusilla has progressed beautifully, especially in artistic matters. Her solo work is wonderful, especially a short suite:

AMERICAN RHYTHMS

1. OF THE BIG PLAIN
2. OF THE FIRST PEOPLE masterful
3. OF THE WANDERING PROPHET ingenious!
4. THE SLAVES
5. OF THE BIG CITY

The two other works do not have quite the same stature, but important because they are a step into new areas! She is a wonderful worker in every respect. AND FIRST OF ALL: A REAL ARTIST!

Florence Gordon — you probably remember her — passed the exam, too. Gifted in her own way, she can create, compose, perform, etc. Unfortunately, there is a certain streak of inertia typical of her southern — Semitic — background. If she is constantly pushed it is okay. But if left to work on her own, she tends to take it easy and is overly self-indulgent.

In general the results of the exams are satisfying, especially the pedagogic results. *Without* exception all of them are able to teach amateurs soundly, freely, and on their own, verbally, and by doing!

It is crazy now. It is the end of the school year with conferences, final classes, performances, and so on. And the follow-up course and the summer course begin immediately. Leslie Burrowes is here with 4 English students. Miss Stewart is here with 4 USA (WESTERN) GIRLS.[4] Pola Nierenstein wants to come, too.[5] At the Vienna dance congress Pola received the first prize for directing (group work) and the second prize for solo dance. And one of Pola's students received the first prize for solo dance. Nice, isn't it?

Crazy situation: we have organizational concerns that are difficult to explain. We (the modern dance) do not quite belong anywhere. On the one hand rhythmic gymnastics claims us, and on the other, the theater organizations.[6] It doesn't work to be torn in two parts. We are working like mad to get all these difficult things figured out. I've been in Berlin for one-and-one-half days of meetings, conferences, four to eleven p.m. without a pause. But there is hope to get official recognition for "THE NEW GERMAN DANCE" and banish ballet back into its proper borders, borders it has penetrated in fantastic ways.[7]

I hope I might still see you somewhere this summer, Hanyuschka, so I can explain to you these difficult things that are damned difficult, interesting, and valuable.

I can't continue now because I have to teach the follow-up course to two students.

Addìo — 1,000 dear, good wishes,

from my heart,
your
Mary

One-thousand dear, good wishes always.

1. Holm penciled *July 4, 1934* at the top of letter and *June 6, 1934* at the bottom.

2. Holm toured the Grand Canyon with her student and admirer Martha Wilcox.

3. Schools of dance offered three degrees: professional dance; pedagogue of amateurs; and pedagogue of professionals.

4. Virginia Stewart organized groups of dancers for study in Europe, and as a journalist she reported on European dance for U.S. readers in the 1930s. The U.S. press attacked Stewart for ignoring the fascist climate in which European dancers continued to work (Ocko 1935:93).

5. Pola Nirenska (1910–1992), a Wigman student, changed her name from Nierenstein; she was in the group that Wigman brought to the United States in 1933. Nirenska then studied with Rosalia Chladek in Vienna and taught and performed in Italy and elsewhere in Europe. Unable to continue her career in fascist Europe because she was Jewish, Nirenska spent the war years in England, working independently and with Kurt Jooss and Sigurd Leeder. In 1952 she settled in Washington, D.C., where she taught, choreographed, and performed. Her last major work was a tribute to people lost in the Holocaust; one section of *A Holocaust Tetralogy* was performed by the Silesian Dance Theatre in Poland and Austria.

6. Many gymnastics systems were popular in Germany for amateur recreation and physical development. Among the dominant systems was one created by Rudolf Bode. Bode's pupil Hinrich Medau developed a second, more lyrical system using objects such as hoops, balls, and clubs. Medau directed 500 youths in games using these objects in the opening ceremony of the Berlin Olympics in 1936.

7. Beginning with the academic year 1934–35, the German government dictated the curriculum of schools of dance and changed the name of Ausdruckstanz (dance of expression) to Deutscher Tanz (German dance). At the time of this letter Wigman was preparing the book *Deutsche Tanzkunst* (German Dance Art), a collection of her essays. The historian Susan Manning reads the book as an "explicit statement of support for fascist aesthetics" (1993:191). After its publication some U.S. writers quoted passages to denounce Wigman as a fascist (Wirth 1935:5). Although without political comment, the essays imply a connection to a collective tradition of national cultural consciousness (Müller 1987:67).

∾

Mary Wigman • Dresden-Neustadt • Bautzner Strasse 107

November 25, 1934 (I)

Dearest Hanya,

To all of you my heartfelt thanks for the beautiful birthday letter.
It has given me much pleasure, and I send you all many, many
cordial regards.

Can you imagine how things are going here, now so shortly
before the eleventh hour? High pressure!

Enclosed is the leaflet of the festival.

Our program:

Women's Dances

1) Wedding Dance
    a) in D major, MW and Ruth Boin
    b) stepping dance, solemn, 4 couples
    c) buoyant part: Chorus

For a joke, I describe it this way: first the bride with the
bride's mother, then the bride with her very best friend, then the
bride with her bridesmaids, and finally the bride and her former
schoolmates.

2) Maternal Dance (solo MW)

3) Lament for the Dead (MW with chorus)

4) Dance of the Prophetess (MW solo with small group of 6
female dancers)

5) Witch Dance (built in three parts)
    1. Chorus
    2. Intermezzo MW solo
    3. Chorus and MW

The dance has become wonderful! Keep your fingers crossed! You
will imagine my sorrows, pain, and agitation. Costumes are not
ready, neither are the dances quite ready for the stage. In short:
well-known circumstances, aren't they?

Dearest regards and kisses, Hanuschka,

from your
Mary

∾

December 8 (I)
[1934 penciled in by Holm]

Dearest Hanya,

We are in the middle of leaving — packing, finding time to take pictures — the craze is complete. But the dances stand! And they have become *very* beautiful. How much I wish you could see them. I, myself, am powerfully fulfilled by this work. Hopefully my girls will not fail on stage!! Two full rehearsals here at the school are behind us.

The order of the dances:

1) Wedding Dance (Ruth Boin as the bridal figure is charming!). First a short duet (black-white) by Ruth and myself, then short transition, forward-backward moving, leading into a couples' dance (four couples all in white with golden yellow belts, the girls look charming). It's solemn, stylized, with many bends and twists, very beautiful spatially — and also very graceful. The dance has the character of a welcome — and leads into a festive, happy, animated round (with Ruth as the center) that is danced very handsomely by all fifteen girls of the group, and which, by the way, compositionally is A-one. Excellent.

2) Maternal Dance — Solo M.W. — it's a kind of Madonna song, silent, simple, restrained, a little baroque in attitude and gesture, emphasizing the costume.

3) Then the Lament for the Dead which has become a real choric dance, very serious, devout, and spatial. Wonderful — silver-gray shirt-like costumes, shiny silk with light and shadows in it. I am the only one who has the same style but in a dark, dove-colored thin velvet.

4) Then comes the Dance of the Prophetess. It is also a solo accompanied by six of the group. They wear gray costumes, gray head scarves, yellow belts, very wide long skirts. I myself wear light yellow with yellow head scarf. The colors are wonderful! The dance has become really perfect, but I cannot interpret it. It is in three phases. First: a walking entrance in two rows — the solo figure builds to an ecstatic (prophetic) state whereas the group is very serious, architectural, keeping and delineating the solemnity. Second

phase: the vision, *seeing* symbolized by the opening up of the two
rows — until now closed, they are torn open — the focus suggests
light — first the search, then orientation, then shock that increases
to fright — the group begins to participate — break down, fall,
solo and group interact. Everything is strongly stylized. Then third
phase: arm swings, victorious, affirmative, heroic — great impact on
space, and so on.

5) To finish: the Witch Dance, which has an absolutely dynamic
character. More of a Walpurgis Night, or witch dancing ground.

I have no idea what people will say about these works. I cannot
guess!!!! Think of us!

Many, many regards to all of you, to you a loving kiss,

from your
Mary

The Nijinsky book has just arrived.[1] I'm very happy with it. I will
send you a novella by Binding that is very beautiful.[2]

1. *Nijinsky*, by Romola Nijinsky, the great dancer's wife, was published by
Simon and Schuster in New York in 1934.
2. Wigman's gift was probably Rudolf G. Binding's *Novella of a Landscape*,
published in 1932 (Forster).

⌒⌣

December 29, 1934 (I)

My dear Hanya,

Time has passed so fast. I don't know how, and with it Christmas.
How I would have loved to have written in time! But I just came
back from Berlin on the 20th, distracted by exhaustion and a
never-ending chain of disturbances that have followed my work
for months.[1]

But one thing I want to tell you. The two festival performances
of *Women's Dances* were incredible. It became a matchless triumph
for me and my work.[2]

The cycle has become five parts:

The Wedding Round as the first has three sections — a duet
(tenderly moving) meeting of two women, an older one (MW) and
a younger one (Ruth Boin) a sort of female dialogue — the older
goes off — and a transition is made through the meeting of the

younger, the bride, with another younger woman, Erika Triebsch.[3] A couple dance begins for four couples. The character is welcoming, festive-solemn. There are many couplings and unions in various ways, and the design of space is very, very beautiful — the couples go off, the bride stays, and immediately part three begins: choric construction, light and playful, serene and happy, almost Mozarty in construction, symmetrical with counter movements. The whole stands wonderfully on stage and the girls look charming. Friedel has dressed them *very* beautifully: plain dress design, very noble, in shining white silk with light yellow belts. Only the bridal figure has a white belt (and I, myself, wear a black dress in the beginning duet).

Number 2. A solo of mine: "Maternal Dance" — kind of a Madonna song — a little baroque in character, very soft, unpretentious, ardent, with a charming, wafting melody by Hasting — I was a little afraid because of the silence, the simplicity, etc. — I didn't know whether a stage effect would be possible — but yes — there was breathless silence in the audience — it worked fully and completely — it was beautiful.

Number 3. The Lament for the Dead — I think you saw the first tryout of it? Here, too, I was anxious! I thought the solemn mood, very much held back, would not affect the audience greatly. Instead, this dance really became my strongest experience of the whole! And it *is* wonderful!!

Number 4. Dance of the Prophetess. For the first time I succeeded in something that I tried earlier in a different form. The solo, absolutely separate, is set against a group of six dancers who represent moving space. They are symbols, all of them. They limit the solo figure, they guard while the dance action is carried entirely by her. The colors are very beautiful. The solo figure is all light yellow, very feminine. The group is in silver gray, with yellow belts, very wide skirts and beautiful head scarves.

[Number 5.] But the most frantic intensification is in the Witch Dance. It is also built in three parts.

1) Group alone, in block like space designs. Through an increasing vibrato of the body (shaking up and down) they dissolve into single figures, then there is a new building of groups with pulling, fleeing,

whisking steps, and so on, symbolizing the *ride* of the witches.[4] With a large circle, group off.

2) Entrance M.W. Short solo (so the girls can breathe) through large circle rhythms turning into the center and then down to the floor, a few wild rhythms there, and up into high movements that fetch the group one by one back in from all sides. Then in the center around M.W. an exciting, actually quite lusty, up and down, back and forth, that dissolves, clusters again, bursts, increases to fury, and at the end is attracted like a magnet into the center. The shaking of the bodies is continuous!

It was funny and beautiful at the same time to see that the audience no longer sat still, but began to shake, too!

Yes — and now it's really over — and we are sitting on the road.[5] The tour that I was forced to agree to has not come about, and now it is too late to work for a tour in January and February, should we organize a private one.

The ministry, however, is paying the group for two months, which means the minimal costs for subsistence are secured.

The sixth and seventh of January we dance in Dresden, the eighth in Bautzen. Chemnitz is next with two performances. Everything else hangs in the air, I with it!

Three of the group are gone; three new ones have to learn everything within *one* week! God, not even a Christmas vacation — not a single day of pause — and the agitation is ongoing.

I am sending you a few press clippings. Maybe you can translate them and make a little P.R. with them. It would be good if people knew something of us over there.

I am also sending you some pictures. We ought to have material of our own already, but the photographers are slow in delivering.

Hearty thanks for your picture! On December 23rd a *sack* of U.S. mail arrived here. Everything arrived together on the Bremen. The "Nijinsky" arrived in early December. I have read the book with burning interest although the interpretation seems to me to be painfully one-sided. Thanks also for this! [Paper broken, a few words lost] . . . for the new year many, many, dear greetings and wishes!

From my heart,

your

Mary

1. In addition to coping with new government regulation, Wigman was facing criticism in the press. Of a solo concert in 1934 a writer in the influential journal *Der Tanz* charged, "Wigman lacks today her former spontaneity — she doesn't excite any more" (quoted in Koegler 1974:36).

2. *Women's Dances* premiered at a weeklong German dance festival in Berlin organized by Rudolf Laban and sponsored by the Cultural Ministry. Dance artists who could prove Aryan origin appeared as soloists and showcased their companies and student groups. Performances were a public success, but press was mixed. Some writers complained that too many outmoded ideas of individualism and expressionism had been on view (Koegler 1974:38).

3. Triebsch danced in the group that Wigman brought to the United States for the 1932–33 tour, as had the American Ann Port.

4. Vibrato was a type of movement dynamic that Wigman used in teaching and in her choreography. In the United States, Holm's vibration classes were among her students' favorites. Holm told the following story about how the vibrato/vibration originated accidentally: During her early study with Wigman in Dresden she shared an apartment with Yella Schirmer and Guri Thorsteinsson. Each day two would go to school while one stayed behind to care for baby Klaus. At the end of the day the two would instruct the babysitter in all that had happened at school. One cold winter day all three, sitting together on a bedspring, began a unified shivering that became a fast up-down movement that they prolonged obsessively. The next morning two of them appeared before Wigman: "Look what we have discovered!" (K. Holm 1994; Siegel 1981:8).

5. By "sitting on the road" she means that they were out of work (Forster).

∽

[Postcard in uncataloged material, Hanya Holm Collection, Dance Division, The New York Public Library.]

February 13, 1935

Dearest Hanya,

Hurried greetings from our tour. Things are great! Seven evenings — one free day —— then 9 evenings, and so forth. But it is fun. Munich yesterday was heavenly! Today Augsburg. How are you, how is the school doing?

Love from your

Mary

∽

Leipzig, Main Station
March 24, 1935 (I)

My Dear Hanya,

Stalwart, we are still spinning on through German lands, small city, large city in alternation. Lately the smaller ones prevail. Not only does this mean stages that are too small, and deplorable changing rooms, it also means guest houses instead of hotels, and therefore life is pretty difficult. Pork chops with red cabbage are always on the menu! The stomach does not like it! Still, I'm amazed that there are enthusiastic people everywhere, and the echo of our work is making us happy. It keeps us going and carries us through.

Last night in Görlitz we celebrated the fiftieth performance of the group and it was charming. Everybody was in top form, a happy reunion with a festive table decorated with Easter eggs (which I got in Bunzlau!).

This morning I pushed from Görlitz to Dresden with Hesschen in my car, had one and a half hours at home to repack, change clothes, eat fast, and off we went!

Now we sit in Leipzig at the main station to go to Erfurt. You see, the tempo is almost American. What's missing is that not

Hanya Holm, just before the debut of her dance company in Denver, November 1936. Photograph by Harry Rhoads. Reprinted with permission of the *Rocky Mountain News*, Denver, Colorado.

everything is geared to this tempo, which is the case over there and makes a lot of things easier.

This scribble will not be a real letter. It is supposed to be a moment's greeting and to show you that I think of you! Very silently spring is coming and the country is becoming beautiful. Cordial greetings to Louise and your students, too.

And let us know more about you, all right? In my thoughts I embrace you and I am with many dear, good wishes,

your

Mary

Gretl Curth and Hasting are sitting here with me and they also send many regards!

∾

April 1, 1935 (I)

Dearest Hanya,

In between — we are still rushing — a greeting. I don't know whether the news has reached you of the sudden passing of Fred Coolemans in Batavia.[1] Pneumonia. I wanted you to know. It touches me. However things went, Fred was one of the "gifted," and close to us through studies and collaboration. Strange fate! Maybe death is good! Maybe not much would have happened, would have grown within Fred. Maybe he was too weak to carry through a task all the way. Who knows? Again, one less in the row.

My God, Hanuschka, how much have we danced!!

It was very beautiful a few days ago in Annaberg in the Erzgebirge. The next morning I went back by car — without chains in the deep snow and ice. But we got to Dresden in time.

Yesterday in Dresden the fourth performance in the playhouse, this time for the winter aid of the German people, very big! High-level visitors on stage: the mayor of Dresden, the Polish Consul General, Prince August Wilhelm von Preussen, the Duchess of Braunschweig. If fate could make it happen for us to go to Warsaw, wouldn't that be nice? In Berlin today only a few hours — early tomorrow we are off to East Prussia. Next Sunday again in the UFA Palace (the eighth Berlin performance!).

How are you? Send a sign of life more often! Just a note is
enough!

From my heart
your
Mary

1. Coolemans was a Dutch-Javanese dancer who trained with Wigman and
worked as an assistant teacher at her school. His New York debut concert had
not impressed John Martin (*New York Times*, January 6, 1934).

∽

September 12, 1935 (I)

Dearest Hanya,

Not a word for an eternity. Why don't you write?

Max Otto visited us briefly after having been over there and told
us that Louise has been painting the walls in the new spaces of the
Wigman School.[1] And we do not even know *that* you are moving,
and *where* to.[2]

If you cannot write long letters, please send short notes or ask
someone else to send word at regular intervals.

Yesterday Tina was here and told me many things. She is as thin
as an anchovy, but quite happy. It is a pity that I can't see her
dances. I was very pleased that John Martin wrote her such an
appreciative review.[3]

Are you back from Mills College? How was it? What does it
look like in New York? My vacation weeks are behind me and I am
supposed to start working mightily. A new group program must be
born. Six-and-a-half weeks for it. Two of the new group members
are invalids and are not yet back.

Elisabeth is leaving the Dresden School to go to Leipzig on her
own. It was not easy, the process of letting go. It had been coming
for a long time and is inevitable. Hopefully, she will succeed. My
hope for her is that with the sheer force of her self-determination
she will set out on her own course, something that she had lost a
little within the last years.[4] Her address will be, as of October 1,
Leipzig Dufourstrasse 6.

And now very dear greetings with many beautiful wishes for you
and the forthcoming work in winter.

Always your
Mary

1. Otto was a German ballet dancer who worked in the United States.

2. While Holm was in Germany during the summer of 1934, Louise Kloepper and Marjorie Forschmer, the school secretary, searched for improved studio space. They found a beautiful, high-ceilinged studio at 215 West 11th Street in Greenwich Village. The New York Wigman School moved there for the opening of the regular session in October 1935.

3. Martin published a long review of Flade's Bennington concert, her first in the East in two years. He found she possessed "the conviction of a genuinely big creative talent" (*New York Times*, July 21, 1935). Flade was representing Holm at Bennington while Holm taught at Mills College.

4. Tension between Wigman's sister, Elisabeth, and others on the Dresden staff, particularly Hasting and Curth, had been building because of Elisabeth's loyalty to Jewish friends and because she objected to government requirements that ballet and folk dance be added to school curricula. In her diary Wigman wrote about a "tragic argument with Elisabeth," and confessed, "I, myself, am feeling confused" (Forster).

∽

Mary Wigman • Dresden-Neustadt • Bautzner Strasse 107

December 27, 1935 (I)

Dear Hanya,

Greetings for the new year and many good wishes. I just received your Christmas greeting and I am enjoying this sign of life, the first in three-quarters of a year. Although your lines sound irritated and nervous, I cannot understand your insistent silence. Why do I have to learn through friends that the school has moved to another location? I don't even have the address of the school that I think is still called the Wigman School.

I do not recognize that you might have too much work, maybe sorrows besides or that you might be in trouble. I mean I do not recognize all these reasons, however serious, as real ones for your silence.

Of course, I am not angry with you! But I demand — as long as you are in charge of this school over there, where you were put in position by me, and as long as the school is connected with mine — the maintaining of personal and business contact from your side. If from your side you do not wish to continue, let me know, but we cannot go on like this. I do not demand that you write often and a lot, but you, as well as I, will find time to keep us informed — be it only through a few short lines — in spite of overwork on both sides and besides the manifold sorrows and difficulties that the profession has for me here and for you there.

So please, Hanuschka, overcome your hesitation![1]

I am spending Christmas with Benkert. He and Frau Renger say hello to you. We are having a beautiful time. Hesschen makes a fourth, and she also sends greetings.

My mother has been sick for a year. She cannot travel anymore. She is in Hanover and has a nurse looking after her. Elisabeth has been in Leipzig since October. She has set up a studio for dance and rhythmic gymnastics, works on her own and already has a nice number of students.

In the Dresden school Hans Huber is working as head of pedagogy, Gretl Curth as the main teacher for dance, Nätsch as the head of the amateur department and at the same time of the practical (pedagogical preparation for examinations in Dance Gymnastics that have to be separated from the dance-art studies). There have been many organizational changes! Huber's collaboration is very pleasing. Gretl's commitment is very positive too. In the group I miss her awfully. On the other hand, our five-week tour (in a stormy tempo, twenty-five evenings of performances one after another!) was very, very beautiful. The group, once again pretty newly put together, worked together very well. The new dances ("Hymnic Dances," a cycle of six dances for group and solo) succeeded in spite of the unusual expectations of the audiences.[2] Wonderful success everywhere. That's a great joy, especially as the labor pains were never as heavy as this year. The bad star of illness stood over us. For weeks several dancers were missing and I was often on the border of insanity because I did not know how to finish in time. But everything on stage was blameless for the dance festival and proved to be a great success.

Benkert gave me a big globe for Christmas. I am going from Berlin to New York with my index finger — and the same way in my thoughts and I am sending you many, many beautiful regards. In old cordiality,

your

Mary

1. Holm's inability, or unwillingness, to keep Wigman informed could have been an assertion of independence, compassion for her mentor, or, more probably, honest confusion about how to respond to declining enrollment and anti-German

feelings in the United States. Bessie Schönberg remembered that Holm suffered "the tortures of the damned" in confronting Wigman about the need to jettison her name (Schönberg 1996).

2. *Hymnic Dances* was the last work for which Wigman received a grant from the government, possibly because of Benkert's intercession. Benkert was a member of the Nazi Party, valued because of his engineering and organizational abilities. He was an executive in the industrial firm of Siemens.

After the December 27 letter, which closes with an image that can be read as an imperialist gesture and also as a sign of friendship at crosscurrent with political implication, there is a break of twenty-three months in the letters found after Holm's death. Walter Sorell remembered that when he was writing his biography of Holm, she showed him letters from Wigman concerning the renaming of the New York Wigman School as the Hanya Holm Studio in the fall of 1936. Sorell said he gave the letters to the Dance Division, but they have not been found. According to Sorell, the letters showed that Wigman herself suggested that her name be dropped when she understood that the school was foundering because of its connection to Germany (Sorell 1969:44).

A picture postcard from Wigman among Holm's personal photographs in the Dance Division proves that the women remained in touch with each other during the break in extant letters. Wigman wrote from Heidelberg on January 14, 1936:

> Dearest Hanya, The Diaghilev book has arrived. I would like to thank you very much for it. I have taken it with me on tour and am looking forward to reading it. We are on tour again, the fourth time for me, and we will be traveling until Easter without a break. In the beginning of February we'll be in Holland. Right now I am with Mrs. Reuther [Martha Wohlenberg Reuther] who sends you her love. I am most cordially yours,   Mary

1937–1941

DRESDEN

In the twenty-three-month break between extant letters, Germany hosted the 1936 Olympic Games. At the opening ceremony, "Olympic Youth," Wigman performed *Lament for the Dead* with eighty supporting women dancers. Her group danced excerpts from *Women's Dances* and her 1935 *Hymnic Dances* in an international dance festival organized as part of the Olympic celebration. U.S. dance companies boycotted the festival because Jewish dancers were banned, but groups from Poland, Hungary, Bulgaria, Yugoslavia, Austria, Switzerland, Holland, Greece, and Italy appeared. After the Olympics, Wigman remained a figurehead of German dance but received no further support from the government. When Erika Thimey, an early student who immigrated to the United States, visited her in 1936, Wigman spoke of her restricted opportunities as a chance to look within, to mature artistically (Thimey 1995).

In 1936 Holm began an independent professional and personal life. Declaring her respect and admiration for Mary Wigman the artist, Holm renamed the school and the dance company that she had formed, and she brought her son, by then a teenager, over from Germany. She also began the process of naturalization. The dance community continued to identify Holm with her German heritage, now in a positive manner: "She brings the graciousness and charm, the profundity of thought, the disciplined approach of her European heritage. These qualities intermingle with the vigorous American motivation and style as she increasingly apprehends them, imparting a new tempo, a new rhythm and a new resonance to the modern dance" (Lloyd 1937). Holm entered her most prolific period as a concert choreographer. After a program of short dances in 1936, she choreographed *Trend*, a work of epic proportions about social destruction and the evils of conformity. John Martin gave it the *New York Times* award for best group choreography in 1937. It premiered less than two weeks after Wigman saw many of her friends denounced in the Nazis' exhibit of "degenerate art" on August 2, 1937. In April 1938 Holm premiered *Etudes* and *Dance of Introduction,* then *Dance of Work and Play* and *Dance Sonata* in August. The popular *Metropolitan Daily* followed. In 1939 she choreographed two responses to catastrophic events in Europe. *Tragic Exodus,* a meditation on displacement, fear, and death, won the *Dance Magazine* award for best group choreography in modern dance. *They Too Are Exiles* was somewhat mimetic and less successful with critics. Holm herself took the role of the "Possessor," who cruelly dominated dancers performing folk themes of various European nations.

After revealing letters about Wigman's life and Holm's career moves, there is another hiatus, between the letter of December 1938 and Wigman's touching letter of February 1941, the last to reach Holm until after the war. This break is easily explained: in 1938 Germany annexed Austria and in March 1939 occupied all of Czechoslovakia; in September Germany invaded Poland and in 1940 took Norway and all the Low Countries, forced English troops back to Dunkirk, took Paris, and began bombing Britain. All German culture became isolated. Wigman performed only solos, and less often.

Hanns Benkert abruptly turned away from Wigman in 1941 to marry another woman. Nazi harassment reached its limit in 1942 when Wigman was ordered to refrain from giving public performances. On March 29 she danced for the last time in Dresden, performing three new solos: *The Dance of Brunhild, The Dance of Niobe,* and *Farewell and Thanksgiving.* Two members of her teaching staff, Hanns Hasting and Gretl Curth, both Nazi Party members, took over direction of her school. Although the Nazis condemned Wigman as an unfit teacher for German youth, an old friend found her a part-time, temporary teaching post in the newly formed Dance Department of the Academy of the Performing Arts in Leipzig. She and faithful Hesschen moved there on April 1, 1942.

∾

January 17, 1937 (I)

Dearest Hanya,

Twenty-four hours in Dresden — what a circus — two school performances yesterday, 5:00 to 7:00 and 8:00 to 10:00. Nice work!! Group dances by the students: Dance cantata in six parts by Gretl Curth, and a tale: "John on the Tramp, or the Coffee Mill Tale" by Gisela Sonntag. Charming, the latter. USA came through especially well with pantomimic talent.[1]

I am only passing by — in one hour the night train to Munich leaves. You can see no more rushing than this.

I have not had a group since summer! I've been very sad about it! But without major funding the apparatus cannot be sustained. I have created a new solo program. At the beginning, the cycle "Autumnal Dances." Order:

Autumnal Gestalt I (Benediction)
Dance of Remembrance
Hunting Song
Dance of Silence
Autumnal Gestalt II (Wind's Bride)

then: from "Dance Songs," 1935/36

The Song of Fate

from "Women's Dances," 1934/35

Maternal Dance

and the cycle of four dances based on Hungarian songs.

I was sick in December, teeth, jaw, head — awful, almost three weeks of pain! You know about that, too!

Otherwise? I am glad, happy, and thankful that the new program is so strong in effect. The tour just took off January 4th; now it continues — pitiless.

This in short:

I am pleased that you — finally — have written. I wouldn't know what to think of your troubles or how to deal with them myself.[2] The main thing is that you — in spite of fights — can maintain yourself, hold the field, push yourself through. That's good.

Many people send greetings to you. Hesschen, Benkert, Frau Renger, Hasting, etc. We have become smaller — not the spaces, though! Hoerisch is gone, too, in Berlin, to Siemens, he is marrying Erika Triebsch.

Thank you very much for the beautiful Christmas parcel. We enjoyed it wholeheartedly!! In every way, Hanya, I am in all friendship, close affection, always

your

Mary

1. A group of Americans continued their study in Germany during the Nazi period. At least two were among the eighty women who danced with Wigman in the Pageant of Youth preceding the 1936 Olympic Games (LaMothe 1996; Houloose 1996). Several did not leave Germany until 1939. Overall enrollment in Wigman's school was declining, however. Jews were not allowed, and many international students were staying away because of unsettled conditions. Wigman had to support the school with solo touring, but the Nazi regime harassed her by canceling engagements.

2. Holm may have written about professional rivalries that she faced. In 1981 she spoke with Marcia B. Siegel about her outsider status in the modern dance community in 1937 (Siegel 1981:22–24).

∾

Mary Wigman • Dresden-Neustadt • Bautzner Strasse 107

September 29, 1937 (I)

Dear Hanya,

I want to congratulate you very, very much on your great Bennington success![1] Potter wrote to me about it, and although he emphasizes not being a specialist, he was very impressed. He also sent me just now some nice photos and a few clippings. I have so wholeheartedly enjoyed the goal you have reached, dear Hanya.

Virginia Stewart brought me your letter and I hope that the awful tooth story is completely in order again.

Now summer — for you an eventful and draining one — has long gone by. A few days ago I came back to Dresden, down from my lonely German mountains. I'm trying hard to cope with the requirements the profession forcefully demands of me, but that doesn't necessarily work.

The weeks of rest were beautiful! Silence and loneliness alternated with all kinds of animation, visits, beautiful car drives, a great many hikes, and alpine climbing. That was not bad at all.

We had a very interesting, but also very demanding summer course. Besides the USA that was pretty well represented, South America, the Balkans, the North; a crazy mix of languages, types and ways of moving.

In the new school year, we have good dance material. It all looks quite encouraging. I must get things done: in five weeks I am supposed to have everything on stage.

Dearest Hanya, many, many, good greetings are coming to you, and also to your boy.[2] I would love to hear from you more often, if you — besides all your work — could find time for a greeting.

From my heart, I am always
your
Mary

1. *Trend* premiered at Bennington on August 13 and 14, 1937. There were two subsequent performances in New York, December 28 and 29 at Mecca Auditorium (later City Center Theater). Part 2 of *Trend* was presented for a benefit, "Dance for Spain," on January 28, 1938. To Wallingford Riegger's score Holm added Edgard Varèse's *Ionization*. For the New York performances she added the composer's *Octandre*. Settings and lighting were credited to Gerard Gentile at Bennington and to Arch Lauterer in New York. Betty Joiner designed costumes. Holm used twenty-two student dancers and her company of eleven, who contributed to the creation of the work (Gentry 1992:24–25, 32–33). *Trend* affected viewers deeply (Kriegsman 1981:161–73). Holm wrote about her choreographic plan in an essay in *Magazine of Art* (1938:137), which also published essays by Arch Lauterer (1938:139, 142–43) and sound engineer Harrison Kerr (1938:143, 184–85), as well as many photographs by Barbara Morgan.

2. Holm had managed to get her son out of Germany just before he turned sixteen and would have been required to register for the draft. Klaus went to boarding school, and after two years in the U.S. Navy he lived with his mother while attending New York University. He then went to Yale Drama School, where he became the protégé of the theater designer Donald Oenslager. Using the name Klaus Holm, he assisted Oenslager with Broadway plays and as theater consultant to cultural institutions in the United States and Canada. Klaus later designed his mother's annual productions in Colorado. From 1970 to 1985 he was associate professor and technical director of theater at Wilkes College, Wilkes-Barre, Pennsylvania. He died in 1994.

ᗏ

[Picture postcard with photo of Wigman and a young woman wearing wings. Wigman holds candles, and both seem to tend a small potted plant.]

January 2, 1938 (I)

Dear Hanya,

Thanks for your Christmas telegram. Are you well? I am thinking of you with all my heart.

On the other side, Christmas celebration at our school — it was so charming this year and reminds one of those festivities that were celebrated in earlier times. You see, I was busy, too!

To you and Klaus from all my heart,

your
Mary

Hanya Holm's *Trend* at Bennington, Vermont, August 1937. Photograph by Bouchard. © Diane Bouchard. Courtesy Jerome Robbins Dance Division, The New York Public Library for the Performing Arts, Astor, Lenox and Tilden Foundations.

◈

Mary Wigman • Dresden-Neustadt • Bautzner Strasse 107

February 19, 1938 (I)

Dear Hanya,

I just returned from a seven-week tour and found this card that had not been mailed. Mr. Potter sent me so many interesting articles about Dance International that it made me sad not to have been able to see any of these things.[1] But, especially, your big success has pleased me wholeheartedly, and I want to congratulate you for it. It is wonderful that you did it, dearest Hanya, and I'm wishing you all the courage and all the energy for going on.

I wanted to ask you something. The American girl that is on the card with me as an angel, from Los Angeles, California, will have to return to the United States rather soon. She is talented, able, and already knows a lot. Her money is going and she has to make some more. She cannot do this here. If you could use her in your group, that would be great, but I have no idea how you are doing money-wise. The name of the girl is Charlotte Sturgis. Please write a few lines, so I know.

God, how much would I love to see your work! *Trend.* I am unable to translate that. What does it mean?

On March 25th Hanns Benkert is leaving for New York. He will stay until mid-May. It is a long research trip throughout the US. He probably will stay in New York only on his way back. Strange feeling that I cannot be there as well. I would so love to be there again.

I send you many cordial regards. Please greet Louise Kloepper for me as well. Often I think of you and am

always

your

Mary

1. Dance International was an ambitious festival held at Rockefeller Center from November 29, 1937, through January 2, 1938. Holm's company performed two sections of *Trend*. Many U.S. modern dance and ballet companies appeared, as did companies and performers with wide international representation. Dance films, lectures, and art exhibitions were included. There were hopes for another festival in four years, but war forced their abandonment.

૨⁀

May 28, 1938 (I)
[date penciled in by Holm]

Dear Hanya,

Jean Houloose will bring this greeting from me.[1] She is a
talented little person. I don't know if you have time to see what
she can do. Her "Golliwog" is really nice.

All my love,

from your
Mary

1. Houloose studied with Wigman from 1935 to 1938 in the last sizable group
of foreigners at the school. When she returned to New York, Holm gave
Houloose a three-year scholarship, and she understudied with the Hanya Holm
Company. She went on to a career as a Broadway dancer, appearing in shows
choreographed by Holm, Agnes de Mille, Jerome Robbins, and others.

૨⁀

Mary Wigman • Dresden-Neustadt • Bautzner Strasse 107

May 28, 1938 (I)

Dear Hanya,

I enjoyed the makeup bands like a child. I want to thank you
for them very much. I traveled to Bremerhaven to pick up Hanns.
The arrival of the beautiful big ship was alone worth the trip, and
to see Hanns tanned, happy, and so excited by everything he had
experienced was especially nice. He brought me your letter and had
a lot to tell me. Then all of a sudden everything separating us was
gone. You yourself, your work — everything stood in front of me,
so alive, so near. Again and again the joy mounts inside me that
you are carrying through so fabulously and successfully, dearest
Hanya. Often I have a great longing for direct contact with you.

Whether it will work out that I can come over? I have no idea.[1]
But I wanted to tell you that whenever you have time and feel like
coming, my house is always open to you and I would enjoy it
tremendously if you would visit once again. A piece of homeland is
preserved in my heart for you and neither time nor distance can
impair that.

From Bremerhaven to Berlin, Hanns had to tell me everything that he had seen and experienced. So when we arrived at Zoo I almost felt I'd also come from over there.[2]

Only this greeting today, I think of you in dear love and attachment

and I am

your

Mary

1. Wigman had planned to make another tour of the United States in 1940 (Forster).

2. Zoo was a train station in Berlin.

∾

1938 (I)
[date penciled in by Holm]

Dearest Hanya,

Shirlee Dodge will bring you this booklet with a greeting from me.[1] She is one of my professional students and is over in the USA for vacation.

All my love!

Your

Mary

1. Dodge, who studied with Wigman until late summer 1939, became a prominent American dance educator, contributing to dance programs at the University of Texas at Austin, Stanford University, and the University of Iowa. Throughout her long career Dodge remained devoted to Wigman and cherished memories of the two years she had spent at the Wigman School (Dodge 1995).

∾

Mary Wigman • Dresden-Neustadt • Bautzner Strasse 107

July 30, 1938 (I)

Dearest Hanya,

Charlotte Sturgis will bring this greeting to you. And with it I want to ask you to take a little time to look at one of her dances. Most probably she will not be able to show you her suite "Indian Dances" because they require a lot of percussion apparatus. A pity! Because the suite was really wonderful. From another dance of hers you will recognize her strong talent and exceptionally clean and considerable technical potential. She teaches brilliant classes and is in general very good professionally. I would love to have kept her as an assistant here, but it was impossible to get a work permit. I didn't even tell her this so as not to make the goodbye more painful. If you see a possibility for her, please help her a little. In practical matters she is a little helpless. I would hate it if she were not to develop her skills in the right way.

It will take a while until these lines reach you. I want to go on vacation and Charlotte will leave before I come back.

Many dear regards and wishes for you.

From

your

Mary

⌒◡

Mary Wigman • Dresden-Neustadt • Bautzner Strasse 107

November 2, 1938 (I)

Dear Hanya,

Thank you very much for the photos that Shirlee Dodge brought me from you. I would give a lot to be able to see your work for myself! You will be on your way by now.[1] "Break your neck, break a leg," is our not very poetic wish for these occasions. I was overjoyed that you had work for Charlotte right away.[2] My problem child! Highly gifted, wonderful worker, reliable up to the last, but having difficulties with herself, and always battling everyday life, which costs her much time and energy. With us she went through remarkable experiences of this kind. I can imagine that in new surroundings many things will go better for her than here, where educational measures had to be taken that will now not be necessary.

No possibility for me to come over this winter! Sometimes I'm awfully sorry about it, but from here I can do little or nothing.[3] I am working a lot in the school and just as passionately for the upcoming solo tour beginning in early January.

The stockings that HB brought me in your name are just great — still in use and not *one run* yet. I am ashamed for not having thanked you earlier!

Here, winter is coming fast. Sometimes I wish one could surrender to the seasons instead of working through them! Sometimes for the weekend I drive to Hanns' little hunting lodge. It is lovely, and there one senses earth and sky with double strength.

One thousand good wishes and greetings for you, dearest Hanya.

From your
Mary

1. Holm was making regular national tours with her company.

2. Holm did include Sturgis on a leg of her spring 1938 tour, but she did not put her on stage. Sturgis played percussion accompaniment and performed other functions. Later she was given a small part in *Metropolitan Daily*. Sturgis did not get along with company members, partly because of her outspoken profascist views (Kim 1995).

3. Wigman was prohibited from performing outside Germany.

ᕪ

Mary Wigman, Dresden N 6, Bautzner Str. 107, Fernruf 50 488

December 28, 1938 (I)

Dear, dear Hanya,

What great pleasure you have given me with your beautiful Christmas greetings and your letter! Thank you from my whole heart. And how Hanns will enjoy the wonderful book of bridges! Tina [Flade], who brought everything, was such a nice surprise. When I came down this morning to work with Hasting there was a silhouette against the window, a small charming person — Tina. It was a great pleasure to see her again after all these years.

And I'm so glad that you wrote about your tour. It is so nice to know that you are battling so bravely and constantly! Sometimes, however, I am sad because I can never see anything of your work. But it is not within my power to change this.

Hopefully, you did have a few quiet days with Klaus! I returned yesterday from a wonderful Christmas. Six hours without a break, through ice and snow — it was damn difficult driving. But Hanns's hunting lodge cannot be reached otherwise. We spent a few wonderful Christmas days there in almost Siberian loneliness. Markische landscape, endless nights, white, wavy fields.[1] Everything snowy, and only for one day the golden sun shown over it. The next day snow fell again. Still, the brave hunter went out on his business and returned at night frozen as an icicle.

Now we are really back to work! In a few days the departure to tour a solo program with several new works.

I am not astonished to hear what you write about Charlotte. It is the same as she was here, only that here she was an American! With an effort I got along very well with her. But I had hoped for her that she would learn from experience, I thought she would pick up on the US momentum. I'd be awfully sorry if she failed. So gifted! Have you ever seen her dances? And such an example as a worker! Besides, she gave fantastic classes when she wanted to. I am curious how things will go with her.

Late, dearest Hanya, but still from my whole heart, a thousand good, dear, heartfelt wishes for the new year.

Always I am yours,

faithfully,
Mary

1. "Markische" refers to the Markbrandenburg region in northeastern Germany.

∽

February 5, 1941 (I)

Dearest Hanya,

It was a great surprise and a very, very great joy when your package arrived just now. Not only because its contents were especially beautiful — you ought to have heard the cry of joy across the ocean! — but because of the sign of life from you. The remembering made me so happy. So much time has passed since I heard from you directly. Silent thoughts and wishes have gone often from me to you! Likewise today, I am wishing you might be well and have a lot of joy and satisfaction in your work and in your son and his development. How wonderful if we could see each other again some day. But as long as the war goes on our personal wishes must be put aside.

What do you want to know from our side? The years are passing, people change, still the school is in the same place and is quite alive. Hasting and Gretl are still working here. Elisabeth is in Leipzig in her own studio. She is doing well. She was here recently, very lively; I am pleased that being on her own is so good for her.

Hanns B. is caught up in his work so much that he often has to pay for it with his health. Frau Renger has become very old, and with that, quite ponderous. Still she does not have real sorrows, and she is very happy about the large garden at the Benkert house.

I myself had a mishap this summer. A fall from my bike and a bad leg injury. Now I am finally at a point where I can work all right technically. There was no question of performing until now, but this has been to the advantage of the school. I am again enjoying teaching very much.

Dearest Hanya, from my heart I thank you for your loving and understanding thoughts.

With these lines, countless heartfelt greetings, wishes and thoughts to you.

I am and always will be

your

Mary

The following poem, which Wigman wrote in the last months of the war, reached a former student just before Allied bombing ceased on May 7, 1945 (Waechter 1945:7–8).

The horror grows.
Ice cold and clammy
it slowly creeps higher
already squeezing at our throats.

The bombs howl, spit, whiz, whistle —
Inferno! Man
stands shaking in torment
in a cellar which is no longer
a refuge.

A primitive angel makes the rounds
and seizes his sacrifice at random
out of the people who are damned.
Man becomes a slaughtered animal
whose fate no God decides.

The majesty of death is canceled —
one no longer dies,
one drops down
exterminated —
without even a burial.

[translation by Ruth L. Kriehn]

1946–1949

LEIPZIG

We are so familiar with the images of destroyed German cities that we find it difficult to picture artistic life continuing during the war and its aftermath. Wigman choreographed and staged Carl Orff's *Carmina Burana* at the Leipzig Opera House in 1943. When the academy where she taught was bombed, she moved her classes to a partly destroyed elementary school and then to her own apartment. Working compulsively, she surmounted enormous privation; Hesschen made domestic survival possible. Wigman had enough students to present a group by the summer of 1946. In 1947 she staged and choreographed Gluck's *Orpheus and Eurydice* for the Leipzig Municipal Opera.

Holm found growth and direction in the war years. From 1941 she stabled her company at Colorado College during the summer, teaching and creating dances that she toured and brought into New York. Three dances, *From This Earth, Namesake,* and *What So Proudly We Hail,* all to the Americanist music of Roy Harris, confirmed her new national identity for a New York critic, who found all doubt about her grasp of the American idiom dispelled (Bender 1943:22). Late in 1943 Holm stumbled, earning bad notices in New York for *Orestes and the Furies,* a large work based on the *Eumenides.* Under financial pressure she disbanded her company early the next year.

Wigman headed most letters with Holm's address neatly printed, no doubt to aid American censors. Holm's family found these letters in their envelopes, the censor's seal broken but clearly visible. Leipzig was under Russian control after the war.

∽

Mary Wigman
Leipzig CI
Mozartstr. 17

November 3, 1946 (II)

My dear Hanya,

I was very happy about your letter (Oct. 14), which I admit I had awaited with longing. All the better that there was so much detail and I can now get at least a general idea of your life. How do you look now? My God, long years lie between our visits! When I look in a mirror unprepared, I am startled. Marked! There is much carved into lines that would not be there under other conditions. It is unimaginable what we have endured, and the worst of it is that we human beings must continue to endure it even still.

Those for whom it is still going well, or should I say, those for whom it is better again, those in the black market, are few. They do not count, even though they dim the picture.

You know that I have worked hard my whole life, but I am sure you cannot imagine how I have to labor now just to live like a human being and to earn money for the school's expenses, or imagine the conditions under which this work proceeds. We do not lack food, but we are never really full and are hungry again one-and-a-half hours after a meal. And we are freezing. That is horrible! We sit in the dark because of the daily electrical restrictions. Simply put, it takes all of our energy just to remain positive. Anyway, the beloved work is there — it helps more than anything else. And I have about 25 young students with whom I work from early to late — good material, with 2 or 3 exceptional talents among them. A few days ago I made my first group trip with them, a 7½ hour ice-cold ride to Erfurt (it used to be 2 hours by D-train). A glance around in one of those trains, Hanya, and you would know the extent of Germany's reduction to poverty! All around my apartment, wreckage. We have endured something terrible.

I can imagine that over there it is also no longer the way it was from 1930 to 1933. And I can only hope that somehow the question of space for the school can be solved.[1]

I have received many kind letters from over there, and have rejoiced at the affection.[2] It is kind of you to think to send me something. It would be wonderful! Because we have *nothing*. I have been given the address of a friend in Berlin who lives in the *English* sector. Dutch woman, architect: Kiek Vander, Bln-Wilmersdorf, Kreuznacherstr. 50 III.[3] But you might also go through Benkert (also English sector) Bln-Charlottenburg 9, Spreetalallee 1. B. is a very controversial person and he is in a very difficult position.[4] I had not seen him since 1941, and I visited him briefly in the cellar of his badly bombed house, where he lives with his wife, mother-in-law, and sister-in-law. Frau Renger died a few years ago. Thank God! She was very sick and did not need to experience the worst. If you send something to Benkert directly, and include a note that it is for me, I would definitely receive it.

I am to send you best wishes from Hesschen, who faithfully stood by me, and whose untiring care I have to thank for the fact that I am reasonably sound. I send love from the bottom of my heart, dearest Hanya; with all good wishes for you, your son, your work I am

your
Mary

1. The owners of the building that housed Holm's Greenwich Village studio reclaimed the space in 1947. Holm retained her apartment there while she taught in various studios in Manhattan. The Primus Studio at 743 Eighth Avenue became a semi-permanent office and studio in November 1948. Enrollment in Holm's New York classes had been small until 1946, when many ballet-trained dancers began studying with her (Shearer 1993:4–7).

2. John Martin announced Wigman's survival in the *New York Times* of August 4, 1946. He quoted a letter that Howard Potter had received: "'Since 1942 I have been living in Leipzig—left Dresden, house, school, everything there because it had become intolerable for me. The Nazis did not like me! Here I live among ruins and have a tiny school of my own where I teach from morning until night. Hard life, but wonderful to be alive, after all!'" The August 26 issue of *Time* magazine quoted Wigman on her personal struggle under the Nazis and her decision to comply with their directives: "We did everything we could to save our little candlelight for the day when we could build a great, warm fire" (61–62).

3. Christina (Kiek) Vander aided Wigman's relocation to Berlin in 1949.

4. The occupation forces denied Benkert clearance for high-level employment on the grounds of his Nazi collaboration. On May 15, 1947, the *New York Times* reported that after the war five nations bid for his talents as an inventor and engineer, but his failure to achieve acquittal for war crimes forced him to take a job in a locksmith shop.

༤

March 3, 1947 (II)

Mary Wigman   To Miss Hanya Holm
Leipzig CI   215 West 11 Street
Mozartstr. 17   New York, 14

Dearest Hanya,

A short while ago your wonderful long letter of January 20 arrived, and I do not want a long time to pass before I write you back because a lot of time passes, too, before a letter from here reaches New York.

I try so often to imagine how your life is today, but behind the ideas lies the knowledge of New York and its living conditions as I knew them when I was there. How much things must have changed! I must admit that I never see you as anything other than active, lively, and strong-willed, right in the middle of the dance existence to which we have pledged ourselves.[1] My burning wish is that you, despite all difficulties, may find suitable studio space because I know from personal experience what it means to get by without it and still get something moderately respectable on its feet.

I was very interested in what you said about the performances for children! And I am amazed at the amount of potential there.

Everything here is under the sign of the last-minute preparations for *Orpheus!*[2] Last week I began working with the singers, after the dance scenes were blocked out. A tough piece of work. All my effort goes just to get them away from "playing" the scene, to have them sing with only the most sparing gestures, so that they do not destroy the style of the whole for me.

I placed the emphasis of the production on dance. The singing chorus is located with the orchestra. Scene I: a large-scale lament with striding figures and lovely groupings set against it, almost ritualistic — a group of priestesses. Scene II: Furies in the underworld. A clearly organized chaos of 45 persons on the stage — for a very strong effect. Scene III: Elysium chain-dance of spirits: suspended, gliding, peaceful. Loose groups detach from chain-dance constructions, a very well danced duo in between. Scene IV: only singers, Orpheus, Eurydice and Amor. Scene V: the most difficult, with which even Gluck failed. Privately, I named it "Triumph of Love." It is a little baroque, like a merry festival, with a few very pretty dance ideas scattered throughout.

I see with alarm that I am almost at the end of the paper, which means I must stop. We have awful weeks behind us, made worse by the unmerciful winter's cold. If I were to tell you everything that has happened in my apartment, you would not believe it possible. I am only amazed that I survived it all. For 8 weeks no usable toilet in the house. Medieval down the line! Of course I have a nasty cough! Thank you in advance for the promised package, Hanya! I am thievishly thrilled about it, and if I can't pick it up myself, Hanns B. will find a way to get it to me. It has not arrived as yet, but the anticipation alone is already wonderful!

Hesschen asks me to send her greetings. She has, like me, completely frozen hands and a nose to go with them! Affectionate hugs and greetings from

your

Mary

1. As the United States returned to a peacetime economy, enrollment in Holm's summer school in Colorado more than doubled. In New York she choreographed *Ozark Suite* to the music of Elie Siegmeister for a mixed company of eight, which she called the Hanya Holm Workshop Group. Performances in 1947 and 1948 met with good reviews, and as some of the dancers—Glen Tetley, Ray Harrison, Annabelle Lyon, and others—were well connected on Broadway, they may have been the link to Holm's first invitation to choreograph for commercial theater. She succeeded handily with *Ballet Ballads* in May 1948.

2. *Orpheus and Eurydice,* the opera by Gluck, premiered March 22, 1947, at the Municipal Opera, Leipzig, with staging and choreography by Wigman. Wigman used mostly students from her school. Although she expressed doubt in her diaries about her ability to undertake complete responsibility for the production, knowing viewers thought she achieved a great realization of choreographic vision (Partsch-Bergsohn 1994:128).

～

April 6, 1947 (II)

Mary Wigman   To Miss Hanya Holm
Leipzig CI   215 West 11th Street
Mozartstr. 17   New York 14

My dear Hanya,

This quiet Easter Sunday should not end without a greeting that shows my most heartfelt thoughts of you. Outside a good-sized storm is raging and it is not at all like spring; it brings back the barely faded memory of bitter winter months.[1]

But in my little room it is warm, and a pair of willow twigs stolen from the nearby park show the very first little hint of green. A pile of wonderful letters lies there, among them yours from the 27th of March. How quickly it traveled! Imagine: today we need 12 or more hours to travel from Leipzig to Erfurt!!! That a letter from or to Berlin only needs 5–15 days is unbelievable.

There is also a note from Benkert with the announcement that your package has arrived. Even if I do not know how it will get here, the joy of expectation is great and my sincerest thanks go to you, dear. I find so much in your letters! To me they are more than what binds us personally, worth so much in their clarity, and in their power of description they provide me much, much more of life over there than other letters, in which so much is always taken for granted that we here absolutely cannot know. You, who know conditions in Germany from earlier, will be able to get an idea sooner than anyone else of what it is like now. The poverty is boundless. A few profiteers, who swim about like blobs of fat on thin soup, may deceive the casual observer. But a single glance behind this false scene is enough! And if I tell you that on every trip to the school through the park I have to bend down at least a thousand times to pick up even the smallest twigs, and proudly bring the prize home for Hesschen to make a fire — that says everything. If I tell you that after the *Orpheus* premiere, with the many out-of-town visitors, none of whom had valid ration cards and who were all hungry, we had exactly half of a turnip left — no potatoes, no bread, that says it all. Even so, we are still better off than a hundred thousand others! If only you could read the letters that lie on my desk. These haunting, unbelievable human fates! They all can and must be borne, and for the most part with a composure which is heroic, not because anyone *wants* to do it, but because they simply must be borne.

Yes, it would be worth it to come here once and take in what a people's fate looks like from the *human* point of view!

It is that kind of day — the first in long months on which one can let the thoughts wander.

I would like to tell you so much, of work, of personal matters, but a piece of paper is always too small for that! Oh yes, Hanya, more than anything we fear — already — the next winter. We have no more good shoes. To have them soled we need everything that goes with it: soles, glue, and nails. God, and if you could manage a pair of wool tights for me, I would simply be ecstatic. Size? Underclothing size, the German one, was always No. 44 — and I have most certainly not gained weight. But they might shrink a little in the wash.

Finished — despite the small writing! Thank you again for everything, dearest Hanya!

I am

your

Mary

1. The winters after the war were especially severe in northern Europe, adding to the misery of survivors.

∽

April 26, 1947 (II)

Mary Wigman   To Miss Hanya Holm
Leipzig CI   215 West 11th St.
Mozartstr. 17   New York City

Dearest Hanya,

If only I could fall around your neck! A note from Hanns B just arrived, saying that a package from you came to him in Berlin. I think someone will be able to drive there soon to pick it up.

And yesterday! The package from Nuremberg promised in your last letter arrived (from Edwin Sears).[1] I am simply ecstatic! The package was badly damaged and had to be bound together by the post office (a bit carelessly packed for local conditions) — but I hope that nothing worked its way out. Contents were: 1 black pullover, 1 beige-colored wool jacket, 4 pairs of socks. Simply fabulous! I do not know if you can even imagine what a *feeling* it is to have something new. For years there was, and still is, no opportunity to get anything. What there was had to be mended, mended and ever again mended. In the war years, night after night, when we waited for the alarm, it was over the mending basket — and when we emerged from the cellar trembling with cold, having once again come through, it was back to the mending. *Now* an old cocktail dress — *at one time* very elegant — will be picked apart. It will produce a proper skirt and will make a stylish ensemble with the black pullover. I am as happy as a child!

Oh, I must tell you that the good Potter sent me a touching package, with men's long johns in it. He included a note that said I should give them away as a present. But Hesschen would not allow it. She said that the pants (wool and *long*!) will be altered and worn in winter. That is the only means by which I will get her through the second winter of poverty.

It is so wonderful that there are *real people*. And to you I would like to send an especially heartfelt thank you, Hanya!

In my own need for workspace I must always wonder if you have found a suitable studio yet. Housing shortage in New York — incredible! The only reason I can think of is that it has been caused by a flood of people who came there in the course of the war years, during which, over there, too, the good of the individual is certainly set aside in the face of the demands of the war.

To you in all love from
your grateful
Mary

1. Edwin Sears, a Jewish German American, was in Germany to participate in the Nuremberg trials. He and his wife, Vera, a Gentile, had escaped Germany in 1939. They settled in Denver and after a period changed their name from its original Sierdaz. Vera studied with Holm in Colorado Springs and New York and then sought out Wigman on visits to Germany. Edwin tried without success to help Wigman obtain a visa to visit the United States (Sears 2002).

❦

May 24, 1947 (II)

Mary Wigman
Mozartstr. 17   To Miss Hanya Holm
Leipzig CI   215 W. 11th St.
                                                          New York

Dear, dear Hanya,

Tomorrow is Pentecost Sunday. Hesschen and I have tried to give
the apartment a somewhat festive character. Vases stand all over,
filled with twigs and flowers, most taken, not to say "stolen" from
the nearby city park. Usually this "home" stands as a testimony to
the profession. It is crawling with students, who always leave
behind the most unbelievable dirt and greatest disorder. But today
it is really back to being a "private apartment." And just as I had
set the last hawthorn twig on the bookshelf with testing eye, an
acquaintance brought your CARE package, which he had picked up
from H.B. in Berlin. God, Hanya, it is simply overwhelming! Like
Birthday, Christmas and all the other holidays of the year together
and all at once! On the table in my workroom I built a pyramid out
of all the things and plundered a few vases to have the reality of
the boxes and packages poetically strewn with flowers. It looks
adorable, and what I would most like to do is dance a dance of joy
around this table! Mrs. Sears had sent me 2 packages *from you*! I
wrote to you immediately, too. The black pullover is my best piece.
I come across as downright elegant! And together with a skirt
finagled out of an ancient cocktail dress it has become a beautiful
ensemble that became familiar under the stage lights more than
once, when I was called in front of the curtain with a loud roar
after one of the *Orpheus* performances.

My heart is so full of gratitude, Hanya! I wish I could prove it to
you and a few others over there! Often it seems that we forget, and
perhaps it is simply necessary to life that one does that; but when
the warmth and affection come, in the form of a letter or a little
package, then it all comes back at once: the war experience, that
which *once* was and *now* is — this unique fate to which we as a
people are appointed, ungraspable despite having been experienced,
the guilt and need which we share, whether or not we wish to.
I try as well as I can to create something decent. And sometimes

I believe I have taken a real step forward. Then suddenly something unforeseen throws me mightily back. But why am I telling you this? You know it from your own life and achievements! The artistic-pedagogic profession is more demanding than anything else. It requires the ever new, purest idealism that gives worth only to the effort and never to the person. With a heavy heart I must let the 4 best of my small 8-member dance group go; they must and can earn their living, and I cannot provide them with this opportunity. Now less than before! My once so promising group work is therefore once again severely cut back. But no amount of complaining will help, and I will lose neither patience nor confidence.

I would still love to tell you much about work, everyday life, of sorrowful and joyful hours. I wonder if a reunion is ordained for us?

Hesschen sends her greetings! And I would like to be able to take you in my arms and say thank you!

Your
Mary

∽

July 7, 1947 (II)

Mary Wigman
Leipzig
Mozartstr. 17

Hanya Holm
215 West 11 St.
New York, 14

Dearest Hanya,

Your letter arrived the day before yesterday (it was dated the 24th of June) and I would have liked to have answered it on the very same day; everything you wrote was so full of life before my eyes. I had also received the book by John Martin a few days earlier and immediately threw myself into the chapter that he wrote about you and your achievements.[1] I was wildly happy about his acknowledgment and at the same time I became very sad at the realization that I know basically nothing of your accomplishments and work.[2] I have not seen even one of your productions! A few words can give no living image! Now I try to imagine how your current work must look — but I fear that I am groping in the dark; the reality is always completely different. It's the same everywhere! In just the same way that you over there, despite your best efforts and despite reports and pictures, can still have no idea of the life that we lead here or of the growing need and the frightening poverty of the people — or of the moral decay to which poverty leads! We here create a false image of your life: the Promised Land, Paradise on Earth! I do know a little — from when I was there — about how hard the fight for existence in the US is. The letters of so many American women confirm it implicitly, and it is also written in your letter, though you do not make much of it.

I need only consider how you must work so intensively year after year in the summer, and that you can only manage a very short vacation, only to throw yourself back into further expenditure of the body, spirit and mind.

I have not had a real break, either, since 1944, except for 10 days last summer when I was ill.

This year I seem to have come to the end of my strength. I do such silly things as fall down faint in the middle of the room (which I have never done before!). Hesschen runs around after me like an anxious mother hen out of fear that something might happen to me.

I would love to travel in the US Zone during the vacation! For weeks we have been trying to get the so-called short-term Interzonenpass, but it seems nothing will come of that. Restricted, they say. I almost have to hope that I don't get the pass. The trip is supposed to be hellish! This is what someone wrote to me from Munich: "After 21 hours standing in the train, the legs of our visitor from the Russian Zone were so badly swollen that we had to take our guest to the hospital immediately." And with me seeing black before my eyes after standing for ¾ of an hour!

So the vacation retreat will be a very humble inn in Erzgebirge (Gottleubatal). Even that comes with strings attached. We have to drag along *all* the food! Strange, but when I write that to you, it seems frightful. From our point of view it is simply a matter of course.

I received the cream and am blissful that something so divine could finally go on my face. I have also received everything else that you had sent along to Vera Sears. She sent me a few little packages herself, which did not seem right to me, as she has relatives here and most likely has to send everything she possibly can to them.[3]

Shirlee Dodge sent a package; Georgia Clarke, too. And Hans Wiener; also a package with clothes, which I found especially touching.[4] (But WOOL TIGHTS were not included.) It is absolutely enchanting how much warmth and affection come to me from the US. And I involuntarily ask myself, "What did you do to earn this? Does your dance really have such an effect that after so many years — and what years! — the memory still survives?"

And now, Hanyuschka, please, please don't *you* send me so much! I know that you had to work hard to earn your living — and really even had to earn the work itself! I know too, that only people in a position such as that can truly understand what need is. They naturally make a sacrifice, while others are content with the usual: "Oh, how very sad!"

Always the same! One speaks in thoughts with the people to whom one turns in letters, and that is how the boundary of what is possible in a letter is *so* quickly crossed. And this is just the start of everything I wanted to tell you!

Dear, good Hanya, I accompany you in my thoughts with heartfelt love and am

your

Mary

1. John Martin's *The Dance: The Story of Dance Told in Pictures and Text* (1946) contained an essay on Wigman as well as one on Holm.

2. Holm supervised major productions in Colorado each summer. She choreographed for guest artists and students after the demise of her company in 1944.

3. Sears sent more than one thousand CARE packages to family and friends (Sears 2002).

4. Wigman continued to use the original name of the dancer Hans Wiener, although he was known as Jan Veen in the United States.

∾

August 19, 1947 (II)

Mary Wigman
3-36 Waldfriedenbaude
Gottleubatal

Dearest Hanya,

We have finished packing. You would laugh at our luggage. Two backpacks and two small suitcases, both bound with cord because they have become so weak that they could burst and surrender their contents at any moment. Two shopping bags and a few beat-up boxes. That is what "today" looks like! What's the difference? I was able to pass a few quiet weeks. That is the main thing. Whether they brought longed-for and necessary rest — that is only determined upon returning to work. Next week I begin again. In the meantime I want to spend a few days in Berlin, where I will meet with Vera Sears. I hope nothing else happens before then.

A short letter from Hanns Benkert: "a CARE package for you from Hanya"!

I am just ecstatic about it. To put it briefly: in these weeks of vacation, we — that is, Hesschen and I — ate everything we had with us because unfortunately there was absolutely nothing else to be had. Neither with nor without ration cards would there have been anything to buy. And we both quickly became melancholy at the thought of a completely empty pantry in Leipzig and at the studio. It seems like a godsend that a little extra came. If only I could express my thanks as I feel it in my heart! But there are no words for it. And my conscience begins to prod: can, may Hanya do that? You don't have it easy yourself and have a son.[1]

I am looking forward to the visit with Vera Sears, who I hope will be able to tell me much about you. Are you back in New York? How much I would love to know about your work this summer, and whether you allowed yourself at least a little rest. And how is it going with the studio in NY? Have you found one?

Winter lies before us like an insurmountable mountain. I have no suitable room, at least none heatable — and the tiny studio in my apartment is heatable, but we have no coal. So this must all be endured a second time, and it really is laughable to think about it in August, when it is such high summer that nature withers. It looks the way I imagine California in summer! Dear, dear Hanya, I greet you from the bottom of my heart, and thank you. I must constantly do that, because my heart is so full of thanks. And always I am

your

Mary

1. Holm had never been well off. Klaus was forced to drop out of New York University for two years because they had no money for tuition. He remembered eating bread and bologna for many dinners (K. Holm 1994).

❧

October 19, 1947 (II)

Wigman
Leipzig CI   To Hanya Holm
Mozartstr. 17   215 W 11th St.
                                                        N.Y.

Dear, dear Hanya,

I was able to pick up the two packages of clothes from Hanns B. in Berlin a few days ago. I am delighted about the contents and ecstatic to be able to help out my students because the cold weather has begun here. Our hands, still frozen from last winter, always hurt, and despite warm clothing the cold goes through to the bone. In the summer we tried to forget all that and we were able to. The high spaces of my apartment mostly face north and are already completely frigid. And we cannot heat them yet, maybe not ever!

It saddens me to think that you no longer have your own studio, and, just like me, have to find shelter somewhere to manage your work. Here it is completely understandable. One look at the ruins is enough to explain the lack of space! And that we can never escape the financial struggle! The situation here has become completely primitive: whoever cannot work, dies! I know that in the end it is no different where you are, and that it takes a great deal of hard work to obtain the amenities of modern civilization that are taken for granted over there.

This morning I thought with mild longing of things like a warm bath, a heated bath towel, coffee made quickly on the hot plate, a slice of freshly toasted bread. GONE, ALL THAT. Hesschen is ill, so I am a Sunday housewife. Because she cannot eat I will skip lunch, too, and remain seated at the desk, as there is much work to be taken care of. We had a lovely performance in Berlin a week ago. Perhaps Benkert will tell you about it! And next Sunday there will be a repeat performance. Two-part program:

1. A talk by me about the dance experience and the development of dance.
2. Group dances.

I was even surprised myself about the impact of the dances, which are dear to my heart: "sketches on the theme of the demands of the time."

Vera Sears came from Nuremberg. She will certainly tell you of her impression.

On October 25th we are doing yet another performance, for the Volksbildungsamt Berlin. There will be only young people involved, and it will be interesting to see how they will respond to this difficult and serious topic.

Uhf, I still have to get a talk ready for that today.

I will write Carmen Rooker and thank her personally![1] To you, dear Hanya, go my special thanks! Will you promise not to spend any money on me? Vera Sears sent the other things to me — they all arrived! — soon after her arrival. The black pullover from you is my favorite and best piece. Except for a once, and in my opinion *still,* very elegant evening gown from the year '35.

I embrace you from the bottom of my heart, Hanya; my thoughts are with you in devoted love.

Your

Mary

The thick winter boots are fabulous —
Hesschen and I will wear them "together,"
She without and I with thick socks.
What more could we want?

1. Rooker (1900–1992) was proficient in many dance styles and danced in vaudeville for ten years. In 1931 Margaret Gage invited her to teach at the Bennett School, and Rooker contributed to the Greek plays that Gage produced. Rooker remained at Bennett for thirty-one years and developed a dance major there.

❧

December 20, 1947 (II)

Mary Wigman
Leipzig CI
Mozartstr. 17

Who knows when these lines will come to you, dearest Hanya. A person always writes out of the momentary situation and frame of mind. Today the view into the future is odd. It is concealed and opaque, at least for us here.

But Christmas is in a few days. And that absolutely particular mood that is bound to the Christmas celebration from many, many years ago has entered my mind again — a mood of which a person

wanted to know nothing because there was no use for it. And if
I *can* celebrate Christmas this year, I have all of you over there who
thought of me to thank for it. So many packages have come lately
and now I can once again bring the joy of Christmas to others.
I will make it as beautiful here as is possible considering — and
despite — the current situation.

Dearest Hanya, I thank you especially, and a very strong feeling
for you is always in me. When a letter from Yella Schirmer came
today many memories were awakened in me and I immediately saw
one situation quite clearly: Königsberg Theater, first performance of
the *Totentanz* (Masks) — all of us racing to the dressing room,
panting, dripping with sweat, masks still on our faces and me saying,
"Whether sick or all right, the dance is our light...."[1] Man is a
strange thing!

We (the school) had a lovely Christmas party here in the little
studio. It was so nice that it was a shame it was not public. But
perhaps the greatest charm of this party lay in the fact that it was
completely oriented toward this special group. I had thought up a
"play," written it, staged it and rehearsed it until it was flawless.
Hesschen insisted it became more heathen than Christian; in any
case the entire Christmas story was represented in dance. But it was
also very current, with a conflict between the dark and the light
angels, with the breaking out of the war and its consequences:
hunger, disease, death. The angel of peace ended the battle, and for
the finish: an "angels' concert" the likes of which none of the old
masters ever painted better. I myself found no end of joy in the
painstaking effort and was especially happy when it ended by being
much, much more lovely than I had hoped.

Did you receive the letter in which I thanked you for the CARE
package? That was a great joy, dear! And now another package
waits in Berlin, but it could not be picked up because the train
connection has become as good as impossible. Even Benkert could
not pick it up because it was addressed to me and only said "c/o
Benkert." But from what I have heard the address of Kiek Vander
was also on it, and because she happens to have my authority, *she*
could pick it up. CLOTHING AND FOOD! Hanya, it is so kind of you,
and my heart is full of gratitude.

How much I would like to hear about you, about your work,
about your big son! But I know that there are excessive demands on

your time. God, Hanya, if you could see me sitting here! Boots out of an ancient blanket, practically torn apart, and a pair of dirty work pants that have experienced the entire war. Three pullovers on top of each other, a shawl around the hips and the whole construction wrapped in an old blanket. It must look like a picture for the comics. And for us this has all become a matter of course, as if it had never been any other way.

Lunch in the kitchen — was there really a red dining room once and a feeling of irritation when the silver was not all perfectly placed?

And is there really a city called New York, in which the towers punch high into the heaven and there are no ruins anywhere?

Hesschen sends her heartfelt greetings. She goes to bed with the chickens because she gets up in the morning *before* the chickens, because that is when there is electricity and light; keeping house has become an indescribable strain!

My wishes, my greetings, Hanya — 1948? — May it go very, very well for you.

In devoted love

your

Mary

1. *Totentanz* premiered in January 1926.

January 5, 1948 (II)

Mary Wigman
Leipzig CI
Mozartstr. 17

Dearest Hanya,

I cannot let the last day of vacation pass by without sending you a greeting. I hardly even noticed that it *was* vacation. There were always people, from early to late, people who came to me in mental, spiritual, or material need. I almost felt like a psychiatrist. But how rarely can one help! At least one is *there* for the people to turn to, to speak openly and have someone listen. It was wonderful that this year I could provide a little joy for so many with the help of the USA packages that came for Christmas. It was simply heavenly. You have no idea how a person can rejoice over a little bag of coffee or sugar, over a little egg and milk powder when one does *not* have these things. To put it plainly, I worked like a horse to distribute my own treasures relatively fairly and justly. But in my whole life I have never had so much genuine and sincere joy to be able to assist other people. The most beautiful and opulent gifts that could be sent before mean nothing beside the spare offerings which can today be bestowed, and thereby bless someone. Naturally, to be able to do that one must have something oneself. And that I had, thanks to the gifts that came from over there.

Today I would like to especially thank you for the package that a truck driver brought with him from Berlin. A properly thick, black winter coat is inside, which I would most like to use myself to help my fur coat "last" a little longer. But this black one will have to be completely redone for me. And where to find someone who can do it and just *so*, so that one does not run around looking like a scarecrow! On the other hand I know so many others who have no winter coat at all that I am getting a guilty conscience over my own egotism!

A letter from Kreutzberg today. He writes ecstatically about the evenings over there.[1] I practically had stage fright for him. I have not seen him dance in so long! And he could have been rejected over there. That that did *not* happen, but rather that he was acknowledged — with complete knowledge of his limits — I find simply splendid!

I wonder what you are working on.[2] I can imagine that you are a little handicapped by the studio situation. I know from personal experience how much time and energy is uselessly wasted when one has many paths to travel and on top of that no personal space, and that only when it is convenient for others.

I have not heard anything from Vera Sears in a long time. She was in Berlin at Christmas. I knew that, and would have gladly traveled there to see her once before her departure, but the traffic situation is so unpredictable that I could not manage the trip for health reasons. Now she is probably already on the way over there!

I am to greet you most sincerely from Hesschen. She was once again on the go so much all day that she is sitting in the kitchen with trembling legs (by candlelight because of the electrical restrictions). I am also writing, quite medievally, by the light of two candles. (Unfortunately one ruins the eyes that way.) The peace that comes with age just does not want to present itself. I am not sorry for that. I am only sorry that I cannot produce any more "written" work. It was so much fun to write "dance histories." I worked out various chapters for my students: Egypt, Greece, Mexico, Peru, and the chapter about Indian dance lies there half-finished. Nothing to do about it! The motto of the present is: work to earn a living, otherwise hang yourself. I am certain you cannot imagine how *complicated* our life has become! For a few envelopes you have to go to 10 different places and then you have to stick them together yourself. And then you have no glue that holds, and smear it all over the desk and have to go running for towels. And there just isn't any warm water with which the damage could be quickly undone. AND SO ON!

This year, though, I celebrated Christmas fervently. And it did me good — at least mentally. My body was less inclined, and the whole time it threatened an attack of inflammation of the nerves in my back. I had it two years ago and it always flares up in times of overexertion. For two days I lay like a wretched dog; the pain was frightful. But I have recovered enough that I can start work tomorrow. If only it were not for that awful walk to the school! Three-quarters of an hour by foot. It is useless to wait for the streetcar. Most of the time it does not even come, and when it does come it is so packed that a person cannot get on.

Dearest Hanya, I cannot say with words what your loyalty and affection mean to me! My heart is full of wishes for you and full of loving thankfulness.

I am ever

your

Mary

1. New York dance critics praised Kreutzberg's performing abilities. Walter Terry wrote of his "buoyancy of body and spirit, his authority of manner, his masterful gesture and communicable love and respect for dance" (*New York Herald Tribune,* November 18, 1947). Critics found Kreutzberg's material stylistically dated, however, and much the same as it had been in his concerts ten years earlier. Robert Sabin found Kreutzberg's themes "threadbare and superficial in light of what has been happening these past ten years" (Sabin 1947:113).

2. Holm created *Windows* in Colorado in 1946 and restaged *Walt Whitman Suite* from the year before, adding men to the previously all-female cast. In the summer of 1947 she staged the Karel and Josef Capek play *The Insect Comedy,* which she then choreographed for a production directed by José Ferrer at New York City Center Theater.

∾

February 19, 1948 (II)

Mary Wigman
Leipzig CI
Mozartstr. 17

Dear Hanya,

How lovely that a letter came from you. If you only knew how often it presses upon me to write you at length, to tell you of everything that fills up and makes my life! But the crazy thing is that permanent, never-ending overcommitment makes impossible what a person would like to do, and in the end even *needs* to do. A letter should really always be relaxing and contemplative, as it focuses on the people to whom it is directed, and should be composed so that the writer is completely present in the other's mind when the letter arrives.

You have the singular talent to be able to do that, and that is why your letters mean more to me than I can say with words. The years that have slipped by since our last meeting do not fade away, space is bridged, and what could be called "closeness of presence" occurs.

A letter from Gabi Poege says so many lovely things about your son. "Kläuschen" — my God — it has been a long time, and *what* has happened in the meantime: beautiful things, odd, horrible, pitiful.[1] This wealth that has been poured into *one* person's life seems hardly believable. Even the most frightening experiences will enrich you once they have been survived and comprehended.

Where did Gabi Poege leave her husband? I do not know if I will get around to writing her any time soon. And *she* wrote of cruises to Belgium and England. Would you greet her for me? It was very kind of her to write!

Quite suddenly bitter winter. Twelve degrees below zero out of the blue, so to speak! And once again we fret over water pipes and heaters. Gone are the few coals we had — the little "ersatz" dirt from the cellar does not burn or heat. And we freeze, freeze endlessly, even though I, for example, am warmly dressed, with blankets and towels to wrap up in. If only this cold spell would quickly pass over! Otherwise the horrible dying will begin again, like last winter!

I really wanted to tell you about my work: school, group, and the restaging of *Orpheus*. Dreadful work this time because the creative aspect is lacking, the reconstructive process has to be in the foreground.

I was indescribably thrilled over the package of clothing (Berlin) and thank you for it. Margaret Gage, in the meantime, sent two packages of food and one of clothing and wrote very kindly. Unique person! A thousand dear greetings for you, and ever with you in my thoughts I am

your

Mary

1. Poege had American and German citizenship because her father was a German diplomat and she was born in the United States. She was the wife of the lawyer who had represented Holm during her divorce. A professional baby nurse, Poege took major responsibility for Holm's young son when Holm toured with Wigman and when Holm came to the United States. Later, Poege emigrated herself, and she helped Klaus and his wife with their young children.

⌒

May 10, 1948 (I)

Mary Wigman
Leipzig CI
Mozartstr. 17

My dear Hanya,

It is sad news that I have to write to you today.

Toward evening when I returned from an hour-long examination — representing the government, I had to evaluate the dance skills of 20 more or less talented girls — Hesschen was waiting for me in tears. There had been a telegram from Berlin announcing the passing away of Hanns B. the night of May 4th. The text of the telegram was so mutilated that I could not figure out the reason for his death, not even guess it. I am incredibly sad, and my entire being refuses to accept this fate. I know you, too, will be touched.

Maybe Hanns's wife will write to you or somehow let you know. I wanted to tell you personally, though, as a couple of days ago I received 2 packages from Frau Benkert, silent ones, so to speak. The contents were unmistakably half a CARE package, and one parcel contained wonderful knitting wool with the necessary tools (needles).

This mailing could only have been sent by you and I want to thank you very warmly. Maybe Hanns had not even had the chance to thank you for the other half — I don't know.

It is incredible that this life, which had by no means been lived to its end, should be extinguished. I had wished so much for Hanns, and believed that fate would again present him with a period of constructive, meaningful activity befitting his character, so that the difficulties of his last couple of years would have been only a pause, a painful waiting. You knew him, too, you know he was not really one to endure fate easily and you also know that his striving was justified because he possessed unusual talents and skills that had to be realized.

Today I cannot write anything else. My entire being is shaken by this news that the heart is not willing to accept.

That you are well — I hope and wish. My thoughts are with you with great cordiality and I am yours

very faithfully,
Mary

∽

May 23, 1948 (I)

Mary Wigman
Leipzig CI
Mozartstr. 17

My dear Hanya,

I wonder whether my last letter will reach you before long, or whether it will ever get to you at all. It contained the news of the sudden death of Hanns Benkert. I went to Berlin for his funeral and stayed for another week to take care of a lot of things that had come up during the course of time. An event like this completely unexpected passing will not go by without its traces. I not only spoke a long time with Hanns's wife, many other people told me about him, too, and confirmed what I knew myself about him, which is that he had grown far beyond what he had been as a personality earlier. For a few months he had not had to go to the locksmith's shop anymore and he had an easier job with more time for himself. He had actually blossomed and become wonderfully mellow both mentally and spiritually. A harmony emanated from his being that communicated to others immediately. And he, who really never could be helped in his difficult situation, stood by uncountable people with advice and action.

So at his grave hundreds of honestly grieving people gathered. It was so beautiful in the Berlin forest cemetery, which feels like an oasis of peace. And it was comforting that the people were forced to keep silence. Actually, Hanns was surprised by death. He was feeling splendid. He worked in the garden after having had a conference with some engineers in the morning. Suddenly a slight nausea came over him and he went to lie down for five minutes. His wife followed him immediately — and fits of choking began that continued until 12:30 at night. He was taken to the hospital at once — he had *all* medical attention and his wife was with him. Supposedly, it was cardiac infarction, a sudden clogging of the large heart artery. The cause is said to be unknown, the heart stops pumping, it idles. The doctors say he would have become a sick man had he survived the attack. So maybe it was good for him that the end came so fast and so unexpectedly. He died believing that sooner or later his life situation would change and that he would again have challenging tasks. There is, to stay the void, a recollection that is transfiguring. Dearest Hanya, you, too, have at one time suffered because of an individual — this one — and I know you, too, will have set up a monument of friendship for him in your heart.

Be embraced by

your

Mary

ᴕ

October 29, 1948 (I)

Mary Wigman
Leipzig CI
Mozartstr. 17

My dear Hanya,

You are so totally silent.[1]

Sometimes it makes me a little sad. I tell myself again and again that you are very busy and that you do not have time to write letters. I had written to you twice this spring right after Hanns Benkert's death. Maybe the letters did not arrive. But Benkert's wife, too, who had sent you an announcement of his death, heard nothing from you.

In Zurich, where I was teaching this summer, Mr. Denby told me that you have had a great success with a choreography and I was so happy to hear that.[2]

I was able to spend a few beautiful, beneficial summer weeks in Switzerland. How far back they are already! And how peaceful they were!

Our life here has hardly changed. Since the currency reforms, it is the financial side of life that is getting more and more difficult.[3]

It happens again and again that we have to wait to send off a letter because money for the stamp is needed elsewhere.

But this winter — at least here in Leipzig — we do not need to freeze. Hesschen is in charge of quite a few CARE packages which arrived over time, so that this matter is now in good hands. I was reckless and gave away too much!

My circle of students has become rather small. Who can afford to pay for studies now? But I will and shall not let it get me down. In November I will give a course for dancers in Berlin. An idiotic idea, really, because there life is a catastrophe and one is no longer allowed to have stuff sent to the western sectors. Otherwise I would have sent a few packages with wood and briquettes of coal so that I need not work in completely unheated rooms.

Just now Marianne Vogelsang is visiting me (formerly a Palucca student) with whom I will be working in Berlin.[4] She has promised to mail this letter there. Maybe it will get to you faster and more safely.

And now I beg you with all my heart for a short sign of life. So often my thoughts are on the way to you and I hardly know where to look for you and how to find you.

The most heartfelt greetings to you — in Hesschen's name as well — and all my good wishes.

Your
Mary

1. Conflicting emotions may have caused Holm's reticence to respond to news of the death of a man she loved and who had betrayed her, but 1948 was a busy and important year for Holm as she entered the high-stakes arena of commercial theater. Her "Eccentricities of Davey Crockett," one third of *Ballet Ballads*, had succeeded along with the entire production and moved from off-Broadway

to Broadway. In June the Experimental Theater Company's production of *Insect Comedy* opened at City Center. Also in June she contributed to $E=mc^2$, a nonmusical play directed by Hallie Flanagan at Columbia University. Holm's summer concert in Colorado included a lecture-demonstration, works by students, and a premiere, *Xochipili*, "concerned with the elemental pulse of mankind: primitive, indestructible, and ever recurring" (program note). Leo Duggan, Marc Breau, Oliver Kostock, and Glen Tetley were featured with a chorus of women, and Holm performed. *Kiss Me, Kate*, for which she was the choreographer, went into rehearsals immediately upon her return to New York and opened in December.

2. The Swiss International Summer Course, organized by the Swiss Association of Professionals in Dance and Rhythmic Gymnastics in 1946, was the first international gathering of dancers after the war. It became the model for other courses of its kind in Europe (Forster).

The American dance writer and critic Edwin Denby (1903–1983) wrote an essay about meeting Wigman in Switzerland the previous summer. It was not published at the time but appeared in *Edwin Denby: Dance Writings* (1986:358–59). Denby had spent part of his youth and young manhood in Europe where he studied modern dance and performed in the company of Claire Eckstein. He had seen Wigman dance and used her as a reference point in his later discussions of modern dance. As a critic Denby came to value ballet over modern dance; he was particularly eloquent in writing about the choreography of George Balanchine.

Denby could have been referring to *Ballet Ballads, The Insect Comedy*, or Holm's concert piece *Ozark Suite*. The critic had never been excited by Holm's choreography, characterizing it as "proper" and "conventional" (Denby 1986:75, 105), and he had given her *Orestes and the Furies* a damaging review in the *New York Herald Tribune*, January 30, 1944.

3. The currency reform of June 21, 1948, in the British, American, and French zones relieved financial hardship there but worsened conditions in the Russian zone. The reform, which was undertaken without consulting the Soviets, was followed by the unification of the three western zones and the establishment of a German government. In retaliation the Soviets began their blockade of Berlin on July 24, cutting the city off from West Germany and necessitating the airlift of food, fuel, other goods, and people into Berlin.

4. Vogelsang was in Leipzig from October 28 to 30 to give a performance, and she taught a class at Wigman's school. Friends helped Wigman arrange to join Vogelsang in her professional school in West Berlin. Wigman was welcomed there with flowers on October 4, 1949, but from the beginning the women were in conflict. Vogelsang left the school to Wigman within a year and opened another school in the eastern sector. Students' loyalty to the two teachers was divided, and ten of them followed Vogelsang to the East (Klein 1996). Although some dancers had thought that Vogelsang and Wigman would form a partnership, Wigman herself referred to Vogelsang as an assistant (Wigman 1950b via Forster; Wigman 1950c). Vogelsang (1912–1973) had a long career as a freelance soloist, teacher, and choreographer despite tense relationships with the fascist government during the war—she spent six months in forced labor in 1944—and the government of East Germany, where she lived after the war (Jeschke 1997:157–64).

❧

undated (I)
[Spring 1949, as contents make clear]
to Hanya Holm
239 Waverly Place
New York, 14

MARY WIGMAN STUDIO
BERLIN DAHLEM
RHEINBABENALLEE 35
Tel. 87 10 45

Dearest Hanya,

Nothing ever pleased my heart as much as your letter that arrived shortly before I once again went to Berlin to teach. Often I was quite sad about your lengthy silence of more than a year. Of course I knew about "Kiss me, Kate." I got appreciative and enthusiastic reports from many sides. And with greatest interest I read John Martin's extensive review of it.[1]

It is just wonderful that you are able to do this, too, and that you can create in a way that is compelling. And what intense effort and patience must have been needed to bring it to this level. And you write: 2nd cast.[2] That means the whole thing again. And in the summer no pause! How is it that again and again we are caught up in obsession that does not allow for a "comfortable" private life!

It is so good to be able to say that you — in spite of all the difficulties of professional life — could keep your energies unbroken, something that for a German artist of your generation here was as good as impossible. All of us here are stigmatized by war misery, by shortages, by everything that is a consequence of this terrible breakdown. And truly, the hardest of everything has been the past 3 years, during which the split between East and West led to a split between the Germans themselves, and in which currency reform brought about heavy setbacks that have made it impossible for the clean working person to recover yet. I have been working as before, but if I'd tell you how, and from what Hesschen and I have lived, you would not believe it.

We are with one leg in Berlin, and the second still in Leipzig. For eight days it looked like the move here would be possible somewhat normally, or legally. But already handicaps are building up. Traffic strike in Berlin. Sounds harmless, but proves to be catastrophic even into the smallest detail. For the journey from L[eipzig] to B[erlin] I needed thirteen hours. You ought to see these trains and the compartments, how people are packed like sardines with their heaps of luggage. One wonders how anyone is able to survive this. But one does! This stationery is the first and for now the only morale inventory of the future Wigman School Berlin. How long I can keep going, I don't know. I, too, have been damaged by the years of want. It cannot be repaired, that I know, but everything is done to halt it. At least when I work I am still quite without handicap. But walking for a long time is not possible. (Reason: the vertebral column. Result: a leg that hurts a lot!) I have to force myself to walk *slowly* because otherwise I have to pay for it.

I hope to be able to travel to Switzerland at the end of July to the International Summer Course in Zurich, where I taught last year as well. And afterwards I *must,* finally, rest for a few weeks so I can begin the Berlin task with fresh energy.

Hesschen, too, has enjoyed your writing a lot. She is also pretty handicapped by several infirmities. But we both have something like skipjack natures and again and again we move our heads toward the light when the dark lasts too long. Dearest Hanya, now again I have to stop telling you stories. What is such a letter, anyway? Outside, the US planes are thundering over the roofs. I wish I could crawl, as a blind passenger, into one of them to be with you very quickly and tell you more.

Be embraced cordially,

by your
Mary

1. *Kiss Me, Kate,* when it opened to rave reviews in December 1948, gave Holm national recognition as magazines and photo journals rushed to capture dance moments of the smash hit for which Holm choreographed numbers in many styles—jitterbug, tap dance, acrobatics, court dance, and modern dance. John Martin led a chorus of critics who marveled at how gracefully Holm had stepped into a new field. Her dances, he wrote in the *New York Times* on January 30, 1949, "have about them the ease and finish of a veteran." He found equally noteworthy that "they have retained the taste, the formal integrity and the respect for movement of the human body which belongs to the concert dance."

2. Holm rehearsed a West Coast company of *Kiss Me, Kate* in the spring of 1949.

Mary Wigman in 1949. Photograph by Wilhelm Reng. Courtesy Jerome Robbins Dance Division, The New York Public Library for the Performing Arts, Astor, Lenox and Tilden Foundations.

∾

September 11, 1949 (I)

Villa la Magliasina
Magliaso, Tessin, Switzerland

My dear Hanya,

For 3 weeks I have been, not quite on the bearskin, but almost exclusively in the deck chair, and therefore would have had enough time to send you a greeting. Thoughts cannot be bound to one spot. They wander and have often wandered to you with 1,000 wishes, greetings, questions.

Now the vacations are ending and with some detours the destination is: Berlin. What and how it will be, I can't even guess at the moment, but at least I will get there with somewhat rested nerves, where one, so to say, dances on a volcano. One can never plan anything more than twenty-four hours in advance. Hesschen and I are still homeless to this day. Provisionally we have found refuge in the house that has been put at the disposal of the M.W. Studio. But for the future this is not a condition that frees energy for work. And winter, once again, will be a private catastrophe under these circumstances. The house is big and cold!

Still, I am glad to have made this step that, considering my "old age," is pretty bold because it means starting all over *once again*.

Through the month of moving, with all its insecurity and the constant nervous tension, I was almost exhausted. I was therefore a little afraid of the summer course work in Zurich. But you yourself know very well how one can grow more than one's own powers allow when one knows that it counts!

It was nice to see so many people once again: Yvonne Georgi, Hans Wiener from Boston, many former students that are scattered all over the world today. I remember that Pola Nirenska must be in New York by now. She was in the group 1932/33 and then pudgy and pretty much of a beginner. But she has become a charming dancer and belongs on stage. Help her, if you can. Usually one can't do much in these cases, but I do not want not to have said it.

I am very happy here in a charming place, in the middle of a landscape that I loved more than any other for more than 25 years.[1] There are no resort goings-on, no traffic, very quiet, and everywhere you look, the wonderful rhythms of vineyards. The blue grapes ripening on the hoisted vine stocks. Everywhere golden yellow corncobs shining, tiny churches of many little mountain villages tinkling for Sunday, and autumnal transfiguration lays over the lake (the lake of Lugano) and the hilly landscape.

I feel personally touched by the wings of the angel of peace. And tomorrow the suitcases have to be packed.

How may you have spent your summer, Hanya?[2] Rushing from one activity to the other? Were I to wish you one thing it would be that the huge success that you achieved through "Kiss Me, Kate" would put you into the position of taking a breath. Will you write once again? Then you must also tell me about your son, all right? And should Pola N. show up, please give her a nice greeting from me! In my thoughts I am embracing you very very cordially and am remembering you very faithfully.

Your

Mary

1. Wigman's life in dance began in Switzerland. She studied with Rudolf Laban at Monte Verita, near Ascona, in 1913. She stayed with Laban in Ascona and Zurich during World War I, and she gave her first solo concert in Switzerland in 1917. Her Swiss student and friend Berthe Trümpy financed Wigman's first tour in 1919 and her school in Dresden. Other Swiss friends and admirers provided Wigman with support during her early career.

2. In 1949 Holm revisited her past at her thriving summer school in Colorado. Assisted by Alwin Nikolais and the conductor Nicolas Slonimsky, she rechoreographed one section from *Trend*, her greatest New World success, and an Old World success in Dresden in 1929, *History of a Soldier*.

1949–1956

BERLIN

Wigman and Hesschen moved to West Berlin on July 4, 1949. Wigman had received authorization from the East German government, yet she found it necessary to make the move clandestinely. In a letter to Holm in the year before he died, Hanns Benkert wrote that he had been trying to advise Wigman about emigrating: "She is being used as a pawn to advertise things she does not want to be associated with" (Benkert 1947). Berlin welcomed Wigman with a small subsidy, but it was not enough to support her, and her American friend Margaret Gage came to her aid with a stipend for her and financial support for her school (Gage 1979).

In the postwar period the dance community in the United States did not consider Wigman to have been contaminated by her work during the Third Reich. Her many champions had always focused on the mistreatment that she had received under the Nazis, and the left-leaning dance press, which had denounced her in the 1930s, was marginalized during the economic boom of the late 1940s and the 1950s and repressed during the McCarthy era. As the charismatic teacher of many women who led university dance programs in the United States, Wigman began attracting their pupils and many other international students at the Swiss International Summer Course, beginning in 1948, and at her own summer courses from 1950 on.

In 1951 Nahami Abbell and Ruth Kriehn were the first Americans to register for the full-year course with Wigman; many others followed.

Shirlee Dodge, one of the last American students to leave Germany before the war and one of the first to return, wrote a paean to her teacher and a report on the first Wigman summer course at the Berlin school, describing Wigman's pedagogic aim as "total human expression in which the physical, emotional, mental, and spiritual entities emerge" (Dodge 1951:36). Wigman's highly individualistic form of dance was less appreciated after the war, however, as Germany all but forgot its former leadership in modern dance and put its cultural resources into ballet. Wigman accepted commissions to stage opera and large-scale theater productions.

Holm choreographed a parade of Broadway hits after her 1948 successes with *Ballet Ballads, The Insect Comedy,* and *Kiss Me, Kate.* This group of letters ends with Wigman's telegraphed congratulations for *My Fair Lady,* the show with which Holm's name is most closely associated. Although Wigman and Holm, at about the same time, accommodated to choreographing with ballet-trained dancers, Holm on Broadway and Wigman in Germany's opera houses, both dedicated all their teaching to modern dance and continued to choreograph concert works for students and guest professionals.

∽

November 17, 1949 (I)

My dear Hanya,

Birthday letter and CARE package arrived; both caused great joy — plus my warmest thanks.[1]

During the summer I had already written to several acquaintances saying that they should not send parcels anymore because, by chance, I heard in the Zurich tram a conversation about "these Germans that still let parcels be sent to them although everything is available there." Well, the latter is true. But it is also a fact that hardly anyone can afford to buy anything as there is no money here. Whereas a year ago, especially in Berlin, we had the food-heat-and-light catastrophe, this year it is the economic catastrophe that causes everything to lay fallow and is handicapping everybody. Really, it is a crazy life that we are leading. Only someone who has actually been *living* here all through the war years can understand it and evaluate it somewhat correctly. The Kurfürstendamm as it now is seems to me quite symbolic of Berlin! In one shop after another the window displays are tasteful and elegant. Once *inside* the shop you ask for something, and for certain it is not available, or the choice is so limited that it isn't worth it. And if you let your gaze wander outside, upward over the level of the shops, the empty window holes in the facades and the rubble behind look at you. There is a lot of bluff, and also a lot of *real dignity*, be it with houses or with people.

It is beautiful, the bustling of a city cobbling itself back together again. Just across from the school there stood a large, badly destroyed residential building. For weeks a lonely man crawled inside — early till late at night — and all at once a huge hole in the facade was rebuilt. Then another. Now it has a roof with cheerful red tiles. It will not be long before it will have windows and doors and in the spring, curtains for a certainty. That's the way we all live. Each nail becomes eventful — "from old comes the new," as is the motto.

For me, at the moment, existence is far too exhausting. For two weeks Hesschen has been living in our future private apartment, a doll's house, and the smallness of its rooms is making me a little anxious. Instead, in the rather large school building, I have one beautiful, large room to myself, housing my grand piano, my old black desk and many other belongings.

God — this school! It is really difficult. There are enough students. Talent however? Average, most of it! How I wish I had at least 2 or 3 very strong, self-willed ones. Besides *no one* has money for studies. Without having the house rent-free from the city and a modest subvention in addition — we wouldn't last 8 days. Still, in no way do I regret the decision to come here, as Leipzig had become pigheaded and one was almost as isolated as during the war years. Here, too, one is not quite the master of one's own decisions. And once you want to leave, the running, the waiting, the begging for a visa begins.[2]

Strange that one gets used to this constant uncertainty, never being able to plan ahead with security.

Mr. Potter writes to me from time to time. His letters are very full and he is really touching in his affection. He sent all kinds of stuff about "Kate," and I have enjoyed tremendously your achievements with this work.

And now another huge task! May you succeed as much as in the first one![3]

Klaus, getting married! Children become grownups. And one ought to realize, therefore, that one is old. But one realizes it in quite different matters.

It has turned out that my back is not the primary reason for my leg pains but that they are caused by pretty strong disturbance of the blood vessels. "The nourishment of the legs is only secured by horizontal rest position," was the medical statement. But you know me and you know that I do not give in so easily, and besides, I am *very* sprightly in all things.

As long as I can crawl I will. Amen.

Dearest Hanya, again I want to thank you from my heart. Knowing that you do not forget me even when you keep silent, it is still wonderful to get a lively letter that brings you close.

Be embraced tenderly

by your
Mary

1. Wigman was born in Hanover on November 13, 1886, and named Karoline Sofie Marie Wiegmann. She was known as Marie Wiegmann until she simplified her name in 1919.

2. Wigman was trying to secure a visa in order to visit the United States.

3. Holm was about to stage musical numbers for *The Liar*. It opened in Philadelphia in April 1950 and in New York on May 18 to mixed reviews.

◠◡

December 9, 1949 (I)
Mary Wigman
private address:
Berlin-Schmargundorf
Warnemünderstr. 26

Dear, dear Hanya,

You have spoilt me incredibly! A few days ago another parcel arrived (and the birthday CARE parcel is not eaten up completely yet, thanks only to Hesschen's chronic parsimony!) and this time the HOLIDAY parcel is full of the most incredible deliciousness, like, for example, a big fat can of turkey, and a chocolate box looking colossally promising and noble. This one I would have tackled right away but Hesschen stood by it: "We'll keep this for Christmas!" I had to agree with her and so she vanished with the parcel under her arm toward the region of the cellar to secure the Christmas goods there.

Oh, Hanya, I wish I could give you a real present sometime! But since 1945 I have been a really poor woman and the low tide in the money chest has become chronic and stays that way.

As long as we lived in the Eastern Zone this was not particularly depressing. One owned nothing and there was nothing that one could have wanted. Here it is a little more difficult! If one has the crazy thought once again to want to have a beautiful dress that one can choose all by oneself, or a coat that one really needs, then one has to control oneself because one can see these things here again and it is possible to buy. Still, these things are not really essential, so one can easily be self-effacing. It is more important to help needy people. Right now Christmas parcels for friends and acquaintances in the Eastern Zone are the priority. There, as far as food and clothing are concerned, it is still desperate. And I am very happy if I get a parcel and can pass on something.

I was sick for fourteen days — bronchitis — it was really bad. But finally I am able to lie in my own bed and enjoy our new little apartment. Our "old-age place," so to speak. I think you would like it, too. It's the first "tiny apartment" of my life, and I have been a little afraid of the necessary "narrowing." But everything turned out to be beautiful, harmonious and comfortable. And I also appreciate that Hesschen has less hard work.

Our HOUSE-WARMING PARTY will be celebrated with Christmas and then we will have your turkey!

Dearest Hanya, I am afraid that your Christmas will bring a lot of goings-on and constant work. Potter sent me all kinds of press clippings about *Kiss Me, Kate*. God, how I would love to sit in the orchestra to see a performance. And already you are busy with another task.

All my tender wishes and Christmas greetings are coming to you and I am, very faithful and always,

your
Mary

Hesschen asks me to greet you and to thank you!

∿

March 2, 1950 (I)

Dearest Hanya,

It was nice that you wrote and your letter gave me great pleasure. Imagine, after 7 weeks I am still lying in bed. The first trials of standing and walking turned out very poorly. The broken ribs have healed quite nicely, *all* on the left side; 4 of them in the back, 3 in front. The healing of the inner injury is taking much longer. There is a lung injury that is taking an extremely long time to heal. Although the pain is still great, I am slowly feeling that I am getting healthier. It looks as if we will not get out of this endless period of illness. Now Hesschen, too, is beginning to have all kinds of troubles. As soon as possible I *must* go for recuperation and follow-up treatment at the sanitarium (near Heidelberg), so then Hesschen can have a general checkup and treatment in the hospital!

You know, it is really a strange fate that after all the years of need and want one cannot breathe freely and just enjoy life, and that only now all the damage surfaces that one suffered in those years. We are all suffering from that damage. As long as we lived in the Eastern Zone, one did everything so as not to get sick. One did not have time for it, but even more, one was in a kind of fearful panic considering the inadequate medical and clinical treatment.

My god, I'd have childishly enjoyed it if I could have accepted the Connecticut College invitation. It didn't work. I could not be indecent to the Swiss, after they have been so charming to me.[1] When I lie around here, like half a corpse, it seems slightly daring to make any plans at all.

Keep your fingers crossed that I will be up and working again soon! You will be working so hard all the time that I can't be sure of getting another report from you soon. But when, from time to time, a greeting flutters by, the joy is very great indeed. Every time!!!

Let me greet you from my heart 1,000 times, dear Hanya.

I am your
Mary

1. Wigman had signed a contract to teach at the 1950 Swiss summer course. She ended a letter of regret to Martha Hill, codirector of the American Dance

Festival at Connecticut College: "I want to thank you, all of you, for your great kindness and loyalty. You cannot imagine what it means to me not to be forgotten in your country and to be wanted again" (Wigman 1950a).

〜

August 12, 1950 (I)

Magglingen[1]

Dearest Hanya,

A cordial greeting first, and then my thanks for the thirty-dollar greeting that Maxine Munt presented to me from you.[2] It is so dear of you! Here the days fly by, although we all are groaning a little. The course is taught in huge gymnasiums and one would like to be on roller skates while teaching to get from one place to another light-footedly and more easily.

Once again, this gathering of so many dancing people is beautiful![3] And especially for me, because Berlin, at least "West" Berlin, has become like an island within the surging ocean. On the other hand, Switzerland is just about the ideal meeting point for everyone and everything that would not otherwise encounter each other.

I am dearly wishing that the people will want to "get" something out of my classes, as the best I have to give I cannot transmit. The classes are too large and the people too different in training and attitude. Still, I do hope I will succeed.[4]

It has taken a long time and an extraordinary effort for me to be able to recover enough from my illness to begin to work again. Now it is twice as nice!

And you, Hanya? Can you go on vacation? I hope and wish it so much! Once a year one ought to take a break from the constant tension that our profession demands.[5]

Whether we can see each other next year? I dare not yet think about it; we had to unlearn making plans so thoroughly.

Be greeted one thousand times and from my whole heart,

from your

Mary

1. Magglingen was the village where the 1950 Swiss International Summer Course was held.

2. Munt was an American dancer who studied with Wigman in the 1930s and with Holm in New York. Holm helped Munt secure a position at Adelphi University on Long Island, where she established a dance major. She married Alfred

Brooks, the first man to dance in Holm's company, and they founded the Munt-
Brooks Dance Studio and a dance company in 1952.

3. In addition to Wigman, who taught choric studies, the faculty of the 1950
Swiss summer course included Harald Kreutzberg, who taught Introduction to
His Personal Dance Technique; Kurt Jooss, Modern and Classical Elements of
Stage Dance; Rosalia Chladek, Method of Modern Expressionist Dance; Hans
Züllig, Modern Technique; Hilma Jalkanen, Rhythmic Gymnastics; and Nora
Kiss, Ballet (Forster).

4. The dancer-journalist Jacqueline Robinson described Wigman's choric movement classes: "None who have taken part, or simply watched . . . could ever forget: twenty persons, utterly different in their personality, style, or aptitude, within
an hour seem to melt together and form an eloquent, homogeneous group . . .
they feel reduced or enlarged to their essential core" (J. Robinson 1997:38).

5. Holm was finishing a busy summer teaching and choreographing in Colorado. In the fall she went into rehearsal for *Out of This World*, like *Kiss Me, Kate*
a show with music and lyrics by Cole Porter. The show was not a hit, but Holm
received good reviews for choreography; John Martin pronounced it "rich in style
and individuality" (quoted in Sorell 1969:117).

ᕀᕦ

April 23, 1951 (I)

Dear, dear Hanya,

Your letter arrived a few hours ago, and it brought me great joy!
I would like to have written to you as well, but during the good-byes
I had completely forgotten to ask for the address. Whether this
greeting will reach you in London, I don't know![1]

Your visit here was the nicest present that I ever received, and
out of my very warm and happy heart I want to thank you for
having come. Each single hour that we spent together was full of
silent knowledge of a bond that is deeper and weightier than all
friendships and relationships acquired later. It is incredibly beautiful
to know that all the years could not mar the sound base of
everything experienced, the bad as well as the good.

I also want to thank you for having taken the trouble with
Burckhard! Will something develop now? Silence on the whole line.[2]

For myself the sacrifice of the US visit would not be too
distressing, but I would be awfully sorry to have to disappoint the
directors of Connecticut College so severely.[3]

Now let me wish you a good journey back. A lot will be
overwhelming you when you get back after having been away for
so long!

Has "Europe" given you a little rest? My love accompanies you. And all good wishes surround you.

Hesschen joins in with her wishes.

I am and will be

your

Mary

1. Holm made her first visit to Europe since 1934. She came to rehearse the London company of *Kiss Me, Kate* for a March 1951 opening.

2. Holm may have tried to intercede with the U.S. consulate in order to secure a visa for Wigman.

3. Connecticut College had taken out large advertisements announcing that Wigman would teach in 1951. In his column in the *New York Times* on January 21, 1951, John Martin predicted that "she will bring with her an unmeasurable wealth of inspiration which cannot fail to stimulate us." In a letter to Pola Nirenska on April 25 (Appendix 3), Wigman expressed deep disappointment that her visa request had been denied, enumerating opportunities she had passed up in order to be available to the American summer festival.

∽

July 2, 1951 (I)

Dearest Hanya,

This morning a letter from Mr. Potter arrived that told me you are already at Colorado College and have begun your summer work.[1] And when are you going to have a vacation?

Although in the end I did not believe that it might be all right with the visa, it was quite a blow when I heard (first from Connecticut College) that I could not go. No one had notified me from the US consulate here. I went there immediately and heard, the visa was "NOT DEFINITELY REFUSED," that the research in my case was not complete yet, that it would take quite a while because I had spent almost my entire life in the Russian Zone. At first, I did not understand; after all, this zone has been in existence only a few years. Finally I understood that there are no legal possibilities for information as there are no consulates or embassies in the Eastern Zone. Besides, I understand that for a year the US has been a country at war and that under these circumstances any country would have grave reservations about all foreigners.

I feel tremendously sorry about the college. They have always written so charmingly that I had the feeling they were really pleased about my coming.

Just now I took Marion Yahr to the airport.[2] She was going to stay only for a few days but she liked it so much that it became three weeks.

Hesschen and I are sitting in our small garden, which has become really exuberant. It was a beautiful summer day today and soon I'll have to get out of my deck chair because Hesschen will get me with the garden hose.

I am waiting to know whether the Swiss summer courses will come through. If not, it will be a little miserable for me.

We have had a few quite nice school performances with works of the students, introduced by a lecture of mine. It is really the first time since I have been in Berlin that I feel the base has become stronger again and the artistic level is beginning to go up.

Dearest Hanya, be greeted a thousand times from my heart. My thoughts are often searching for you and uncountable good wishes are coming to you from

your

Mary

Hesschen, too, sends her regards.

1. Holm choreographed two works in Colorado, a quartet called *Prelude* to music of Armas Jarnefelt, and *Quiet City* to Aaron Copland's music of that name.

2. Yahr, who was from a prominent family in Milwaukee and ran a ballet studio there, took summer courses with Wigman before and after the war. She spent eleven Christmas holidays with Wigman and subsidized some of her vacation trips.

∽

December 5, 1951 (I)

My dear Hanya,

One never finds a really quiet, contemplative hour for writing! The day passes, the week passes, even "holy" Sundays, to Hesschen's disgust, are not exceptions anymore. One asks oneself why and *what for?*

Nothing changes and probably one does not *want* to do anything about that. I must quite honestly confess that, at the moment, I quite revel in the frenzy although it leaves me totally "shot" every night when I fall into bed.

It is the work on new group dances and larger choric studies that is captivating me — work that has to be done *besides* the work at the school, with its cumbersome side effects.

Typical of our situation: after a 2½-hour evening rehearsal, a crying pianist because her small son was at home with a high fever; a desperate girl who is going to be late to Valeska Gert's nightclub where she is making a few marks per month by sacrificing her sleep; on the stairs to the first floor a waiting assistant who is unsuccessfully trying to arrange our own rehearsals besides the ones in the theater at Kurfürstendamm.[1] (There are a few others trying to make a few marks for survival.) All this will hardly move you very much!

A grim Hesschen has been waiting to fetch me home. But the secretary did not allow it. She had worked out the budget for 1952 that has to be presented to the senate. And we are already trembling about *whether* it will be approved or simply rejected and therefore we would be standing in front of nothing and would have to close down because in *this* city no institution can exist without subventions.

My stomach was turning over and the figures danced in front of my eyes while within me the rhythms of Honegger that we had been working on shortly before were still twitching.

In mid-January a school performance. No money to pay the pianists for the necessary rehearsals, no money for getting a few costumes for the work. No money, no money, no money! It is enough to make one sick! And yet this chronic situation of deficiency does not take away from the real beauty of the work and from one's self, nothing of the inner impetus.

And, you see, Hanya, this *is* beautiful!

I celebrated a quite glamorous 65th birthday. Thank God it is a while ago. Now, Christmas celebration is approaching — it's a little depressing. Connected with it the traditional sentimentality wants to be attended to. A beautiful Advent candle has an honorary place in the greenery on the living-room table, and a proud, red poinsettia is shining under the window. I am rummaging through my closets to see whether among my clothes, linen, shoes, something can be found that one can do without and others might need.

Most probably this year our Christmas celebration will be in honor of American visitors: 2 US students from the school, a little US soldier who is detailed to Berlin, a young couple from Chicago, and maybe in January one from Milwaukee.[2]

— Now I must ask something very fast: Today a message came about the arrival of a HOLIDAY CARE parcel, sender *Elsa Rainer,*

SECRETARY.[3] — Is it from you, Hanyuschka? If so, I want to thank you affectionately, but again also say: You should not, need not, do this. You know that everything is available here — and you also know that between the two of us such proof is not necessary. All right?

A very warm heart is pulsing warmly for you, year in and year out. It loves you dearly.

Your
Mary

1. Gert (1892–1978) was a dancer-actress-mime famous for her outrageous and grotesque cabaret performances in Berlin in the 1920s. A Jew, she came to the United States during the Nazi period and ran a nightclub in Greenwich Village called the Beggar Bar, where her performances may have influenced emerging avant-garde theater figures like Tennessee Williams, Judith Malina, and Julian Beck, who were entertainers and servers there (Anderson 1997:139).

2. Inviting American students for Christmas became a tradition with Wigman. Joan Woodbury described the 1955 Christmas party in *Dance Observer* (1956:39).

3. Rainer (née Reitzenberger) and a sister were students of Wigman's and Jewish. They escaped from Germany with Wigman's help in 1937. Holm and Rainer worked out an arrangement for Rainer to be her school secretary. She performed her duties faithfully until the end of Holm's private teaching lessons in 1968.

❦

November 19, 1952 (I)

My dear Hanya,

After so long a time, once again a letter from you. How much I enjoyed it! And as a sign of remembering my birthday it touched me especially. Thank you! Absolutely, I understand that there is never enough energy and time to write letters. It is the same with me! At the moment I am sitting here bewildered in front of a huge heap of birthday mail, having the most noble intentions of answering and sending letters of thanks, still knowing that I will never make it through, that slowly and steadily one envelope after the other must disappear into the wastepaper basket.

But a few regards are especially touching and then it is not duty but the heart's demand to send an answer. Dear, hopefully you will completely cure this lung catarrh. It is too bad, to have to carry on with something like this, not being able to take enough time!

My God, how much I burn with desire to see your work in "My darling Aida." Even the title I find delightful. But what you tell me about the mixture of style is enough to confuse me. How difficult must it have been for the choreographer! I am glad you have finished this work and I am convinced your dances are excellent.[1]

Hesschen asks me to greet you very warmly. After 8 days of birthday hurly-burly and a flood of visits from abroad, she has fallen into bed dead tired. I, too, am somewhat done in. This combination of professional and private life is more than exhausting.

I am trying very hard to create a number of choric studies that I want to show in public in January. *Only* students. And it is damned difficult because one doesn't get from them exactly what one wants, how it ought to be. And where to get money for "costumes?" Even if they are very simple ones, they would have to be in multiples of 20! Crazy, that one is driven again and again toward "creation" although the exterior circumstances are 100% against it. Each time I swear: Never again! And then it catches me suddenly and I can't help it.

Dear Hanya, so many, many, good, ardent wishes want to reach you. I think of you in faithfulness and love and I am

your
Mary

1. *My Darlin' Aida* opened on October 27, 1952, and ran for eighty-nine performances. The show used the music of Giuseppe Verdi, and the book was based on his opera but set on an American plantation. The critic Arthur Todd wrote, "Miss Holm's sixth major venture on Broadway again demonstrates this choreographer's taste, integrity and innate theatrical craftsmanship" (1952:153).

◰

January 2, 1953 (I)

Dearest Hanya,

I just sat down at my writing table a total Christmas, New Year, and professional corpse. Hesschen is shaking her head and says: You belong in bed! — It has been snowing for 12 hours already and our rural Dahlem has become an enchanted winter fairy tale.

I would have liked so much to have written earlier, Hanyuschka! But it never worked. Behind me is a time that could be called: "black weeks," in the real sense of the word. *Everything* went wrong, as if everything and everyone conspired to make my life hell, healthwise, financially, and professionally. Therefore I began the new year with a huge sigh of relief. One knows from long experience that the low will sometimes be followed by a high.

And still, Christmas was charming. An old friend of mine, head of a big ballet school in Milwaukee, came flying over to celebrate a real GERMAN CHRISTMAS with us. Therefore, I made a special effort and decorated everything very nicely. For the first time in our Berlin apartment there stood a real Christmas tree, a delightful thing. Its only possible place was at the foot of my bed and at night more than once I had to pick needles out of the soles of my feet. Hell knows how, in spite of all precautions, those crazy little things got *into* bed!

On January 11th our performance is supposed to take place. It had to be placed earlier at the last minute — 10 days earlier. That means an incredible finish because we were on vacation and the students will return to work only on the 5th. I mustn't start thinking about it. Group and solo dances and choric studies, everything new. Compositionally, surely okay — but how will it be performed? How can one know when one has to work only with students?

In addition, I absorbed myself in costumes so much that I am scared to death. I made debts!! And I will be able to perform the entire program only *once* because part of the more advanced students have signed up for an operetta tour in western Germany. Exactly the ones that I cannot possibly replace. — Strange, that besides all resistance, one *cannot* give up. You will understand this the best because, like me, you belong to the fighter type that never has it easy because one stands up 100% for what one does.

Dearest Hanya, your food package arrived. I was touched and overjoyed. I thank you from my whole heart. We did with it beautifully. For Christmas eve 9 people were with me, MOSTLY AMERICANS. On the first holiday, 25 people.[1] I had invited our Eastern Zone students who could not dare to go home. But then all the others were begging to join, too. God, did they tuck in! They can never do otherwise.

Your letter shows me that you, too, have not had a "vacation." And the knees, Hanya! I am keeping all my fingers crossed that that hell of a TREATMENT will help!

And now let yourself be embraced from my whole heart. Although the new year is already two days old, the wishes for it are still red hot and fresh.

May it become a good year for you. This I wish you hotly and affectionately and Hesschen joins me with her wishes. Be embraced

by your

old and faithful

Mary

1. In Germany, December 25 is the first Christmas holiday and a second is celebrated on the 26th.

∾

February 28, 1953 (II)

Dearest Hanya!

My birthday wish so wanted to reach you on time. And just now I realized that it is already Sunday evening, that February does not have 30 days, that the mail does not go out on Sunday, that the letter can only go out on Monday, and that that is the 2nd of March. And your birthday is on the 3rd! I have been thinking about it all along, and in my thoughts I have sent my most heartfelt wishes.

My only excuse is that I have been sick for 5 weeks: flu, and to top off the whole painful matter, a serious jaw infection set in, making things difficult for me. As a result I am in a state of total idiocy! Hesschen attempts to comfort me, calling this misery a "creative pause." So let's hope for the best!

How thrilled I was with your lovely letter, Hanyuschka!

Yes, and the performance was also lovely. I was very happy. Naturally, the worst came right after, most of all because of being sick.

Is it really your *60th*? I can hardly believe it! On Yella's birthday we will celebrate yours along with hers! Dearest Hanya, my wishes for you are innumerable and come from deep inside, where the heart beats the warmest.

May the new year of life be good for you.

I send you all my heartfelt greetings

and am

your

Mary

Hesschen also sends her heartfelt congratulations!

∾

March 26, 1953 (II)

Dearest Hanya,

You in Italy. Splendid! I wish I could climb on the next airplane and be with you for a few days! I hope the film proposal will not take up so much of your time that you have no chance to relax.[1]

It appears that my strength is slowly returning, thank God. It was in no way pleasant to crab around so laboriously all these many weeks.

Of course, I *must* be back in form. On Good Friday we will give a repeat — finally — of our January performance. Under difficult circumstances! My "soloists" can be here only on April 1, and that means 3 rehearsals at the most. They have to perform both with the "choir" and "solo" in all parts and each has a solo dance in the program. And there will even have to be changes, as 2 boys have been engaged at the theater in Hanover and had to go there immediately. Hopefully I will get the whole thing back the way it was and how it has to be according to my standards.[2] How lovely it would be if you could be there! But you will be in Rome, and hopefully in accommodations without insects and other crawly things.

I am to send you Hesschen's warmest greetings. When I told her that you have run off to Italy, she said very approvingly: "At least *that* woman is sensible!" God, if only I could be sensible in *that* sense. But with what? Now, finally, spring has unpretentiously appeared and the first little spring flowers are blooming in our garden, which is still not in very good shape.

Funny, how rumors are created. Everything here is completely unchanged. Nobody worries any more than they ever did, though the refugee problem must naturally be dealt with, as it pervades both professional and private life. I have to send my sister a large package of provisions every 14 days. They not only have it hard, they also have too little to eat.[3] So fat heads of cabbage also find their way into the box, since there are no vegetables there either. In the school the most tragic scenes are played out, but one person can do nothing to help.[4]

It is about time for me to set off for school.

I would love to have some tiramisu, but I am afraid there is not any here! In any case, of all my flu infections this last one — jaw and frontal cavity — was the worst. It still bothers me a little.

Addìo, carissima! Thank you again for your letter. I hope things go well for you. Greetings to Florence and Rome! All my love —

your
Mary

1. Holm was working on the musical film *The Vagabond King*. Paramount Films released it in September 1956.

2. Wigman made a cameo appearance in the choric work. She moved minimally but projected with great intensity and control the figure of a prophetess. The audience responded with many minutes of applause (Kriehn undated:12).

3. Elisabeth stayed in the eastern zone of Germany after the war. She did not have enough students to continue to teach so she worked in a factory, spinning wool with primitive materials and methods.

4. Some students were able to cross from the Russian sector of Berlin to study at the Wigman School. The East German government subsidized their education but with such a meager allowance that Wigman charged them half the tuition that Westerners paid. Some depended for nourishment on the lunch provided at the school. Stories of harassment and threats against these students and their families by the East German government reached the ears of U.S. students (Kriehn undated:38)

~

November 22, 1953 (I)

Dearest Hanya!

So much birthday mail that I am scared stiff. 200 "official" greetings can easily be met with official, printed cards of acknowledgment. But all the rest, the same amount, I am convinced, ought to be answered personally. That means: night shift. Today it is Sunday, and Hesschen went to a concert, I am alone and if someone rings the bell repeatedly, even then, I will *not* open the door. It is a real November day, gray, cloudy, a little foggy. It's a good day "to snuggle at home." I have been digging into the stack of letters and fished for yours; therefore I am traveling to you, knocking on your door and saying: dear, dear Hanya, thank you. (I really wish this would not be an illusion!)

I try to imagine New York. There are still a lot of images when I can raise them, but a slight mist has overlaid them and, besides, one asks oneself: What does it look like *today*? It is good to get a letter from you, such a rare bird! But I understand only too well, that with a 100% professional life one cannot often spare energy and time for writing a personal letter.[1]

I had a wonderful birthday this year, the 5th in Berlin, and the first that was in no way shadowed. It was very harmonious, especially in the school. For the first time no troublesome hidden divisions, no envy, no jealousy, no repressed egotism.[2] This gave the "festivity" a special atmosphere of clarity and purity. Besides, the students had thought out something that touched me deeply. I had been a little sad about not being able to get the large choric works on their feet again, or to continue with this idea on the level that I had already reached. *All* my best, longtime, most talented students have gone into engagements! Those *now* creeping and crawling are more or less kindergarten and average talent. And then, all these children, who carry the characteristics of their generation, had rebuilt the "Temple" (one of my choric works) exactly like the original, architecture with bodies, except that each of the 28 figures held a burning candle in her hands and they did not make the steep pyramid suddenly collapse, but developed it into a very well-composed light parade.

Otherwise, from my end as well, there is nothing special to be mentioned. School work, once in a while a lecture, and the everlasting fight for future existence. Here, too: ballet, whether good or bad, is very big. Therefore, I regret especially that I cannot go on with the line of choric works, which had the only chance of standing against the mainly decorative effect.

Hesschen sends you many dear regards. And I myself take you into my arms in my thoughts, and in my wishes I am with you, as

> your faithful
> and loving,
> Mary

1. Holm was preparing *The Golden Apple*, which opened in April 1954. The lyricist John LaTouche and the composer Jerome Moross retold the Homeric legend of the Trojan War in the American Northwest. The show was in operatic format with no spoken dialogue. John Martin recognized Holm's shaping influence in the staging of musical production numbers without interruption by anything "that looks like a dance 'routine'" (*New York Times*, May 2, 1954).

2. The atmosphere at the school was sometimes tense. Her students had never seen Wigman perform and, enamored of the athleticism of visiting dance companies from the United States, they were impatient with her image-based teaching. Vogelsang's departure in 1950 had been ugly, and other staff members felt that they needed more latitude in their own work (Partsch-Bergson 1994:126; Müller 1986:282–85).

❧

December 16, 1953 (I)

My dear Hanya,

My thoughts are with you, my greetings and wishes yearn to come to you: Yesterday I suddenly realized that Christmas is ahead and I will have to make a big effort starting today to meet the expectations that are asked increasingly of me right now. When the purse is not particularly swollen, fantasy and craft have to stand in, and Hesschen is giving herself quite a headache in order to create the diverse festive meals *without* saddle of venison, roast of hare and Christmas goose.

Hanyuschka, I am so sad about Yella and Guri.[1] Maybe they have written to you. They both stand under such heavy shadows that I am afraid they will not hold out. Guri's husband has been very sick for months. I cannot believe he will get well again. Looked at clearly, it is really delirium tremens. Guri, with the 3 kids, is standing as if in front of nothing if a miracle doesn't happen, and some insurance or pension lights up the situation a little.

And Yella's husband is struck very seriously in a different way. Although in general he hardly had anything to do with the matter, his name has been brought up in connection with embezzlement at the Technical University and publicly he was made to look bad. He has not lost his nerve, but Yella is totally done in and is hiding in her apartment like a sick dog.

I wanted to ask you to write to them a few lines soon without letting them know that I told you. I know very well that *each* word of friendship is a blessing in such dark times. And what about sending them a parcel? (*I* don't need anything, Hanya!) I can hardly believe that both of them have to suffer so much at their *age*. How cruel life can be! Where is the "sense" of it all?

Dear, are you well? My very very cordial regards are coming to you, in Christmas colors, and I am

your faithful
old Mary

1. Guri Thorsteinsson Nöllen, like Yella Schirmer Kuhnert, a classmate of Holm's at the Wigman School, also danced in the first Wigman group.

∽

December 30, 1953 (I)

Dearest Hanya!

The new year is already sitting on our skin so closely that I am almost frightened. Of course my greetings and wishes for a *good* 1954 ought to have been on their way a while, as well as our thanks for the 2 divine Christmas packages from you.

God knows, it *would* be wonderful if you could be here! Because we *had* the Christmas goose, we *had* the most charming Christmas tree and we even *had* champagne, a real French one. Besides, our *German* Christmas had an American touch. Marion Yahr came in from Milwaukee, two other Americans studying here were invited. One of them brought along her 10-year-old boy, one of those entirely unconcerned guys, drilled in liberty, who gave our festivities a special note. He was glowing with enthusiasm and ecstasy.

As I, however much I'd want to, cannot spend much on presents — it would be so much easier — I plunged into wild decorative activities and worked like a maniac. Result: for one week my apartment has been a fairyland. You would be amazed! And each time I look around I am astonished myself, and pleased.

It is almost an art by itself to live within this mixture of needles, golden glitter, small and large figures. 168 candles were burning, from high church candles to fat decorative ones, to miniature decorative ones from the Erzgebirge, Bayern, Tyrol and elsewhere. God, now I am, in the truest sense of the word, a Christmas corpse, and I would love to disappear from the picture for a week. Not possible! On January 4 the school will begin again. I *must* be present.

And you, dear? Thank you so very much, and I was especially pleased about Klaus's greetings. On New Year's Eve — and this is tomorrow already! — Hesschen and I will toast you!

Unfortunately, I have not seen Yella in all these days. She has hidden within her 4 walls. But I still hope that she finds courage and trust in the future!

Dear Hanyuschka, my very, very affectionate wishes are flying across the ocean with these lines, I am, very faithfully and from my heart,

your
Mary

[In Hesschen's handwriting]: From my heart, also, a very tender embrace and a kiss of thanks from

Hesschen

I am now always cooking strong coffee for my "lion."[1]

1. Hesschen often called Wigman "my beloved lion" (Gage 1979).

∽

February 27, 1954 (I)

Dearest Hanya,

March 3rd is your birthday. Although I had a stupid series of accidents — or unpleasant surprises— that came over me unexpectedly, I remembered, so you may realize that you are close and present and very loved!

Right in the middle of the coldest weather — the second time this winter! — we discovered a defect in the school's heating system. Of course there was no money to fix it! So: either close down indefinitely — which is *impossible* — or find a way to manage. And that is what we did! Don't ask me how.

Then the Ministry of Finance wanted 2,000 marks in extra taxes from me, completely unaccountably. The tax collector did not want to take me to jail although I would have gladly gone just to get away from this awful business. So I went to various Senate offices 3 times until I finally got the miserable scrap of paper I needed to let the whole tax business drop. Isn't it enough to make you sick?

Now, at least, I have worked out a decent and, I think, an actually very good speech, which I will deliver in Hamburg March 6th and 7th.

Besides that, I plunged into Handel's "Saul," which I will stage in May in Mannheim as "*Szenisches Oratorium.*"[1] All by myself! My old friend, Niedecken-Gebhardt, whom you certainly remember, suffered a severe stroke and is still in the hospital, paralyzed on one side.[2] We were supposed to stage the production together.

I wish you joy on your birthday, Hanyuschka, from the bottom of my heart.

Hesschen also sends her best wishes.

I am ever

your

Mary

1. *Saul,* an oratorio by Handel, premiered June 18, 1954. In letters to Margaret Gage during the rehearsal period, Wigman complained about the inability of opera ballet dancers and singers to understand and execute the style of performance that she wanted (Wigman 1954). Planning her productions, Wigman sketched in charcoal, pencil, colored pencils, India ink, and pen, drawing floor plans, stage sets in perspective, and small well-rendered figures in action. She wrote out ideas, commented with approval or rejection, and added more ideas. Many are reproduced in *Mary Wigman Skizzenbuch Choreographisches, 1930–1961* (Wigman 1987).

2. Wigman and the stage director Hanns Niedecken-Gebhardt were connected in many ways. He had arranged a performance of Wigman's group dance *The Seven Dances of Life* at the Hanover State Opera in 1921, and he then became a proponent of modern dance. He was the organizer of the celebration of Olympic Youth preceding the 1936 Berlin Games. He made it possible for Wigman to find refuge and a teaching post in Leipzig in 1942.

∾

November 23, 1954 (I)

My dear Hanya!

I would like to thank you from the bottom of my heart for the lovely birthday letter. How happy I was to know you were thinking of me!

The "festivities" in school and at home, with many visitors from out-of-town, are, thank God, finally over. Even though it is terribly stressful for me as well as for Hesschen, we are deeply thankful for the fact that on *one* of the 365 days there is nothing but love and kindness, so that the heart is warm and a person can be truly happy. That is what I was for 24 long wonderful hours.

Guri has her 50th birthday behind her. Her husband is doing so much better, thank God, that he is once again able to work. The Kuhnerts are beginning a disturbing time because today the difficult trial began in which Kuhnert is involved. I just hope that it will go off without any problems. It is not a question of *guilt*. The way things are now, though, his full rehabilitation *must* be granted to him *publicly*.

At the moment I am teaching at the school more than ever and it is great fun.

That is a sign that I relaxed this summer. It was a heavenly and completely "private" vacation with Hesschen in Ascona. We had a jungle home and plenty of personal freedom. It did us good!

Berlin is an odd place. There is never true peace here. Everything always seems to be thrown back into question.

But the school is full of life. It is also nice that there is a group of Americans among the German students: 5 girls and 2 boys, one of them a very talented, cute fellow who used to work as a FREE CLIMBER. My mouth hung open as he told me about it. It remains to be seen if his very promising talent can be developed.

The other is Paul Reck (from Radebeul, near Dresden).[1] He is as much a Saxon as ever and is still the nice person and good friend as before. Eventually I will have to get to the piano excerpts of the two works that I will stage next year in Mannheim — [Carl] Orff — beautiful and very danceable music.

Hanyuschka, dear, I thank you again and embrace you tenderly. And do come visit us again!

I am ever your
Mary

1. Reck was born in Dresden and spent much of his youth in the United States. He returned to Germany in 1936 to study with Wigman, earning a certificate in 1939. He worked professionally in Europe until March 1940, when he returned to the United States and joined the Graff Ballet in Chicago. He served in the U.S. Army in the Pacific and then rejoined the Graff Company. In Mannheim in 1954 he assisted Wigman with her staging of Carl Orff's *Catulli Carmina* and *Carmina Burana* (Hamm 1993:3–4).

⌒∾

December 19, 1954 (I)

My dear Hanya,

It is Sunday evening, the 4th Sunday of Advent. It's really going to be Christmas soon! From the kitchen comes the aroma of freshly baked cookies. In the living room all the books have disappeared from the bookcases. Instead, the nicely decorated Christmas parcels form a row: for the colleagues at the school, for the newspaper woman, the postman, and especially for the four ashmen who empty the garbage bins and are especially keen to get their christmasy consideration. WHAT A NUISANCE! And still: They are all so nice, genuine Berliners with big mouths and good hearts.

Every year I swear not to continue this silly hullabaloo, but when it comes to it, I cannot resist. To be quite honest, I am having fun again doing it.

Yesterday I taught the last exercise class at the school, with lots of energy on my part and enthusiasm on the part of the students. In the window niche the four Advent candles were burning between the strong-smelling mountain "Latschen" that our "holiday farmers" had sent.[1] When I was about to close the class with a solemn walk, the pianist began to play "O, Du Fröhliche . . ." and all of a sudden all the young voices arose in choir, and it *had* become Christmas.[2]

Julie Hamilton was here and brought me a pair of lovely gloves from you, Hanyuschka.[3] I enjoy them so much and want to thank you from the bottom of my heart!

Christmas Eve it will be very American here. I have invited the USA students, so they will not feel lonely, but also to have them experience a "German" Christmas celebration.

Tonight in the windows along the street candles will be burning for the first time for all the war prisoners of the world. It is a beautiful custom, and our otherwise rather dark street has become very charming. Nothing pompous or showy, only silent memory.

Tomorrow I will have an onerous day. In the morning, a meeting at the Senate. We are supposed to move out of the house at Rheinbabenallee by the fall, and plans are to "merge" all kinds of things: Conservatory, acting school, MW studio (modern dance), Tatjana Gsovsky (classical dance).[4] If they had the guts to build a great academy out of it, there would not be any point speaking against it.[5] But they only want to save money and space! In the afternoon, meeting with a tax expert. Help me God — it will be dreadful!

Well, *today* the christmasy "peace on earth and good will toward men" has spread within me and around me. And, in my thoughts I take you into my arms very firmly and tenderly and greet you with all the love in a warm heart.

Your

Mary

1. An aromatic mountain pine and also a slang word for old, worn-out shoes.
2. The carol "O, Du Fröhliche . . ." translates as "Oh, Joyful One."
3. Hamilton, an American dancer, studied with Wigman for four months in 1954. She went on to dance in the companies of Alwin Nikolais and Murray Louis.
4. Tatjana Gsovsky (1901–1993), a Russian by birth, was the senior force in the postwar renaissance of ballet in Germany. With her husband, Victor Gsovsky, she had established a professional school of ballet in Berlin in 1928. During the

war she worked in Dresden and Leipzig. She choreographed Carl Orff's *Catulli Carmina* for the 1943 program at the Leipzig Opera House for which Wigman choreographed *Carmina Burana*. After the war Gsovsky worked in East Berlin, briefly in Buenos Aires, and then came to West Berlin in 1954. With a vision of dramatic ballet, she is said to have written one of the most important chapters in the history of German dance (Steinbeck 2001:19).

    5. Nothing came of these plans.

∾

February 1, 1955 (I)

Hanyuschka, dear,

I have thought of you so much. I could literally *see* you juggle on the slippery ice of the Hollywood film production. But I also know that it will succeed in spite of the unknown territory.[1] You belong to the few who know that to say A has the consequence of saying B within itself! Besides everything else, my confidence in you is unshakable.

In the last few days I have begun to get down to my staging of "Carmina Burana" and "Catulli Carmina." Once again, every single hair stands up when I think of the difficulties of bringing them to life.

Last year, Handel's "Saul" drove me to the border of suicide — but to create *this* to one hundred percent *rhythmic*, dancy music with the 100% "classical" ensemble of a provincial theater? Dear god! Would that I had a "theater" at my disposal with all the technical possibilities of shifting scenes, a lot could be done to emphasize and transform the dance.

But it is just a dressed-up *concert hall*.

Well, we know, one does one's best!

Hesschen sends her greetings! She has been miserable for several weeks: a secretion problem with a nasty rash!

The separate copy I add comes from a lecture I gave last year in Berlin, Hamburg, Mannheim. Maybe you have a moment to read through it.[2]

    toi — toi — toi

Dearest, someone here is thinking of you, someone for whom you are always present and close, and this is

your old
Mary

[Enclosed, a small card with a hand-drawn cartoon of a woman holding flowers.]

HAPPY BIRTHDAY
DEAR HANYA,
HAPPY BIRTHDAY TO YOU
MARCH 3RD, 55

[on the other side in Wigman's hand]

all the warmest congratulations
toi toi

                                        Hesschen

1. Walter Sorell quotes a passage from Arthur Weller, a *New York Times* film reviewer, lauding Holm's dances for *The Vagabond King* (Sorell 1969:146).
2. The lecture to which Wigman refers was not preserved with her letter.

∽

                                        July 7, 1955 (I)
                                        Mannheim
Dearest Hanya,

On July 2 the child was baptized, and it was so splendid a christening celebration I would not have dreamed it. What relief after weeks of pain and superhuman effort![1]

Of course I am totally done, exhausted, burned out. But what does it matter if one can say: it was worth it! When I sit now and let the two works roll over me, listening to the music and visualizing what occurred on stage, I still cannot grasp that everything was my work, the invention, the creation, from the stage design down to the detail of the gestures.

I would have thanked you a while ago for your dear letter, Hanyuschka! But there was no free moment for anything but work. You will be in Colorado, also at work again.[2] Vacation? I could do with that now, but tomorrow back to Berlin and 8 days later to Switzerland, for the Zurich International Summer Course.

Hesschen, who has been taking care of me here during the "finish," is already back in Berlin and will be taking me under her wing tomorrow for a short time. Without her I probably could not work like this anymore.

Dearest Hanya, 1,000 greetings and affectionate wishes for you — from the bottom of my heart,

your
Mary

1. *Catulli Carmina* and *Carmina Burana,* with music by Carl Orff, premiered on July 4, 1955. The Wigman sketchbook (Wigman 1987) contains fifty-six plans with rehearsal notes for the production.

2. Holm's annual production in Colorado was informal. No program was printed, and she introduced her dances and those of her staff and students from in front of the curtain, "giving the outline of the problem the choreographer was intending to solve" (Kostock 1955:131). Holm was also preparing choreography for the Broadway musical *Reuben, Reuben.*

Mary Wigman's Christmas party for American students, Berlin, 1955. Anni Hess (Hesschen) is in foreground. Behind her, from the left, are Emma Lewis Thomas, Betty Bowman, Joan Woodbury, Wigman (seated on floor), and unidentified students. Photograph by Charles Woodbury. Courtesy Joan Woodbury.

༄

December 14, 1955 (I)

Dearest Hanya,

For my birthday *you* were my most beautiful gift for which I
have wanted to thank you for a long time.[1] Now you are coming to
us as a kind of Christmas angel. I want to thank you before I get
eaten up by the usual Christmas hullabaloo. Strange, that all good
intentions are of no use! As soon as December is here one gets
caught up again. The first priority is always the Eastern Zone,
where some more things are available again but only a few can
afford them. Hesschen inevitably comes up with a list that carries
on top the name of my sister. And when I revolt at the names that
follow, the answer is "But she was so good to us during the war!"
One digs farther and deeper into the purse. Deep enough it certainly
is — unfortunately not full enough, though.

On Christmas eve our American students will be with us again,
and I will try to make it beautiful and festive. For the time being,
no "idea" has yet come to mind for the transformation of my living
room into a Christmas chamber. But something will come.

My god, *you* will not have any time to deal with these typical
German things. I see you before me, vivacious and active in your
wonderful steadfastness. Oh, dear, it was too lovely that you were
here.

When we celebrated Hesschen's birthday, Yella brought your
Christmas presents. We were not to have opened them and only to
have looked at them, but, as we were women alone together and
very curious, we peeked at them. It was beautiful! The stockings,
the article most in demand, that always need to be bought at a
moment when the money is gone! Now I feel wealthy again, with
this treasure in the closet. And then, my favorite eau de cologne! It
is a little too irresponsible, when one makes one's money the hard
way. But I don't deny that the pleasure is great and thanks come
from the heart.

How are you coming with your Pygmalion preparations?[2]

For a few days I was a little sad because when I visited
Mannheim it became clear that the Stravinsky evening I was to
direct next summer will not be possible. It costs so much money
that the city could not allow it. Because they are building a huge

new theater, everything is concentrated toward this new building and the opening season, which will begin January '57. They would like to have me for *that*. So in 1956 the beautiful task is forbidden me, but — as always — it may make sense. I can concentrate more on the school. And we will again offer a summer course here and I hope it will be worth the effort. If you can, please promote it a little. Maybe the work would be interesting for those who are planning a trip to Europe. We are always grateful for each recommendation.

Dearest Hanya, if only you could be with us for Christmas, too! We will think of you; you are dear to our hearts, and all our good wishes are with you and accompany you into the new year.

Let yourself be embraced

by your

Mary

1. Holm visited Germany in the fall of 1955 from London, where she was researching the upcoming Broadway show *My Fair Lady*.

2. Wigman sometimes refers to the show as "Pygmalion," as it was based on the George Bernard Shaw play of that name.

ॐ

February 26, 1956 (I)

My dear Hanya,

March 3 is your birthday. My most affectionate wishes want to reach you. How nice it would be if Yella, Guri, and I could knock on your door, a good bottle under our arm (like *you* three on my birthday!) and a big bouquet of spring flowers with it. As this cannot be, greetings and wishes come your way in writing instead, and are by no means any less heartfelt.

Time is rushing — however, not always at the same speed. For weeks we have had a shamelessly cold and hard winter, which has not yet let us guess at a coming spring. Our quiet Dahlem is shining in untouched splendor, white and glistening.

I am quite proud of my achievement: *every* morning, whether 18 or 25 centigrade below zero, through snowstorm or ice, I pushed on to the school, on a narrow path between meter-high snow banks. It was difficult for me. And in the school it was by no means peaceful. Each time coming home was a treat — and most beautiful, then, was a slightly prewarmed bed and a sip of cognac. After a while, I became "human" again. Strange, though, that thoughts and feelings circle so insistently around "winter" and that narrows down the extent of experience, whether we like it or not.

The school so far is doing well. I am curious to see if the summer course we have planned, and which was announced in the US dance journals, will be something of a success.

We would have liked to have known the result of your work on the musical "Pygmalion." I am sure it was a wild work time for you, and we hope it was worth it and rewarding.

All good and lovely thoughts go with these lines, and want to be with you and around you for your birthday.

From my heart

your
Mary

ॐ

March 21 (I)
[Telegram]

Dearest Hanya,

Letter from OLD MR. POTTER AND HE RAVING ABOUT YOUR SUCCESS IN "MY FAIR LADY."[1] A very good review of the piece as a whole included.

Delight here is immense.

All love, all the best and most heartfelt, and in addition a kiss for Easter

from your
Mary

Berlin
beginning of spring

1. *My Fair Lady* was the most successful Broadway musical hit up to that time, running 2,717 performances. It combined a substantial story—George Bernard Shaw's *Pygmalion*, adapted by Alan J. Lerner, who also wrote clever lyrics—music by Fritz Loewe, staging by Moss Hart, and the stars Rex Harrison and Julie Andrews. Holm's deft use of movement to tie the show together and make situation and character vivid won her respect and praise.

1956–1964

BERLIN

Wigman staged three more major productions and basked in the reverence of her country and the world on her seventieth and seventy-fifth birthdays. Her letters to Holm chronicle common themes in their careers. Their shared obsession with work and success is exposed as Wigman unself-consciously celebrates her own successes and honors Holm's. In household rituals the older woman displays her nationality proudly; Holm's domestic life becomes interesting with the marriage of her son and the arrival of grandchildren.

After the delirium of Wigman's seventieth birthday subsides, she reports a meeting with the dancers Martha Graham, Agnes de Mille, Doris Humphrey, and José Limón during a Berlin Festival Week. Modern dance was an American export by the late 1950s. Dancers just finding their way in 1930, when Wigman toured the United States, were now the acknowledged titans of the field. As younger women and men challenged their hegemony, dance was constantly renewing itself in the United States, the undisputed center of modern dance.

∾

November 15, 1956 (I)

Dear dear Hanya!

Here I am with an overflowing heart, and I don't know what to do with this exuberant feeling that awakened in me, and, at the same time, was given to me by others. Could anyone ever have dreamed of turning 70 years old? And now I *am* that, and am looking around in awe, being celebrated (and how!). I cannot grasp that one could be *such* a famous woman. The German press is suddenly reveling in the highest tones, and the press from the USA is not holding back.[1] My sister got a kick out of counting the telegrams and letters. Of the first: 230; of the latter: 380. All the packages and flowers have not even been counted yet. Vases, preserving jars, buckets, washtubs, all full of colorful delights! Celebration at the school quite lovely, very lively, full of dance, and *talent*. Youth ruled. In the afternoon, to the oak gallery in the old royal Prussian castle in Charlottenburg for honor and appreciation organized by the Senate and the Academy of the Arts. I had every reason to be happy, and *was*. My poor little heart held up bravely. And that was something! Because I have to admit, it *was* a strenuous day.

Now comes the duty of thanking everyone for the thoughts, the love, the honor, and the recognition. Quite a task! But I can't dispatch *you* with a printed thank you note. You are among the first I must thank personally.

Good old Potter sent me your wonderful article in Dance Magazine! But I am ashamed that you would want to give me yet *another* gift. I cannot imagine *you* as a well-to-do woman; I am sure you are not. So you should not send me anything, dear! And if you have not mailed it yet, I ask you please not to. Instead, take me out to dinner when I come over to USA, all right?[2] It would have been heavenly if you had been able to come for my 70th! But we *have* to see each other again on this earth, don't you think?

My thoughts are with you with great warmth, and I love you very much.

Your

Mary

1. In anticipation of Wigman's seventieth birthday, the November 1956 issue of *Dance Magazine* ran an article by Holm, "Who Is Mary Wigman?" It used a full-page contemporary portrait photograph of Wigman and photos from her U.S. tours. An essay by Wigman followed in the same issue. In "My Teacher, Laban," Wigman emphasized her role in helping Laban to formulate his theory of movement. A large photo of Laban was augmented by informal pictures of Wigman and her colleagues, including Holm. The December issue of *Dance Magazine* contained a news report of the birthday festivities, noting Wigman's

special pleasure that an American student had organized a celebration at the school (3). John Martin devoted his column in the *New York Times* of November 11 to a "Salute to Mary Wigman in Fresh Perspective on Her Seventieth Birthday." He wrote that people all over the world were thanking her for the "incomparable revelation she has made to [the] true nature and practice of the art of dance."

2. Wigman's trip to the United States became possible in 1958. Her American student, Nahami Abbell, believed that she was instrumental in clarifying misperceptions about Wigman that until 1958 were blocking a visa. Abbell, whose father was close to the Eisenhower administration, visited the State Department and talked with officials there. According to Abbell, the government had kept a dossier on Wigman since the 1930s. Some early entries hinted at communist sympathy, and her residence in the Russian zone when partition was formalized was another problem in the cold war period (Abbell 1996). In a letter to Pola Nirenska, Wigman wrote of Abbell, "Her father . . . was the one who backed me for my USA visa" (undated c).

∾

December 1, 1956 (I)

Dearest Hanya,

For hours I have been sitting in bed writing thank you letters. My back is already completely twisted and my hand is beginning to tremble. I'm doing penance! If you could see this stack of birthday mail you would turn away with a shudder. Two hundred and sixty-five telegrams, 700 letters, and hundreds of notes that accompanied flowers, packages, and other niceties. After being a voluptuous flower garden for a while, my living room is now an *office*. Everything is organized in nice little piles: West Berlin — East Berlin, West Germany — East Germany, Europe, overseas. I'm working like a conveyor belt!

This afternoon I had to get my official letters out of the way. This is the hardest for me, so I am recovering by writing to *you*. I would have done it a long time ago if there hadn't been so much that had to be taken care of right away.

Oh Hanyuschka, it was *lovely* to turn 70 and somewhere, deep inside, I feel truly blessed, though I always have to ask myself: What did you do to deserve this? So much love and affection all *at once* is hard to bear. So I am *doing penance* and trying as much as possible to thank everyone who thought of me. In most cases a printed card will have to do, but even for those I had to write more than 500 addresses myself.

My birthday was a beautiful day. The celebration in the school was charming, talented, carefully and splendidly done, and so heavenly *young*. Old Redslob (formerly Reichskunstwart and until a few years ago rector of the Free University of Berlin) — perhaps you remember him from Dresden and Ernst Schlegel's time — came and recited a self-composed sonnet. That was the festive opening in the morning. Then there was dance: solemn, lyrical, serene, comical.

In the afternoon the official celebration was held in the beautiful old oak gallery of the Charlottenburg castle. It was very impressive with the glow of candles and the flowers, with beautiful *old* music (harpsichord, shawms, etc., played masterfully) and then: tributes with many beautiful speeches — as is customary. I was *uncritically* happy.

Because I still have to be a little careful, there was no party at my place, only a few out-of-towners would not give up and came over, since they were leaving the next morning. Among others was Yvonne Georgi, who brought me an invitation from the Oberbürgermeister of Hanover to visit my hometown. Of course the topic of conversation was old times. And your ears ought to have been ringing!

Dearest, now let me thank you first of all for everything you sent me. My conscience is still not quite at ease with the 500 marks you sent. It is entirely too generous a gift, and it bothers me that you could have used it yourself. How wonderful the article you wrote in "Dance" was.[1] It took a lot of effort that you had to squeeze out of your precious time.

My god, how much did we — Hesschen, Yella and I — wish you were here!!! I've been so busy with this birthday mail I just can't comprehend that tomorrow is already the first day of Advent. Christmas stands in front of the door. Time is rushing once again.

How much would I like to send you an especially lovely present. I cannot, dearest! Just a book, the "Festschrift" put out by the Akademie der Künste, will be sent to you as soon as I receive an extra copy myself.

I embrace you tenderly, dearest Hanya, in all my devoted love I greet you

and am

your

Mary

1. Wigman refers to the November 1956 issue of *Dance Magazine*.

∞

January 28, 1957 (I)

Dearest Hanya,

A short while ago Dance Magazine arrived — your picture right there on the cover stepped toward me.[1] And then there was the beautiful article with more pictures. I passed it on to Yella, who will be just as pleased as I. And that man in the background of the cover is your son Klaus! How well I remember when he toddled around us just a little squirt! Probably in connection with the name Klaus, I remember that I was going to tell you about the passing of Mrs. Knippinger a while ago. Extinguished, and quite calm in the knowledge of her passing.

Here everything is very lively, and without care or regard for matters of health. I am not as strong as I used to be, but I forget or do not notice.

In mid-January I went to the opening of the new Mannheim National Theater. Those were truly festive days — and the strongest *artistic* impression was left by a performance of Schiller's *Der Räuber,* directed by Erwin Piscator on the new "Arena Stage." Next week I am going — or rather, flying — to Hanover (taking advantage of the birthday invitation of the city) and will see 2 ballet evenings for which Yvonne Georgi is responsible as resident choreographer and ballet mistress. I am very eager to see them as I have not seen any of her work for years.

At the moment I am working on a new lecture that I am supposed to give in Düsseldorf in mid-April. It is going very slowly because I am so very busy and really only at night can I find the concentration that is required for these deliberations.

My sister is coming for a week in order to visit my doctor again. Beautiful concerts, an occasional visit to the theater, on February 1, a dance performance of Dore Hoyer, who has continued to develop wonderfully and today is first rank. She is at a point now where she ought to dance over there in the States.[2]

If only I knew how the summer and fall will turn out for me! Once again it is quite intricate. I was supposed to, and wanted to, stage a Gluck opera in the new Mannheim Theater in late fall, but now Berlin has come in between. If *that* were to come through (for the Festspielwochen in September) then I would have to do it because I would never be forgiven if I declined. Although, as I see it, there is no plausible reason to accept it.

This could put my trip to America in question! If I can manage it timewise, I would like to fly in mid-April (right after the Düsseldorf lecture). But I do not want to work on *anything* over there. I do not want to appear "officially" in any way. Will you let me know how long you are going to be in New York? I must see *you* there and "My Fair Lady," too. But I don't want to stay there long, as my visit is really meant for California (Los Angeles, Margaret Gage — San Francisco, Catherine Austin-Müller; the 2 invited me and it is they who are making the luxury of the trip possible).[3] I can put New York either at the beginning or at the end of the trip. I have no more than 6 weeks for the entire undertaking. I ask you very earnestly for the time being not to tell anyone about this as I myself don't know yet whether I can come or not. Don't even tell our good Mr. Potter who could not resist his PUBLICITY obsession.

Please, write me briefly as soon as possible and just mention whether it is better to be in New York around April 15 or near the end of May.

It is lovely and stimulating to make plans, even when we know that only a small part may be realized.

Are you healthy and happy? You should be more than happy, dearest! We here, who love you, are very proud of you.

Greetings and a tender embrace from

your

Mary

1. *Dance Magazine*'s January 1957 issue carried a cover picture of Holm and an article written by Walter Sorell, "Hanya Holm: A Vital Force," subtitled "From Convent to Wigman to *My Fair Lady*." Sorell summarized Holm's education and early career and honored her for her contributions to American theater as a choreographer and stage director, finding it natural that she should have codirected the premiere in 1956 of the Douglas Moore–John LaTouche opera, *The Ballad of Baby Doe*, at Central City Opera House in Colorado. He lauded her teaching, writing that it had had "far-reaching influence, particularly on dance education in colleges throughout the nation" (22).

2. Hoyer (1911–1967) had been a student of Palucca's, and she danced in Wigman's group in the mid-1930s. She began a solo career in 1933 that she continued during the war. She ran her own school in Dresden from 1946 to 1948 and then directed the ballet of the State Opera in Hamburg for two years. Hoyer was one of the few German soloists to receive international attention in the 1950s. She performed at the American Dance Festival at Connecticut College in the summer

of 1957, where she premiered *The Great Song*. The critic Doris Hering wrote, "Miss Hoyer was to us a revelation in pure movement-intuition. Watching her was like revisiting the essence of modern dance—movement rising from a deeply personal source to assume universality" (quoted in Anderson 1987:47).

3. Catherine Austin (Mueller) was among the last group of Americans to study with Wigman before the war. She reported that she had urged Wigman to emigrate, but her teacher replied, "I am German" (Mueller 1996).

༄

February 25, 1957 (I)

Dear, dear Hanya,

March 3 is your birthday, and the days are rushing away under my hands and feet; I can only catch up by breathing heavily. But you see, you are not forgotten. On the contrary, again and again my thoughts turn to you, and a flood of warm and tender love is on its way to you and cannot be weakened or cooled down by the distance or the waves of a wintry ocean.

There is so much that could be said, but in the end only a heartfelt birthday wish comes out. In front of me lies a small picture that I not only find charming, but also love dearly. I fear that Yella will snatch it from me when we celebrate together in the time between your birthday and hers, when we put something special on the table to honor you and open up a bottle of Sekt to your health. If only you were here! The little picture was sent to me by Shirlee Dodge; it shows you with one of her two "daughters"![1] Was it nice there? Or *just* exhausting? God, *what* a distance just to teach one class! As God knows, we here are behind the times!

I feel a little frivolous for flying to Hanover for a few days, as guest of my hometown, and to see Yvonne Georgi's work, as she is ballet mistress there. Guess who I ran into after many years: Dr. Reinhold Schairer. Does the name ring a bell? Dresden, his wife from Denmark, a writer. They were with us often and always very lively, interesting. They spent many years in exile and just returned 2 years ago. They live in Denmark, but he is director of an institute in Cologne that gave him the task of fostering and promoting *talent* in all areas, though mainly in technical and scientific fields. Now I am to write a paper about the artistic area, that is, the field of dance. Actually, I should not take on the job, as I am working on another lecture, but the topic does interest me and the work would be comparatively well paid — as much as I would receive for staging an entire opera! Therefore, let the *brain* steam and unleash *its* power!

That is not all. Today I had a meeting with the director of the Städtische Oper. The senate invited me to do Stravinsky's "Le Sacre du Printemps" for the Berlin Festwochen. There was nothing but to say "yes" for the sake of the existence of my school and myself. But it will be a difficult undertaking, I am almost afraid of it. And it tears my whole summer apart. I will have to start as early as the beginning of June (with the *ballet* group of the theater!), pause in July and go on in August! I do not like that at all. The only time left for the USA is from April 20 to June 1! You write "in April we are in Los Angeles, etc." Does that mean I will *not* see you in NY on the trip *over*? But will you be in NY at the end of May?

No, I *do not* want to work over there. But whatever else, I want to visit Margaret Gage, who again and again has invited me with the utmost sincerity. I could also fly directly to Chicago, and after a short break continue to California.

A very short note from you is enough; just let me know if I can reach you somewhere and when. A detour to Colorado would probably not be ideal.

Tjüs, darling — I wish you a beautiful and 100% *healthy* birthday, which I will open in the morning with thoughts of you and a "serenade."[2] A tender embrace from

your
Mary

1. Dodge, who was teaching at the University of Texas at Austin, had three daughters, then ranging in age from nine months to five years.
2. *Tjüs*, also spelled *tschüss*, is slang for "bye" (Forster).

∽

November 1, 1957 (I)
[dated by Holm]
Ascona, Ticino, Switz.
c/o Mme Bara
Castello San Materno

Hanya, love!

Your letter followed me here, and full of enthusiasm, I jumped in the air thinking of a reunion at Christmas time.[1] What a terrific person you are!

I'd give a lot to watch you working, silently and secretly sitting in a dark corner. I hope everything turns out the way you want it to.

Well, for my part, I cannot complain as far as the spirit of enterprise is concerned. It makes me inexpressibly happy that the "Sacre," that almost indigestible piece, was such a success.[2] As a matter of fact I was so blissful that I did not even think that I needed a rest.

Then, all at once all kinds of health problems made their appearance, and Hesschen and I made a quick decision to come here for a break of at least 2 weeks. I stopped in Stuttgart to speak at the USA consulate's press conference on American Dance (in particular about José Limón) in preparation for the upcoming guest performance of LIMÓN AND HIS COMPANY.[3] I hope my appearance contributed suitably to the PUBLICITY.

At any rate, thanks to that invitation, two-thirds of the trip there and back was paid for. The Berlin Festwochen were very interesting for me! For the first time I was not only part of it, but I also saw myself the center of interest. Of course, the unending demands on me were a strain, but I made it through quite well.

It was nice to see so much AMERICAN DANCE. And to meet the dancers personally:

Martha Graham
Agnes de Mille
Doris Humphrey
José Limón

In addition to the artistic impressions, the personal encounters were delightful. I hope to renew them in the spring of '58.

But first, the most important thing: that *you* are coming to us! All hot wishes for the success of your "English" project.

I embrace you, Hanyuschka, and 1,000 greetings come from the heart of

your
Mary

Hesschen also sends her greetings and adds her wishes to mine.

1. Holm was in London in the fall of 1957, staging a production of *Where's Charley?* As she was needed there in early spring to help prepare the London company of *My Fair Lady,* she spent the Christmas holidays in Germany. Klaus

paid his mother a surprise visit while she was with her family. During the visit he met his future wife, Heidi Büttel, a distant cousin. She came to the United States in April and the two were married in May. (Klaus's earlier marriage plans, to which Wigman referred in her letter of November 17, 1949, were unfulfilled.)

2. *Le Sacre du Printemps* premiered September 9, 1957, at the Berlin Municipal Opera, paired with *Maratona di Danza* by the Italian film and theater director Luchino Visconti and starring Jean Babilée. A British reviewer, impressed neither with Wigman's choreography nor the performance of Dore Hoyer as the Chosen Virgin, remarked on the two works' common theme of sacrifice—Babilée's character sacrifices his life to win a dance marathon (Crichton 1957:125). Other observers considered *Sacre* a masterpiece, "an uncompromising statement of Wigman's artistic beliefs" (Partsch-Bergsohn 1994:129). Paul Moor called Hoyer's performance of the Chosen Virgin "vital, raw, almost violent" (quoted in Anderson 1997:233).

3. In the fall of 1957 José Limón and his company toured Europe and the Middle East under the auspices of President Eisenhower's special International Program for Cultural Exchange. In a lengthy report to friends, Limón wrote that the company's reception in London and Paris had been inauspicious: "The Parisian press disliked us intensely and wrote of us with derision and mockery." In Germany, however, he and his company were well received: "Berlin was our first triumph." He wrote of his meeting with Wigman, "It was a rare privilege to know this great generous woman, this rich all-encompassing maturity, this loving spirit" (Limón 1957).

∼

Mary Wigman
Warnemünderstr. 26
Berlin-Dahlem

January 31, 1958 (I)

Dearest Hanya,

You must forgive me for not letting you hear from me before your departure. I have a very uneasy conscience about it.

But I was dog-tired and my temperature began to rise gradually. Result: apathy, down the line!

If only I could get over this bronchitis! I can't walk around New York coughing like an old GRANDMA with one foot in the grave!

And you will have to work in the narrow and foggy London halls again. I think of you with pity!

Mary Wigman's *Le Sacre du Printemps,* 1957. Photograph by Siegfried Enkelmann. © Siegfried Enkelmann/ARS, New York, 2003. Courtesy Jerome Robbins Dance Division, The New York Public Library for the Performing Arts, Astor, Lenox and Tilden Foundations.

It was so wonderful to see you here, dear, and to have met your son. Thank you!

And I embrace you fondly. With all my best wishes,

your old
Mary

෴

February 21, 1958 (I)

Dear dear Hanya,

It is still far too early for your birthday letter, but I am afraid that if I do not write it now it will not get done. The days are rushing by and I have so awfully much to take care of before my departure that my head is already buzzing. But to whom do I say this? *You* know better than anyone else what it means to get one's stable in order for a long period of time. And you also know that — no matter how well it was organized before — one finds things a little upside down when one returns.

How often my thoughts have wandered to you, dear! Are things going as you wish there? I am amazed at your unswerving dedication and steadfastness, and my heart is full of warm, loving wishes for you, your work, and your well-being.[1]

I wish Yella and I could be with you for your birthday, to make it a nice occasion for you and to drink to your health from a bottle of something good!

On March 3, the day of your birthday, I am flying to Frankfurt to spend a few days working a little more on my fall Gluck production in Mannheim. On the 7th of March to Zurich, and on the evening of the 8th I will board the "Atlantic Super Swiss" airplane to land in New York on the 9th in the morning. My New York address: The Beverly Hotel, 125 E. 50th Street. IT IS ALL TAKEN CARE OF NICELY AND I NEED NOT WORRY.[2] I am a little bit afraid, however, to think of all the many people that I will not be able to avoid. NEVER MIND, I'LL FACE IT ALL! Your Elsa Rainer wrote me a very kind letter, and so did Arthur Todd.[3] My dear old Mr. Potter — maybe he is already a little senile! — is getting so agitated and I am having the hardest time trying to distract him from his publicity madness.

On the 17th I will continue to Chicago, the "Midwestern Wigman Meeting" is to be on the 23rd of March in Chicago and IN BETWEEN

I must visit Marion Yahr in Milwaukee.[4] On the 24th of March, though, I want to go on to California as quickly as possible. Sun — I hope! — and a little peace and quiet, for which I am really hoping.

Crazy! Other people fly to the 4 corners of the earth without batting an eyelash, and to me this journey looks like a huge adventure. What's nice, though, is that the lust for adventure has gripped me, even if the adventure will be limited to Margaret Gage and her milieu. I admit, the thought of the *wide* world does have its fascination.

Too bad that my flight does not go through London! I could drop in and spend a few hours secretly watching you work in one of the drafty rehearsal halls![5]

Darling, a little *sweet* birthday wish went off to you today. Hammans Pralines, the best Berlin has to offer. I hope you enjoy them!

Now I embrace you, beloved birthday child. With loving thoughts of you

I am your

Mary

1. Holm had had a full year in 1957. After her Colorado Summer Institute, where she choreographed two works for guest artists and students and restaged her *Ozark Suite,* she choreographed *Pinocchio* to the music of Alec Wilder for NBC television and supervised the road company of *My Fair Lady.* In England her production of *Where's Charley?* opened in Manchester in November and in London in February 1958. In 1957 she also contributed to a production of the Canadian Broadcasting Company.

2. Nahami Abbell made the arrangements for Wigman's New York visit, met her flight in New York, and accompanied her to Chicago, where Wigman was a guest of the Abbell family for several days (Abbell 1996).

3. Todd was associate editor of *Dance Observer* and the American correspondent for *Dance and Dancers.* In New York on March 16 he gave a party in Wigman's honor. The May issue of *Dance Observer* covered the event and noted the many distinguished dance figures who attended to pay tribute. Wigman was pictured with Todd and Martha Graham in a photo by Jack Mitchell (69).

4. The Midwestern meeting occurred in Milwaukee, hosted by Marion Yahr at her home. Attending were Louise Kloepper, Ruth Kriehn, Ellen Moore, Mary Fee, Jayne Poor, Betty Pease, Lisbeth Ebers Hoope, Georgia Clarke, Shirlee Dodge, Ione Johnson Cope, Margaret Erlanger, Nahami Abbell, Inga Weiss, and Nancy Brook.

5. Wigman and Holm did not meet during Wigman's visit to the United States because Holm was in London working on a production of *My Fair Lady* that opened in April at Drury Lane Theatre.

～

March 11, 1958 (I)

Dearest Hanya,

How I miss you! Even though everybody here has been simply divine to me. Especially Elsa, who has done so much to make this all possible and to ensure that I am not transported back to Europe as a corpse after 1 week of NY. Still, I am enjoying it fully.

Thank you for the "welcome" gift in the name of Hanya, Klaus and Elsa that waited in the hotel room to welcome me. I am almost bursting with bliss, thanks to you!

So much thrives here that *we* began a long time ago, changed, developed toward this or that direction. Even within the almost rigid aristocracy of Martha Graham's schoolwork, some of it is evident.

I saw "My Fair Lady" and I was overwhelmed. From the choreographic point of view it is a masterwork. Absolutely superior is the handling of scenes into which dance is placed as a completely organic element, so wonderfully relaxed that one hardly notices the transition from gesture to pure dance. Marvelous! I am overjoyed, Hanyuschka, proud and deeply grateful.[1]

I hold you dear and greet you tenderly. With you in my thoughts,

I am your
Mary

1. Wigman also saw a production of *West Side Story* and was impressed by Jerome Robbins's masterful handling of hostility between ethnic groups. "It was painful, reliving that," she told Louise Klocpper (Kloepper 1996a).

～

April 21, 1958 (I)

Dearest Hanya,

It is the height of summer. I am lying, comfortably placed, in the shade of a cool tree in full bloom, and looking at hundreds of roses bursting with grandeur. And I am *alone,* and cannot just think of you but also finally *write* you a greeting.

While I am lying here as lazy as a sun-drunk lizard, you are in the middle of furious work: Final rush?! Your son is getting married sometime soon. You won't have time to envy me.

To experience this country at this time of the year is the nicest thing that could happen to me.[1] And, of course, I am having a wonderful time in Margaret Gage's care. Everything before, God knows, was hard to take. Interesting, fascinating, shocking, pleasant. But almost too much for such a short time. In the end it is the people that do one in, so that a person can't dig oneself out. Even now I get dizzy when I think of how overwhelmed I was from New York on. I don't want to write all that. You don't have time for letters, anyway. But you should know that I think of you and have the highest hopes that your work will turn out well for you.

How much I would love to come to London! But I won't be able to. First for financial reasons — and then Margaret invited me for a trip to the Grand Canyon. I can take a plane to Chicago from Phoenix and without any extra cost fly directly to Frankfurt. And to see the Grand Canyon is one of the dreams of my life.

Dear, I send you all my fondest greetings and embrace you.

With all my heart

your

Mary

1. Gage's home was in the Pacific Palisades near Santa Monica, California.

Mary Wigman visiting the Henry Street Playhouse in New York City, 1958. Photograph by David Berlin. Courtesy Nikolais/Louis Archive, New York City.

❧

Dearest Hanya,

My thoughts are with you so often. That is where they are now in this quiet evening, when the setting sun colors the heavens golden red and illuminates the rows of Brandenburg pines.

It was a stressful workday, and the bus trip into the city — necessary for household shopping, as tomorrow is a holiday — finished me off.

Were you able to work in a few days of rest somehow or somewhere after your return to the States? I am sure you desperately need them, but I can imagine how you were bombarded from the time of your arrival at the airport until your departure for Colorado. I suppose you have been there already for a while and are hard at work.[1]

I wonder whether I will see you in August when you come with Klaus. It is around the time of my summer vacation.

"My Fair Lady" is still with me, and every now and then I play the record and enjoy myself. I know how there is a good feeling when something has succeeded and when you were the person responsible for it. But I also know how much has to be put into it, and how you would need a long rest afterwards.

I am trying to bury myself in Gluck's "Alkestis" — diligently learning music and text. I am trying to get a feeling for the scenic, spatial and choreographic development and above all else to find a line that carries through from the stylistic angle. For modern man the conflict in the work of a composer like Gluck lies in the rigor of the material, a Greek tragedy, which tends toward the archaic and comes across musically in the lamenting chorus, and the 6/8 and 4/4 exhilaration of festive and buoyant music, which is baroque through and through. I have decided to hide the singing choirs in the orchestra pit again and to leave only the soloists (singers) on the stage, and to use the dance group of the Mannheim National Theater as a dancing chorus. Through three long acts nothing much happens. Cross your fingers that something at least pleasant and perhaps even moving comes to me.

It is still a long time until fall. But even *then* I will have only 4 weeks rehearsal time altogether. That is why I must get all the preparations out of the way, including setting the forms so that I will not need to experiment any further.[2]

It is getting dark, and I am going to treat myself to a cognac to try to calm this somewhat nervous stomach. Because it is a very good French DRINK I will drink it to your health.

Greet your son for me!

You, though, I embrace in all love, and with tender thoughts

I am your old
Mary

1. Holm choreographed a brief opening dance for her annual concert in Colorado, and she closed the program, as she had done the summer before, with her 1947 *Ozark Suite*. Other choreography was contributed by her assistants, Oliver Kostock and Molly Lynn, and by advanced students, among them Bernadine Madole and Jayne Poor, both of whom had studied with Wigman.

2. One hundred thirteen drawings for the production were published in Wigman's sketchbook (1987).

∽

December 11, 1958 (I)

Dearest Hanya!

I wanted to have written to you earlier to thank you for your dear lines. But "Alkestis" in Mannheim did not give me time for one private gasp. And in Berlin? Well, you know yourself how it is when one gets back to the stable after a long absence. *Everyone* is happy that you are back; still, fodder is not prepared so you need to mobilize even more energy to produce it for others as well as for yourself.

The human being is, and always will be, a strange thing! As long as a person squirms in creative agony before one's demon, he is ready to sacrifice *everything* so the work can succeed. But once it *is* a success, keeping one's promise is not easy.

"Alkestis" was a colossal bit of work that had to be conquered in a few short weeks. It was of course done. But don't ask me what it cost in effort. I was just about ready for the sanatorium. But the name of the sanatorium is Berlin, and that is another piece of work in itself.

How often in my life have I experienced this blissful relief that a newly created work bestows upon us when it is fulfilling for oneself

and the public. And each time it seemed more pleasant than ever
before. It was the same with "Alkestis." Perhaps even more so
because, in this case, completely unique problems came up in the
struggle to create a contemporary and effective production. My own
personal and deeply felt joy lay in the successful mastery of concept,
material and music, of space, scenery and presentation.[1]

The choreographic background before which everything was
played out, and which also carried the entire production, proved
itself 100%. And the representation of the underworld through
dance became the crowning achievement of the whole.

By the way: many friends and former students came to the
premiere. Dotzler with her husband, Bibi [Trümpy] with her "son"
Roberto, Mltoda from Yugoslavia among others.[2] Therefore, the
reception that the city of Mannheim gave after the premiere was a
colorful and moving picture of great splendor.

All of this seems like a long time ago, though. Christmas is
pressing me hard and I don't know how to manage the demands
that come with it.

Tomorrow Elizabeth Selden (very early Bennett School!) will
visit.[3] The day after tomorrow is the school Christmas party, with
more than 30 people in my small apartment. Today we celebrated
Hesschen's birthday with Yella and Hilde Klemm and we thought
very warmly of you. Then Marion Yahr is flying in. The chain will
not break until after New Year.

And 1959? I hope the political situation does not affect my school
negatively.[4] Of course, we *in Berlin* have no fear. We are used to so
much. But the others? No one knows!

How are things with Klaus's marriage? Has his young wife settled
into the rhythm of New York?

And you, dear, how are you? So often my thoughts travel to you.
And today they bring my most heartfelt wishes and greetings for
Christmas and the New Year. In great devotion

I am your
old
Mary

1. *Alkestis*, opera by Gluck, opened in Mannheim on November 23, 1958.
Although all of Wigman's productions succeeded with the public, critics were
not kind. Of *Alkestis* Willy Werner Göttig wrote in *Frankfurter Abendpost* on

November 28, 1958, that Wigman's production was "outdated by a quarter century" (quoted in Müller 1986:297).

2. Roberto was an adopted son (Forster).

3. Selden was a dancer, choreographer, teacher, and critic who was European by birth but a U.S. citizen. She studied with Wigman and Laban in Europe and with Humphrey, Graham, and others in the United States before teaching at Bennett College. Judith Alter calls Selden's 1935 book, *The Dancer's Quest,* the first inclusive technical discussion of modern dance theory (1991:47).

4. The Soviet-controlled East German government made increasingly threatening moves in the late 1950s to stem the flow of migration to the West. Finally, the Berlin Wall went up on the night of August 12–13, 1961.

౮

January 1, 1959 (I)

Dearest Hanya!

The new year has begun, and I had made up my mind to send you a proper "Prost Neujahr" letter, most especially in remembrance of our New Year's celebration last year.

I was very touched when your flowers came for Christmas: five charming red poinsettias in a planter, surrounded by tender spring primroses. Simply lovely! Thank you for thinking of me, dear!

Just like every year, the Christmas season was very lively here with us, with many visitors from the West and East and the USA. It was a little too unsettling for me, as I do not feel at all well, and would have much rather spent a few quiet days in bed. But now the hubbub has passed and made way for our very stable everyday life, which is, yes, more monotonous, but much more manageable than constant celebrating.

I am sure you spent Christmas with Klaus and Heidi, whom I thank for their greetings; hopefully their marriage is off to a good start. And you will not have been able to enjoy much free time yourself, Hanyuschka, would you?

On January 15 I am going to fly to Mannheim, accompanied by our USA students, to see another "Alkestis" performance. I really miss the piece, which I really only experienced once, at the premiere. I am excited to see how it will be as one of their repertory productions.

Mr. Potter sent me a huge packet of newspaper clippings, all of which I cannot, of course, read. One, marked with a thick red pencil, discussed the projected receipts of "My Fair Lady" and he scribbled underneath: "I HOPE HANYA GETS A FORTUNE OUT OF THIS." By God, I wish it were so! But I do know all too well, that the naked truth looks damned different.[1]

Hesschen sends 1,000 greetings, and wants to tell you that she drank a sip of Sekt to your health (usually she stays with fruit juice) after the dying away of Beethoven's 9th Symphony on the radio and while Berlin bells were ringing in the new year.

May this portentous 1959 be a good and peaceful year for us all, despite everything! All my best thoughts are with you, dearest Hanya! I greet you from afar

in devoted love,

your

Mary

1. Royalties from *My Fair Lady* put Holm in a secure financial position for the first time. She bought a townhouse in Greenwich Village just one block away from her first studio on West 11th Street and Waverly Place.

∾

February 28, 1959 (I)

Dearest Hanya,

Where are we to direct our birthday greetings? We heard you were in Australia, and Yella talked a while ago about the Fiji islands for your recuperation.[1] And now our old Potter just wrote: "MY FAIR LADY OPENED IN SWEDEN. AND I HOPE HANYA IS ON THE PAYROLL." I'm sure you were up to your ears in work, and just couldn't write.

However and wherever you may be: I greet and embrace you in loving thoughts. The good wishes are many, sincere and genuine: may you remain healthy and full of zest for life.

There is not really much to tell about us. I'm going bravely to the school and looking for a new apartment with growing pessimism. Everything that's not too far from the school is too expensive. The rents are too high. And what is farther away would cost so much in taxi fares driving back and forth to the school that I wouldn't be able to handle that, either. So I keep looking and secretly wait for a miracle. Of course, the "Berlin crisis" is throwing its shadows on all of us. A person wants to keep out of it and does everything possible to do so, but such things simply cannot be wished away. And for me there is always the question of the extent to which this political situation will affect my school.

Will the enrollment of foreigners decrease or cease again entirely? We don't know yet. What a contrast to last year, when I could make my USA trip so expectantly and without hindrance! Well, nothing is eaten as hot as it is cooked! It is not that I am particularly discouraged or unhappy. But we will not be completely safe as we enter the spring, which sent us its first sign today with a beautiful sky, radiant sun and the first snowdrops in the garden. I wish I could lay them freshly picked onto your birthday table!

Hesschen, too, sends you her fond birthday wishes. She worried me because she has been very sick. Flu with a terrible middle-ear infection in both ears. My poor little one has been in terrible pain. And the fever just did not want to go down. But now I guess she is over the hump, but she is still very weak, and worst of all, does not hear well yet. We can understand each other only when we shout.

Dearest Hanyuschka, once again my ardent wishes and greetings. And *how* we here all wish for a reunion.

Always

your

Mary

1. Holm had been in Australia for another production of *My Fair Lady*.

❧

May 18, 1959 (I)

[dated by Holm]

Whitsunday, a most beautiful day, almost like the height of summer and that makes the approaching farewell from this familiar apartment very difficult.

Of course, it is late at night now, but you must know where we will be living as of June 1st, dearest Hanya:

Berlin-Grunewald, Taubertstr, 2-4

I was in Heidelberg for a week. Mrs. Reuther died.[1] Although I know it is good the way it is — in the last weeks she was hopelessly sick — my heart is hurting. All the wisdom of age does not protect from the selfish pain of loss.

Hesschen has been sick again, too, another flu attack. She is by no means at her best yet — and as I myself am not, either, I am a little afraid of the upcoming move. At the moment I do not really have a relationship with the new apartment. But this will come, as soon as we are living there and find our rhythm.

How are you, Hanyuschka? Are you in Vancouver yet?[2] And terribly hard at work? And are your children all well? Are they happy with each other and looking forward to the coming generation?

Dearest, this is just a short letter, telling you that I am thinking of you, that my wishes are with you.

From my heart

your

Mary

1. Wigman always referred to her lifelong friend, Martha Wohlenberg, by her married name.

2. Holm staged and choreographed *Orpheus and Eurydice* at the Queen Elizabeth Theater in Vancouver, British Columbia. It premiered in July 1959.

∽

July 5, 1959 (I)

Berlin-Grunewald

Taubertstr.2-4

Dearest Hanyuschka,

Highly honored Mrs. Grandma! The grandchild was born.[1] Yella told us, and Hesschen and I congratulate you on your new dignity. Whether you are still fluttering back and forth between Vancouver and Colorado I don't know. But I do know how intensely you work. And therefore don't wonder about a long silence.

Just imagine: I could have spent my summer vacation this year in the COLORADO MOUNTAINS. I was invited by the mother of a student (Nahami Abbell) who has a large hotel there. But I refused because I didn't want to be completely dependent. Mama wanted to pay for the flight, too! And that's what kept me from accepting the invitation. Our move cost a great deal, of course. I would not like to be over there without a penny.

A pity that I cannot show you our new home in the first freshness of its existence. I think it is most beautiful with all our old goods and chattel. At any rate I am happy about it and am amazed in hindsight that we 2 old bags pulled it off. Now that the stress is over we are fast recovering.

Summer course is in full bloom. As suspected, not as well attended as in previous years because of the Berlin situation, but nice people who are good to work with. Two more weeks, then finally a pause for me, also.

Hopefully not only you, but Klaus and Heidi and grandchild, are well. Our most cordial wishes are with all of you.

It is Saturday, we are living on our very big, covered balcony and think it is wonderful. Hesschen has chosen the sun while I rest in the shade on a newly acquired deck-chair. Prima! A little lazy — therefore the letter might be a little goofy. But it brings you my love, and I embrace you warmly

your
Mary

1. Holm's first grandchild was born June 27, 1959. She was named Karen Marie.

∾

November 29, 1959 (I)

Dearest Hanya!

It was very sweet of you to write me on my birthday. Thank you very much. I am very much indebted to you. I still haven't answered your last detailed letter. But you must forgive me!

I have been so ill and in so much misery for so many weeks that it was impossible for me to do or think anything that took effort. I did not want to send you just such drivel.

I am glad that the "Belshazar" staging for Mannheim has fallen through. I couldn't have handled all that work in my current condition.

It was aggravating that after I was up and merry once again I had an ugly setback. But now it seems — thank God — that I am finally getting better. At least my own therapy (infrared lamp and bright sunshine) has done me good, and I am relieved from the raging trigeminal sinus pain. It brought me to the border of insanity.

But I could celebrate my birthday quite well and happily. The students made the morning very beautiful. Among their performances one group dance delighted me especially. It was *so* good as a composition and in addition very well rehearsed and performed. Occasionally the deeper meaning of pedagogical work is revealed!

In the evening with me were: Yella (with Helmut), the Klemms, Cora Waechter, and Mrs. Dotzler who had come especially from Nuremberg.[1] (Of course a few more, too.) Your ears ought to have been ringing, Hanyuschka! And there was a lot of hearty laughter!

Now Christmas wants to come again! Although the air is like spring in Berlin. I wish we could once again celebrate together.

I am very interested in your opera project. And I must laugh, as I have often laughed about myself, because the fact is, we are given the opportunity to do these stagings although basically we have no connection to the musical, operatic form. I am curious to know how you deal with this new opera, without dance, without chorus.[2] Toi, toi, toi for it.

My school at the moment is an international hotbed of races and therefore very active. Two Egyptians with state scholarships, 2 Chinese from Hong Kong, dainty creatures that put on the European ballerina smile like a mask over their Mongolian faces, 2 totally gay young men from Greece who do not at all remind one of the noble Attic type.[3] Five girls from the USA, among them a chocolate brown youngster from the South. In addition, the Germans. A colorful picture.

Beloved little grandma, do you ever see your little granddaughter? Hopefully Klaus's marriage goes well. I think of you with great fondness and send you thousands and thousands of dear regards and the warmest wishes for Christmas and the coming year 1960 as well.

HUG AND KISS,
Mary

1. Waechter had been Wigman's student in 1926 and became a theater director in Wiesbaden before the war. The two women renewed their friendship after the war.

2. It is not clear whether Wigman is referring to *Orpheus and Eurydice,* for which Holm did use dancers—two ballet soloists plus a group—or to another project that did not come to fruition.

3. Wigman used the word *schwul,* used casually for *homosexual,* as is the word *gay* in English (Forster).

❦

January 1, 1960 (I)

Dearest Hanya!

Your poinsettias are still shining in my room and their beauty
pleases me every hour. My warmest thanks for your wonderful gift.

I hope you have been able to celebrate a beautiful Christmas
together. I'm sure your little granddaughter had sparkling eyes, and
I don't doubt her parents and grandmother did, too.

And now, the new year has already begun and stands with its
first demands. We welcomed it last night with a glass of Sekt and
this morning with the 9th Symphony. A splendid performance! And
each time my entire being vibrates when the soloist stands and
sings "O Freunde, nicht diese Töne, sondern lasst uns angenehmere
anstimmen, und freudenvollere."

I am sitting here with a gravely demolished hand (left) and am
in raving pain. Bad luck! With my childishly blessed Christmas
preparations I slipped on a piece of glazed paper and fell lengthwise
on the floor. Nothing broken, but the hand is so beaten and battered
that it will be a while before it is back to normal.

That's a shame because I have to fly to Bonn on the 6th, where
I have been invited to a gala dinner by our President of the Federal
Republic. I only hope I am able to strap my shoes on and zip up
my evening gown.

Dear, all my greetings and my most beautiful wishes for 1960 are
coming to you and your children.

Hesschen sends her love. And I embrace you,

lovingly and thankfully
your
old Mary

❦

On the third of March, 1960(I)

Hanyuschka, beloved and dear
Once again it is that time of year.
If I could have my way March third
When the day of your birth is observed,

I would be there to bring a bouquet
Of loving birthday wishes your way.
An ocean separates us, it's true,
And to quickly fly over is not hard to do.
But I must admit, though it makes me sad,
The money for tickets is not to be had.
So I reach for the airmail paper again,
To congratulate you by fountain pen!
And from within my heart I wish you might
Be blessed with the bountiful harvest of life.
May you be surrounded with kith and kin
And be happy as your new year of life begins!

and a kiss in addition
from
Mary

Hanya Holm teaching at her summer school in Colorado, 1960. Photograph by Myron Wood. © Pikes Peak Library District. Courtesy of Pikes Peak Library, Colorado Springs, Colorado.

∽

undated (I)

[late 1960, as content makes clear]

Dearest Hanya!

It was wonderful to finally hear from you personally. I was ecstatic over your letter! And of course I can understand 100% that in times of such overcommitment a person has neither time nor desire for personal reports.

Will you ever put your legs up and rest?

Yesterday evening on the radio: music from "My Fair Lady." I saw everything clearly in front of me, and I had to think about everything that goes with organizing such a musical and *what* then determines that it is a great success. I am curious to see how "Camelot" will do in the long run.[1]

It will be a melancholy Christmas celebration for me this year because for three weeks I have been lying in bed and at this point may only leave it at the most for 10–15 minutes at a time. I caught a cold, and then an abscess developed on my upper right lung, which made life difficult for me as well as for my doctor.[2] Certainly these things can be taken care of these days, but it is a tedious process and more than anything the chronic weakness is horrible to bear. In any case I hope to be relatively fit by the beginning of the new year.

Hesschen is not in good condition either; she is tormented with eczema that has spread over her entire upper body. At least until now it could be contained!

I was immensely thrilled with Klaus's personal success and congratulate him most sincerely.[3] And what a strapping little thing your granddaughter is! The picture is delightful.

Now I will have to lay my head down on the pillow again. But I will be with you in my thoughts a little while longer with sincere wishes for a beautiful Christmas and a *good* new year that will hopefully bring us together.

An embrace from my heart, Hanyuschka,

from your old,

true

Mary

1. *Camelot* premiered on December 3, 1960. The same team that had produced *My Fair Lady* had trouble this time, and the show went through many changes. Nonetheless, it had a run of more than a year, propelled by its stars, Richard Burton, Julie Andrews, and Robert Goulet. Before *Camelot*, Holm choreographed *Christine*, which opened in April 1960 and had a brief run.

2. Wigman was a heavy smoker for most of her life. The story goes that early in her career she was offered a cigarette to calm the violent agitation that she worked herself into while rehearsing her group and that she immediately started to smoke two packs a day (Kriehn: 10).

3. Klaus received special praise from a critic for his execution of dramatic pinpoint lighting in *Advise and Consent* on Broadway.

∾

January 4, 1961 (I)

Dearest Hanya

It is already pretty late for a real new year's greeting. But as wishes coming from the heart never stop, mine will not be too late.

My energy doesn't quite want to last to do what existence demands. I have been sick for so long that it will be difficult to find connection to *active* life again. Until now the passivity has not been too great — but physical weakness is ruling more than I would like. It was a bad story, this abscess that developed in the lungs. It is healing now, but the doctor says there must be no relapse. Briefly, existence consists of lying, getting up and lying again. In spite of that we have busily celebrated Christmas, as far as possible.

Are *you* getting some rest, love? It would be necessary after all that lies behind you.

So beautiful, the holiday flowers that came from you. I want to thank you warmly for them. Please thank Klaus and his wife for their Season's Greetings. I enjoyed their thinking of me.

May 1961 be a good and satisfying year for you, dearest Hanya.

I embrace you in my thoughts and Hesschen unites her greetings with mine.

Your

old

Mary

⌒

February 23, 1961 (II)

On the 3rd of March our beloved Hanya has her birthday. Will she celebrate it in New York with children and grandchildren?

We will think of her very affectionately here and guaranteed we will drink a bottle of very good German Rhine wine (vintage 1959) to her health. Hesschen made certain that just enough was left over from a Christmas gift.

I hope you do not have too much planned and are not so busy that you are forced to take no notice — or hardly any — of your birthday. It would be even better to know that you would finally take some time for relaxation and true rest. What craziness don't we pursue! I have been, God knows, ill for more than 3 months and must once again waste weeks in convalescence.

Shortly after your birthday we are going to Ascona, Switzerland, and I hope to be healthy and strong enough afterward to step back into my artistic role: to choreograph Gluck's "Orpheus" under the direction of [Gustav Rudolf] Sellner, the future director of the West Berlin Opera. It is the first time in my life that I will work under a different director than myself.

Innumerable loving thoughts, wishes and greetings will be with you on March 3rd, darling, and embracing you is

your old
Mary

⌒

May 16, 1961 (II)

Dearest Hanya!

How wonderful it was to hear from you. I had been longing to see your handwriting, but I know all too well how it is with writing letters when obligations demand 100% of a person. I am just happy that you have not already taken on another of these monstrous productions, as musicals can be! Are you taking a long break now? Colorado is not exactly a sanctuary![1]

At the moment I am in the middle of the first "Orpheus" rehearsals. It is work to which I am completely unaccustomed!

I would find it easier to stage the whole opera, which is what I did in Leipzig right after the war. This time, though, I must answer to someone else, but I am 100% prepared for it as my BOSS (Sellner) is a splendid man. Conversations with him are wonderful! But getting things carried out is another matter. The ballet in the opera is overworked. I have to fight for every rehearsal. The reconstructed Charlottenburg Opera House is by no means finished. It is suicide to rehearse there, especially for me, whose doctor's orders run thus: "You may not catch cold!" I do not know how to resolve this chaos! I also do not know how I can bring the performance about correctly and relatively well under these conditions. It is not possible to improvise with the purely classically trained opera dancers.[2] So, for me the whole affair is basically a leap "into the blue."[3]

The Kuhnerts, lucky ones, took off for Ischia. I hope it is nice for them there. I absolutely loved the island because it had something "Homeric" about it, even though there are no visible remnants of Greek culture left.

I have recovered very nicely from my long and difficult illness. Only physical weakness remains; the rest break was not long enough for that. Tant pis — I must endure for a little while longer.

I think of you in affectionate love, dear Hanyuschka. I wish you a good summer, and I think of you often. Greet your children and Elsa for me. I am and remain

your old

Mary

1. After the labors of *Camelot*, Holm directed and choreographed a major production in Colorado. It starred the ballerina-actress Vera Zorina, who read the Edith Sitwell text of William Walton's *Façade*, and Janet Collins, who danced an extended solo to *Six Psalms* by Heinrich Schütz and appeared with Don Redlich and Elizabeth Harris in Virgil Thomson's String Quartet No. 2. Collins had been Holm's lead dancer in *Out of This World* in 1950.

2. Both Wigman and Holm favored using improvisation to elicit movement from dancers, then molding it to their purpose. This was difficult for ballet-trained dancers who had no background in improvisation and may have resisted the practice. Wigman confessed in her diary that there was "yelling and crying on both sides" as she tried to get dancers to respond to her direction (Müller 1986:296). Broadway dancers discussed their attitudes toward Holm's improvisation with the critic Marcia B. Siegel (1993:42, 43). Sharry Underwood wrote of Holm's choreographic process in *Ballet Ballads* (1986:322–25).

3. *Orpheus and Eurydice* premiered on October 8, 1961, in Berlin. It was the last of Wigman's opera stagings.

∾

November 25, 1961 (II)

Darling Hanya!

The ecstasy of a wonderfully festive birthday has faded away, but the deep happiness that it brought still vibrates in me. I need only look around this room in which I am surrounded by so much love, friendship and respect, and pure joy rises up anew. True, the huge sea of flowers has lost its bloom; only the arrangement from Willy Brandt, our mayor, still blooms in all its glory. Because it is composed mainly of impatiens, it continues to bloom steadfastly and reminds me to be steadfast in response to my birthday mail. You have no idea! This year it is in the thousands.

Dearest, I have long wanted to thank *you*, but I needed a peaceful moment, and that is something that has not come until today. How, though, can and should I thank you? There stands the precious wish from Hanya WITH FAMILY AND STAFF before me, as full of life as if you had all come directly to me. There is a generous birthday gift of a $100 dollar check! I have opened an extra account so that I will not simply pounce upon it and spend it on Christmas presents. A $1,000 check also came, which Jan Veen apparently scraped together! I am truly a wealthy woman!

But I would like to put the extraordinary amount away for a vacation, and am naturally eyeing a trip to the USA.

Did Yella tell you a little about the wonderful birthday party that the Kultursenator and the Akademie der Künste threw? We old-timers wished you were there!! It was not just a great honor for me, it was inspired by much human warmth and genuine affection, and was joyous and free of any problems. I swam in bliss and forgot all my physical ailments.

There were many speeches: Yvonne Georgi as representative of my hometown, Hanover, Kurt Jooss from the Folkwang School Essen,[1] G. R. Sellner from the Deutsche Oper Berlin, Tatjana Gsvosky from the Opera Ballet, Dr. Schüler, director of the National Theater Mannheim. He spoke about his memories of the war and the first postwar years in Leipzig, and of my staging of "Orpheus" there. He also said that Hesschen was as loyal to me as Sancho Panza to Don Quixote, at which the 500-member audience broke out in thunderous applause. The main speech was given by my old friend Will Grohmann.[2] It was special because after all the acknowledgments of personal and artistic acquaintances, it gave a three-dimensional picture of the personality of M.W., awarding her an appropriate position in the epoch to which she belonged and was a contributing factor.

At the reception afterward Yella was a little tipsy and from time to time wobbled into my arms saying, "Oh, Mary, it is heavenly!"

There were pre- and post-parties because many visitors from the East came, including my sister, and of course Dotzler, who set her big mouth, always in the Saxon dialect, in motion. Do you remember Ilse Jacob, who was in our group? She is the wife of one of our eminent bankers, lives in Hamburg and has three splendid children. She was also there, as a result of which we will have enough Sekt for Christmas and the New Year! If only I could drink a bottle with you in all peace of mind.

A long letter! Will you find time to read it? I must thank you for the charming gift, the book that included all the letters, good-wishes and memories: "To MARY WIGMAN ... FROM HER AMERICAN FRIENDS." God, that is kind of you, Hanyuschka! I can imagine the effort and trouble that you went to get it together and make it so nice.

I sing with Orpheus: "Great gods, how should I thank you" — because this 75th birthday was almost like a gift of the gods, even if it was humans who brought it to me.

I can take you in my arms only in my thoughts, darling, but I do that in all tenderness, in all truth and affection and tell you once again of the love in my heart.

With all good wishes I am ever

your
Mary

[Photograph enclosed of Wigman studying her sketch of floor patterns for *Orpheus*, September 1961.]

1. Jooss (1901–1979) came back to Germany in 1949 from self-imposed exile in England. The Jooss Ballet, performing his blend of ballet and modern dance movement, had been touring internationally, but he received little support in Germany for his choreography and found it difficult to front a touring company (Partsch-Bergsohn 1994:147). Through his mentoring and teaching he was a significant influence on dance in Germany and the United States nonetheless. Lucas

Hoving and Jean Cebron were among his students, and from Jooss's school in Essen sprang, in the 1970s, a revitalized German modern dance form, Tanztheater. His 1932 masterpiece, *The Green Table,* has been reconstructed and performed by both ballet and modern dance companies.

2. Grohmann was a teacher, writer, and historian who promoted new art in Dresden in the 1920s. He included Wigman in his circle of artists — Paul Klee, Wassily Kandinsky, Lyonel Feininger, Ernst Kirschner, Oskar Kokoschka, and others (Howe 1996:104–5).

∾

December 15, 1961 (II)

The little Julklapp presents for students and employees are sweetly packed and stowed in the shopping bag, since tomorrow is the last school day before the Christmas vacation. Now I can start to breathe again, to begin the preparations for the Christmas party in my own house.

Dearest Hanya!

Thank you for your Christmas greetings, and I send Klaus and Heidi my thanks for their greetings and the little picture that they included. A handsome family, which hopefully gives you great joy. I imagine how you will celebrate Christmas together and how little Karen's eyes will shine.

Yella will have told you that she will be in Munich with Helmut for Christmas. So one of the traditional visits here will fall by the wayside.

Yella told me about your Christmas money for flowers, and for that I would also like to thank you warmly. I will invest the money in white lilacs, which at Christmastime speak so much of spring.

Oh, I am so thrilled this year at all the Christmas lights I will light on Christmas eve! It is simply magical here then.

Marion Yahr, our traditional Christmas angel, will fly to us again, and a group of "homeless" students will also be here.

I wonder if next year I'll be able to manage to come over to you? I would so love to! But it depends on so many things, not the least of which is my physical condition. But we'll see!

Hesschen just looked over my shoulder and asked me to send her greetings.

And so we two old ladies wish you not only a joyful Christmas, but also a happy, healthy, and *good* new year.

Embracing you tenderly I am

your
Mary

∾

January 17, 1962 (II)

Dearest Hanya!

Yesterday Yella was here, and we had a genuinely merry "girls' night," the first after a very long time, and we thought most affectionately of you. And I all the more when Yella gave me your New Year's gift for flowers in the form of 2 bills, for which I thank you a thousand times!

I am in a quandary whether I should use the money for flowers or a pillowcase. Hesschen pleads for the latter, while I am irresponsible enough to get two stalks of the red-blooming amaryllis. They bloom so beautifully in the windows of the flower shop, and I have a vase in which they would look especially decorative. Granted, their blooming time is short, while the white pillowcase will have a very long life span. I am excited to see who wins the battle!

Actually, I wanted to come over there now, in spring, stay in New York a little while and then wend my way through the different states to California, to relax with Margaret G. But all that requires time! And at the moment I am more tied to the school than ever.

I think everyone would fall asleep during a long absence. One of my best, longtime assistants intends to go out on her own — I thoroughly approve — and that of course means that her performance with me is not 100% what it would otherwise be.[1] So I will just have to wait it out.

For that reason I would only too gladly run off, as my physical condition, except for a cold, is good. The financial situation is also excellent. The ticket is from M. Gage, and then I have set aside my birthday mail, yours, and that from Jan Veen, for that purpose.

How are things going for you, Hanyuschka? Are you doing "Orpheus" in Toronto?[2] Yella told me. Are you enjoying it? Are children and grandchildren OK?[3]

Your charming card is still on my bookcase: "HANYA WITH
FAMILY AND STAFF." I just cannot tear myself away from it and am
happy every time my glance falls on it.

Please send Klaus and Heidi my greetings, and your ever-true
Elsa, as well. I embrace you, thank you from my heart and envelop
you with many, many good wishes

from

your old, true
Mary

1. Til Thiele and Manja Chmièl were Wigman's assistants at this time. It was
Chmièl who left. Thiele had toured with Palucca before the war, and after the
war she joined Wigman's staff in Berlin and lived at the school for almost twenty
years (Thiele 1996). Chmièl had hitchhiked through war-torn regions and ille-
gally crossed borders in order to reach Leipzig and study with Wigman in 1946.
She became Wigman's assistant in Berlin in 1952. After leaving the Wigman
School, Chmièl opened her own studio in Berlin and had a dance company into
the 1970s. She rejected the subjectivity of Wigman's training yet remained faithful to the aim of freeing the individuality of her students. She is said to have
been a link between Ausdruckstanz and its modern incarnations (David 1997:56).
The Japanese American dancers Eiko and Koma, who developed dramatic expres-
siveness through stillness, found guidance in Chmièl, who, according to a former
student, "had penetrated to the dramatic essence of movements" (Sieben 1997:57).
Hellmut Gottschild replaced Chmièl as Wigman's assistant and remained until
1967 when the school closed. He came to the United States in 1968 and embarked
on a career as a dance soloist, choreographer, and co-artistic director of the Zero
Moving Dance Company. He became professor of dance at Temple University
in Philadelphia.

2. Holm's 1959 staging of *Orpheus and Eurydice* in Vancouver, British Columbia, was repeated in Toronto in May 1962.

3. Holm's second granddaughter was born November 2, 1961, and named
Angela Susan.

❧

Mary Wigman, Berlin-Grunewald, Taubertstrasse 4

February 26, 1962 (II)

Dear Birthday Child!

We send our best wishes your way, and we are waving to you
from a distance. HAPPY BIRTHDAY, DEAR HANYA, HAPPY
BIRTHDAY TO YOU.

You will most likely celebrate the 3rd of March in a whirl of activity, and hopefully also in the best of health. How much I would like to be at the party.

If it were not so difficult with the school here in Berlin I would have definitely found a way to come over. Margaret Gage has invited me to California again, and I had saved my birthday money for that purpose anyway, but even though wanderlust has set in to my bones and I feel well enough for the trip, my conscience and a feeling of responsibility tug at me. Berlin is an odd place. We never know how it will look the next day, and even if we here are not afraid, others are, indeed. We notice that. Now my best and longtime assistant would like to establish her own studio, which I understand. However, I cannot afford to pay a replacement, who must come from out of town. That means I cannot presume to take anyone on permanently because I do not know whether or for how long I can afford to. As a result, I must tighten my belt. Well, we will see what becomes of it all!

As a substitute for California, Hesschen and I will spend the Easter holiday in Ticino, where friends from Hamburg have placed their cottage at our disposal. It is available for a short time, and at the end of April spring will have already arrived there.

On the 11th of March we are going to celebrate Yella's birthday here; that is, *pre*-celebrate. Then we will drink a glass of Sekt to your health, Hanyuschka, in *post*-celebration of your birthday.

I am sure your children will be with you, and I send them warm greetings. I think of you with great love and embrace you in my thoughts!

Your old
Mary

⌇

Mary Wigman, Berlin-Grunewald, Taubertstrasse 4

on the 3rd of March, 1963 (II)

The seventieth birthday is a marvelous affair —
And our Hanya in New York has finally made it there!
I thought how nice a voyage on the third of March would be,
And was determined to board a plane and fly across the sea

To personally bring the happy wishes in my heart
By joining with the birthday choir to sing my little part:
    HAPPY BIRTHDAY, DEAR HANYA, HAPPY BIRTHDAY TO YOU!
Alas, a nasty sickness came and ruined the little dream,
So I won't see Hanya face to face when she turns seventy.
But my heart is opened wide, and the words I say are true:
Hanya, dear, a year of health is what I wish for you.
I ask you not to try too much, enjoy your home, and rest.
At this age — heaven knows! — we all could be a little blessed.
And since you are beloved over there as over here,
A celebration on the third is guaranteed, my dear —
Take me up into your dances, though it must be from afar!
With a happy somersault I swing into the stars
And wave from up above as a flicker in the dark.
And you, my old companion, save me a corner of your heart!

Sending my greetings
And congratulations,
Honoring you
And holding you very dear

your
Mary

[The short verse at the end is woven into a drawing of a person in the shape of a five-pointed star holding flowers in one hand and a wine glass in the other.]

༄

August 31, 1963 (II)
[Picture postcard]

Dearest Hanya —

   A greeting should have come to you from Greece long ago. I spent 6 unbelievably hot but unbelievably wonderful weeks there and am still full of everything I saw and experienced. I hope you were also able to relax in the summer. 1,000 loving wishes and greetings to you from

your
Mary

❦

Mary Wigman, Berlin-Grunewald, Taubertstrasse 4

December 31, 1963 (II)

Dearest Hanya

Only a few hours separate us from the new calendar year, which will carry the number 1964. I am sitting in my beautiful Christmas room enjoying the quiet, but sooner or later our guests will appear and when the moment of truth arrives, and the bells begin to sound, and the first toast to the New Year rings through the streets, I will raise my glass in the direction of Israel and drink especially to your health.[1] How is it going for you? What is it like to work there? I am sure there is enough *talented* material. I hope that it is not too taxing on you.

We were able to have a wonderful Christmas party, and I am very thankful for that. My thanks go also to you, dearest! Your incredibly generous gift went a long way toward making Christmas Eve festive.

I sent you my recently published book, "Die Sprache des Tanzes."[2] It was by regular mail, not airmail, so you probably would not have received it before your departure. I hope, though, that you will still enjoy it later.

All my kindest and warmest wishes go with you into the New Year, so that it may be a good, a successful, a "blessed" one for you. With all my heart

your

Mary

1. Holm was in Tel Aviv for a production of *My Fair Lady*.
2. *Die Sprache des Tanzes* (The language of dance) was published in 1963 by Ernst Battenberg Verlag, Stuttgart.

❦

On Board the Lufthansa Senator-Service

April 3, 1964 (II)

Dearest Hanya

Time races by so quickly. I can hardly grasp that I have already been in California more than two weeks. It is wonderfully beautiful here in all the blossoms — and Margaret Gage's garden is a stretch of paradise. The weather is admittedly not so heavenly: rain, storms and cold weather off and on.

I will be in New York on the 21/22 April. How I look forward to the reunion!

Martha Graham let me know through Arthur Todd that I could use her apartment; she herself is not in NY. I do not want to accept the invitation, though; I do not know Martha well enough to know if it would be right.

I also do not want to be a burden to you, dearest. You have to work and have other obligations. And anyway, long ago a former student, Dr. Masami Kuni, invited me to be his guest at a hotel.[1] He is a big name in his homeland of Japan — lives in the USA part of the time — and is giving a course in NY at the moment. He hopes to go to Europe over Easter and be back in NY by mid-April. So I hope everything works out with the accommodations. In any case I will let you know when I will arrive in NY.

I embrace you in my thoughts today; how lovely that I will soon be able to do it in person!

Margaret Gage sends her love. And so do I.

Your

Mary

1. Kuni, a graduate of Tokyo Imperial University with a doctorate in aesthetics, directed the Kuni Institute of Creative Dance in Tokyo. He had gone to Germany in 1936 and studied with Wigman, Laban, and Max Terpis, then toured Europe as a solo artist and taught in London, Denmark, Argentina, and Brazil before returning to Japan in 1956. In 1961 he was brought to Los Angeles to co-direct the New Dance Theatre at the site of the former Lester Horton Dance Theatre. John Dougherty reported that Kuni brought "contact with original sources of European modern dance movement" (1961:15).

∽

April 14, 1964 (II)

Dearest Hanya,

Your letter just came, and I thank you for it from my heart.

I wrote to Arthur Todd a while ago to decline. I will not be accepting Martha Graham's offer, for the same reason that you mentioned: Todd is a bit of a busybody. And if Martha G. were completely serious about her invitation, she could have found time for two personal words.

I would most prefer a hotel, and so I wanted to ask you to get me a room, if possible, in the little one you mentioned. If it is a *quiet* room, all the better.

I did not at all like the hotel I was in before!

Originally I wanted to come to NY on April 22, but because that is the day the World's Fair opens — and, as I found out, your president is also expected at the airport that day — I will arrive on the 24th, from Boston.

I have not yet booked a flight; I will do that in Milwaukee, where I will be flying *tomorrow*. In any case my address there is: c/o Marion Yahr, 2233 N. Lake Drive, Milwaukee, Wisc. I will telegraph the arrival time in NY, airline and flight number from there. *Departure* from New York on the *29th or 30th* of April.

How kind of you to send the theater announcements. I am confused, though, because I do not have the slightest idea what it is all about! In vain I looked for "Camelot" on the list! Is it no longer running? Or just not listed?[1]

I would love to see it, because it displays *your* work!

It is up to you, then, to choose something.

I am moved that you are going to so much trouble, dearest. But on the other hand I am as happy as a child about being in New York again *with you*.

Affectionately

your

Mary

I would like to be with the *entire* Holm family at least once!

1. *Camelot* closed May 1, 1963, after a run of 874 performances.

∽

On Board the Lufthansa Senator-Service

May 2, 1964 (II)

Dearest Hanya,

THIS IS BERLIN AGAIN — I had completely forgotten how green it is here — the sun shines in the room, and the freshly washed curtains glow in bridal-veil white.

God, I am tired and have put myself to bed — the flight was very stressful. Mostly because of the delay. Not only did the connecting flight in Frankfurt not arrive, there were no other planes we could take. So I sat for 3 hours in the Frankfurt airport thoroughly irritated. There someone told me my bags had gone on to Berlin. But upon arrival there, they were nowhere to be had, and I waited again for a long time — Hesschen was not there and the little room for baggage was packed full of people. When I called the house, Hesschen said as cool as you please that my bags were there — she had brought them home. It was beyond me why my bag had to go through customs. But an old skycap spoke for me, claiming that he knew me — so everything was all right.

I landed in the afternoon in lightning and thunder and pouring rain.

Now the towers in New York are no longer there, one's gaze is no longer drawn upward by their seemingly unending rows of windows — it all becomes a memory!

Beloved, I thank you! You made everything so lovely for me and I was so happy to be with you — also happy to experience you in your own milieu — in the lovely house that carries your mark. And now you will concentrate completely on your work, and I fervently hope that it is not too much and not too exhausting. Because it is a huge amount that you have to do. I am so happy that you told me about it![1]

Greet Elsa from the heart for me.

You yourself I embrace in my thoughts, in all love and, with my loveliest and sincerest wishes and very thankful heart,

your

Mary

1. Holm prepared a revival of *My Fair Lady* at New York City Center Theater.

❧

Mary Wigman, Berlin-Grunewald, Taubertstrasse 4

June 16, 1964 (II)

Dearest Hanya,

I was so indescribably happy that "My Fair Lady" has once again been such a great success — and I congratulate you with all my heart. I can still see you sitting across from me and saying

thoughtfully, "I have exactly 14 days to do it" — how in the world
did you pull it off?

And now you're probably already in Colorado and have begun
your summer work. Oh, dearest, should I envy you? My innermost
activity, I think, is still unweakened — but the outer possibility for
movement is rather "LIMITED."

50% of my students left for Bayreuth today. They have a very
well-paid engagement there for the festivities and will perform as
a dance group under the direction of Wieland Wagner and the
choreography of Gertrud Wagner, his wife.

Earlier today I was completely dismayed to determine that the
classes are made up only of bloody beginners, and I have to adapt
myself and work completely differently.[1]

Thank you from my heart for your last letter, and thank you
from me for taking on the translation of my book.[2]

Yella has — oh, my heart — gone to the Eastern Zone. But I
hope she will have a wonderful time there despite all reservations.
Today I'm already sad that the Kuhnerts will be leaving Berlin
soon — it's as if the last living tie to one's own past is being
completely severed.

With all my heart I wish you a lovely and not too stressful time
working in Colorado. The 25th, right? But you should also celebrate
appropriately![3]

Fondest greetings, dearest!

And a loving kiss from
your
Mary

1. Only Wigman's amateur classes were enrolling sizable numbers. Dancers
of the 1960s, calling themselves "the skeptical generation," thought Wigman's
teaching was based on old values and spoke the language of the 1930s. Wigman
had trained soloists to engage universal themes, but young artists were interested
in concrete ideas and in the collaborative process (Gottschild 1996). Susanne
Linke, who was in the last generation of Wigman's students, acknowledges, "We
didn't understand her." Nonetheless, Linke speaks with reverent excitement of
her teacher: "We got the spark of her personality ... dramatic, rich, profound"
(*Evolution of Wigman's Dance* 1986).

2. Walter Sorell translated *The Language of Dance*. Holm took no role in its
preparation (Sorell 1996).

3. The summer of 1964 marked Holm's twenty-fourth in Colorado. Her program consisted mainly of student works.

❧

undated picture postcard (II)
[Summer 1964, per content]

Dearest Hanya,

We are on an indescribably beautiful spot. Only one shadow.
Hesschen broke her leg and is hobbling about in a walking cast.
Fond thoughts and loving greetings from us both.

Your

Mary

❧

November 2, 1964 (II)

Darling Hanya!

For many weeks I have wanted to write to you, especially after
I received the card from you and Gretchen Wallmann. It was
relatively hectic here for a while, though, and I had much to take
care of that was absolutely no fun.

Hesschen broke her foot in the Swiss Alps, where we spent part
of our summer vacation. Even back in Berlin she still had to limp
around with a clumsy walking cast. Things were especially critical
after the cast was removed because she received no bandage, even
though the break had not completely healed.

In addition to being school director and dance teacher, I was
busy not only as head of the household but also as shopper, kitchen
help and messenger. And naturally, because the string of visitors
never broke off during the Berlin Festwochen, I also had to
function as HOSTESS and ENTERTAINER.

Today I received news of the death of Gabi Poege. For a little
while time seemed to stand still, as if the deceased herself were
claiming her moment of thought and reflection before life could
again proceed. Quick as lightning, images from the past surface,
alternating, often springing forth. Gabi was a good friend to you.
You will feel her loss more deeply than I. Yet, her image is
intermixed with so much that has to do with me, too; I hope she
did not have a hard death.

Dearest, how is it going for *you*? So often I send my loving thoughts
over the Atlantic; I often think of the happy days in New York
when we were together. I have not heard another word from Walter

Sorell since giving him the official rights to the translation of my book.[1] As far as that goes, though, the editor of the Wesleyan University Press has written to me a few times, and I take it that the negotiations with my German publisher are in progress.

I received a long letter today from Yella in Rome. All in all she and Helmut have had an interesting time there, full of experiences. She is already excited about "Girls' Night" on Taubertstrasse and a thorough gossip!

I dread the long winter to come. I could probably give talks all over West Germany, but decided not to because I know I would not be able to endure it; during this time of year my lungs and heart are not stable enough for such extensive strain. So, I go to the school daily and attempt to get across to the students something of the "SPIRIT OF THE DANCE." We have another group of strangely talented USA students here.[2]

Will you ever tell me more about what you are doing? Since you belong to the group of "die-hards" I know how difficult it will be to find time for a letter, but that would make the joy all the greater if you wrote.

Hesschen put the list of all my November birthday children on my desk. There are 17 — and 4 of them will be 70 years old! It is unbelievable how time flies.

It has grown late. The light should have been put out long ago. But my thoughts continue to wander, and I greet you affectionately with many good wishes for your well-being.

Also greet your children and Elsa for me.

I am your old,

true

Mary

1. Sorell (1905–1997) was from Vienna and immigrated to the United States in 1939. He worked as a book reviewer and translator and became internationally known as a dance writer and reviewer, also publishing poetry, essays, and plays. He met Wigman in New York in 1958 and became an admirer, and an admirer of Holm's, whose biography he wrote (Sorell 1969). After *The Language of Dance* was published, he gathered some of Wigman's lectures, essays, and interviews and translated and published them as *The Mary Wigman Book* (Wigman 1975).

2. To many German students it seemed that Wigman favored American students throughout the postwar years because of the financial support that they provided. Another factor in her favoritism was the memories that she savored of her tours in the United States (Gottschild, quoted in Brooks 1979:15).

∽

December 3, 1964 (II)

My dear Hanya!

Today I was finally able to return to my desk, after a time of so much unrest and turbulence that I always had to have my date book within reach, so as not to get all muddled. Somehow, though, it was all so lively that the rounds of newspaper, radio and TV interviews were actually fun. The school was visited by groups from the near and far Orient. Something that also interests me: a seminar for students of the Free University here about choreography. It is being arranged by the institute for theater studies. The young people all want to be opera directors.[1] Things are unusually active in my school, as well. The group of students is quite internationally composed. Along with the pitch-black boy from Africa are the greenish-yellow Japanese boy, the brown girl from Indonesia and the white-as-wax boy from Texas, who went wild this morning when a few pitiful snowflakes fell from the sky. The nicest thing about it: among them are a few very talented dancers with whom it is going especially well, and this allows for diverse projects. On my birthday I was ecstatic that temperament has broken through the abstract stubbornness and extreme coolness that our avant-gardes have favored for the last few years, and the very young now have their courage back. They are once again dancing the way they want to, without imitating others. It was a simply wonderful birthday. I was happy and grateful to be able to once again experience and enjoy it totally and completely. Hesschen and I walked around for two days with aching backs and trembling legs, but the joy won out over the manifestations of age.

I am thankful, dear, that you thought of me. It was so good to hear more about how things are going and how things look for you. By now you have learned how to be a grandmother. I am also anxious to find out which sex No. 3 will be. Greet your children dearly for me!

Everything here speaks of Christmas! I really hadn't been thinking of it before; but now a precious little pine tree stands in my room with 4 Advent candles, a few little gold balls, and a tinsel star on the top. And so we come to realize that a long year is coming to its end and that the festival of lights, love, peace, and, LAST NOT

LEAST, the winter solstice, have yet to be celebrated. It makes me very happy to think that the days will now become longer.

Today my German publisher sent me a letter from the Wesleyan Press, and apparently the business proceedings are in progress. Unfortunately, Walter Sorell remains completely silent, and I would so much like to know how he's coming with the translation.

Another card from the Kuhnerts in Rome came today. Their time there has ended, and they are gradually working their way home. We are already looking forward to seeing them again.

So, darling, I should really close, as Professor Taubert (Musikhochschule) will be arriving in a few minutes.[2] He is going to hold a few lectures in my school, and we want to discuss the topics — and this has become a rather long letter.

The day after tomorrow the "Advent celebration" takes place in my apartment: 35 people, counting all the students and instructors! Uhf — but the "children" wanted it, and so we must go through with it with good manners and grace.

I embrace you in my thoughts with love, Hanyuschka! Thank you again for your birthday letter. Stay healthy, and please don't try to do too much. Have a lovely Christmas and New Year celebration with your family, and go cheerfully into the new year.

Affectionately,

your

Mary

1. Wigman influenced many prominent opera directors. Wieland Wagner, grandson of Richard Wagner, Oskar Fritz Schul, and others consulted her; Peter Sellars claims to use her principles in his work (Weiss 2002; Thomas 1996).

2. Karl Heinz Taubert was a dance historian.

1965–1971

BERLIN

Wigman taught during windows of time when her health permitted, but a heart attack in 1967 forced her to close her school. Discouraged by the lack of financial support for modern dance and by students who wanted quick and, in her opinion, superficial training, Wigman advised her last assistant to go to the United States (Thiele 1996).

Holm closed her New York studio one year after Wigman did, citing similar reasons: "Few young dancers are willing to take the trouble to spend months, let alone years, to learn. They want to learn everything in a hurry" (Estrada 1968:53). Holm sustained a summer dance program in Colorado until 1983, where as many as one hundred students, most of them amateurs, enrolled each summer.

❧

[Dated January 1 and January 3, 1965, two letters cover the same topics in much the same language. The second letter follows.]

January 3, 1965 (II)

Dearest Hanya!

I wanted to write much sooner, to send you my greetings for Christmas and wishes for the new year. And more than anything to thank you for your generous Christmas gift, which came in the mail from Frankfurt.[1] But things are not always as they seem.

1964 was a *wonderful* year for me — except for the last two weeks of it. Right in the middle of the happiest Christmas preparations I tripped in the apartment and broke 2 ribs. That wasn't so bad by itself. We have plenty of those curved sticks! But a few hours later a nasty lung infection appeared. So things weren't just painful, but dangerous.

But I was in good hands and have come through it all once again. We went through the whole schedule of visits nonetheless — the festivities centered around my sickbed. On New Year's Eve the doctor said to me, "Now you don't have to worry about 1965."

I am still in bed and am terribly weak — but my "spirit" is well and is leaping about.

How are things with you, dearest? First let me give you the fond wish that you are and *stay* well, feel good in your skin and have fun and joy!

Has the grandchild come in the meantime? Hebby Binswanger has become a grandfather.[2] He was shocked that it could happen without his noticing it.

Now we are waiting for the Kuhnerts, who have invited themselves over to watch television. A film is being shown that Guri's son-in-law made. And we are all interested in it. We are the new owners of a television set. Actually it belongs to *Hesschen*. We received it together as a gift, and I handed over my half to her.

A few days ago I finally received a letter from Sorell with the first draft of the translation. I don't see any major problems with it. But I must admit, I haven't quite processed it yet. My first impression was that it was *too* true to the original.

My God, a person goes on for pages and doesn't say a thing! How lovely it would be if you could come to us!

My fondest thoughts are with you, they surround you with heartfelt love and the best wishes that one person can have for another.

A beautiful, a good, a blessed 1965 and a dear kiss from

your

Mary

1. Holm kept funds in German marks in a Frankfurt account. Wilhelm Büttel, the father of Holm's daughter-in-law, managed the money according to Holm's wishes.

2. Herbert Binswanger and Wigman had been lovers for six years during the height of her career. He was a medical student from a prominent Swiss family and fourteen years her junior. His family accepted the relationship and the two traveled openly, spending many holidays together. Binswanger, who became a prominent neurologist, and Wigman remained friends until her death.

❧

Mary Wigman, Berlin-Grunewald, Taubertstrasse 4

January 23, 1965 (II)

Dearest Hanya!

Even in so-called convalescence, time flies entirely too quickly. The first month of the year '65 is already over, and so much that I wanted to do and should have done remains unfinished. Well, a person has to come to terms with the fact that in advanced age, recuperation after sickness lasts a little longer every time. I go to the school daily and give my complete curriculum, but I am happy when I can make my way back to my bed. Actually, it is very good therapy! At least a person knows why she is exhausted and can accept in good conscience the passivity of lying still.

We were ecstatic at the announcement of your third grandchild.[1] In the meantime he has become an accomplished baby, who is demanding his share of life. We hope his mother has recovered from the strain of the long pregnancy and the process of bringing him into the world. And you, dearest? Have you fully recovered from that awful virus?

I am a bit confused about the translation of my book. The few pages that Sorell has sent do not give the complete picture. What there is is very good, that is, translated true to the word, but I don't know if, for English readers, it bears the mark of having been translated. I would have liked to send you the text, as a control, but I did not want to do it without Sorell's knowledge. If you would be so kind as to call him and ask, it would relieve a great burden for me.

At the moment Wallmann is here to stage "Turandot" by Puccini at the Opera and it is not easy for her. Tomorrow she and the Kuhnerts are coming to visit. We will think of you with great affection and have a good drink to your health. Hesschen sends her greetings and so do I, in all love.

Your

Mary

1. Jessica Christine Holm was born December 12, 1964. She was delivered four weeks late and arrived a strong, healthy baby. Wigman got the gender of the child wrong.

∿

February 25, 1965 (II)

In a mere few days the third month of the year begins. And on the third day of this third month, our dear Hanya has her birthday. And because she lives in America and with Americans, we will not ask which year of her life begins on March 3rd. Well, love does not count years, either! It comes to us from the depth and warmth of the heart and surrounds you with its fond wishes. You will have American birthday wishes, but you will also have the German ones that Hesschen sings to me every year on my birthday:

"Good luck and blessings
Wherever you go.
Good health and happiness
Go with you, too."

I hope you can celebrate the day healthy and happy. With your children and *three* grandchildren this year. I will be there, too, in my thoughts. And *here* we will drink a bottle of Cordon Rouge to your health, a good-bye gift from Gretchen Wallmann, whose Puccini staging for the German Opera went off with grandeur and great public success.

I hope Yella can drink the especially good drops with me, and then our loving thoughts of you will make your ears not just ring, but resound like cathedral bells.

It has been snowing nonstop since this morning. The world is white and cold. But it is still February. When March comes, perk up your ears, the first snowdrops begin to pop up and we can feel spring start to sniff around. May the spring sun shine on you on your birthday, dear Hanya, and may you be happy! In heartfelt love, an embrace

from your old
Mary

∾

April 24, 1965 (II)
Marbella

Dearest Hanya,

Easter vacation in Spain. We are staying in a charming bungalow; only the palm-surrounded patio with lovely flowers separates us from the sea. The Costa del Sol is living up to its name. We have had wonderful, sunny days and are very happy here. Unfortunately this time of utter laziness must come to an end. I hope the relaxation is evident when everyday life claims its due. We have thought of you in love often and sent a greeting your way through the Gate of Gibraltar and over the Atlantic. I hope from my heart that things are going well for you and your children — and now I really have to write "and children's children!" Don't do too much — and don't forget us.

Affectionately
your
Mary

∾

September 25, 1965 (II)
Magliaso

Dear Hanya!

Summer is over — autumn has long since made its stately appearance. Hesschen and I are still in Ticino, and I am still a convalescent — and even if I am on the road to recovery, I am still too weak to make the trip back to Berlin.

Bad luck down the line! And I had so looked forward to a few relaxing weeks in this beloved place. But I was hardly here and taken in by a beaming Hesschen before my misery began — high fever, coughing — lung infection. And this time it hit me very hard.

In a week Hebby Binswanger will pick Hesschen and me up and take us in his car to Zurich. There I will see a doctor. And then we will see how it goes from there.

In the meantime, you will be hard at work in New York, and I hope not only that it is not too stressful, but also that you have a little fun.[1]

I was so happy about the 25th anniversary celebration in Colorado that was given for you — my God, I would have loved to have been there![2]

Yella and Helmut visited us here briefly on their return trip. Wallmann came over a few times from Milan — and Bibi [Trümpy] was here, too. Mostly *lovely* visits. Lively past in the living present.

Yes, and Walter Sorell was here, too — that was nice. Cross your fingers for him as he works on the translation of my book![3]

Dearest Hanya, we two old ladies send you uncountable loving greetings and the best wishes.

I embrace you lovingly in my thoughts and am

your

Mary

1. Holm was working on the Broadway musical *Anya*, which opened November 12, 1965, and ran for sixteen performances.

2. Colorado College celebrated the twenty-fifth anniversary of Holm's summer program there with a gala concert by prominent former students. Performing were Valerie Bettis, the Nancy Hauser Dance Company, Don Redlich, Elizabeth Harris, Murray Louis, Phyllis Lamhut, and the Nikolais Dance Theater.

3. Sorell described this visit in his introduction to *The Mary Wigman Book:* "I had the distinct impression of him [Death] sitting there at her bedside, waiting for a few more moments before calling her." He heard a cough "cutting into her heavy breathing and a relentless pounding at her weak heart" (Wigman 1975:15).

∽

October 9, 1965 (II)

Dear Hanya,

Your letter reached me while I was still in Zurich — it moved me deeply and my heart is full of gratitude. But I have to ask you not to send such large gifts of money. If it were needed, I would accept it with great joy! But I really do not need it. Hebby Binswanger and another friend helped me through this summer marked with illness. And now I am back home, where everything is so much more easily and simply arranged than in a strange place.

I admit I had wished to come back "healthy" and I am a little put out that the doctor's examination in Zurich confirmed that although my heart and lungs are no longer in danger, now I have an intestinal and bladder infection. That means I have to keep taking this damned medicine. I hope the condition will pass soon.

The meeting with Walter Sorell and his wife was lovely, and I hope that it has a positive effect on how the translation turns out!

It is not good to lie in bed for such a long time. We just got back yesterday — 5 hours late. But Yella the true was still there at the airport to take us both in.

Hesschen asks me to thank you for your letter, also. If she doesn't thank you herself, it is only because she has to first bring the household back in order. She was toiling like mad, and now she has gone shopping.

Dearest Hanya, I wish you a good winter and complete satisfaction with your work on the new show. Stay healthy! If you can do *that*, work can also be fun.

I embrace you with love, in my thoughts, and thank you again from my heart.

Toi-toi-toi!

Your

Mary

❧

November 1965 (II)

Dearest Hanya,

Because of the unimaginable mail I received for my birthday I will not be able to write a real letter, but even if my thanks to you must be brief, they still come with all the warmth in my heart. How wonderful it would have been if you could have come! Yella and I were beside ourselves with joy at the thought alone. Toi-Toi-Toi for the work!

And 100 dear greetings — from Hesschen, too!

Your old

Mary

[The above letter is on the back of a printed card with the following message:]

For all the many signs of affection, for all the greetings and wishes that came to me on my 79th birthday, I thank you out of the warmth and fullness of my heart.

Mary Wigman

Berlin, November 1965

Mary Wigman, Berlin 33-Grunewald, Taubertstrasse 4

December 31, 1965 (II)

True, the year *is* over — only a few hours separate us from the moment when a five turns into a six, to mark the 365th day of the year 1966. I have always loved to have something behind me, to move into another unknown. And so the big question mark that a new year places before me is always something exciting! This time, too! And perhaps even more than ever because behind all the questions that *life* raises, the last great question stands. We call it Death — He has often been close, and we have become good friends.

Hanya, dearest, I don't know why I wrote that. This is the first sane hour I've had in weeks and it should begin with a greeting for you, a fond thank you for your thoughts and for your overwhelmingly wonderful gift. I'm sure Yella has thanked you long and exuberantly. I am a little behind, but my thanks are no less sincere. This year the money order will go into a bank account. If my physical condition allows, I want to give in to my wanderlust and spend a few weeks in the south this spring.

Yes, I am flirting with the idea of New York! I am certain I would not be allowed to travel alone, but Hesschen is not familiar with NY — oh, well — dreams, but it is certainly good to dream!

And what is the fate of the new musical? It seems an abomination to just let it drop. But one must probably think as producer, not as an artist.

Dear, I greet and embrace you in loving thoughts — may 1966 be a *good* year for you — for us all.

Your grateful
Mary

Mary Wigman, Berlin 33-Grunewald, Taubertstrasse 4

January 23, 1966 (II)

Dearest Hanya!

I truly enjoyed the Colorado book, with all its many pictures of you. Thank you for sending it.[1]

I took it to Yella in the clinic. She also enjoyed it. It's not going at all bad for her now that the wound on her backside has healed.

Because of her back pain, though, she has been put into traction again, and she will remain in the clinic a bit longer than was at first expected.

We visit her often and cheer her up by telling stories in between vermouth and cigarettes.

A few days ago Wesleyan University Press sent me a preliminary print of my book.[2] There is an odd finality about it, as if the matter no longer had anything to do with me. I do hope that the book will be well accepted over there. I cannot judge how much success Sorell has had with the translation; I have only seen a little of it, and that only in the beginning stages. Let's hope for the best!

The book was a wonderful success in Germany; it received good press and sold well. What a person earns as author is actually not much more than spare change, but when that is multiplied by a few thousand a very nice sum comes out of it.

I hope you are in good health, darling! The nasty winter climate we have here naturally makes it difficult to handle an old body. Nevertheless, I go to the school every morning and teach.

Klaus and his family must be back in New York. The photo in which the oldest grandchild gives you a kiss, with son and grandchild No. 2, is simply adored.

I embrace you in my thoughts and greet you tenderly. Hesschen also sends many warm wishes! From the heart,

your
Mary

1. In the fall 1965 issue *Colorado College Magazine* ran an article by Barbara M. Arnest, "In Celebration of her 25th Summer at the College, Hanya Holm Gets a Dance Festival." Several photographs accompanied it, including one with Klaus and his daughters.

2. Wesleyan University Press published *Mary Wigman: The Language of Dance,* translated by Walter Sorell, in 1966. A paperback edition appeared in 1974.

༦

Mary Wigman, Berlin 33-Grunewald, Taubertstrasse 4

February 24, 1966 (II)

Dear Hanya!

Your birthday is around the corner. We don't want to be missing from the birthday chorus. All my fondest wishes are on their way to you, to surround you with love. Have a lovely, festive birthday! We will celebrate it here, too, as Yella and Helmut Kuhnert will be here the evening of March 3. I have already put aside a bottle of extra fine French champagne (a birthday present from Gretchen Wallmann, that was waiting for a special occasion to be drunk).

Now the occasion has come. In addition, Yella left the hospital today. *That* event will also be celebrated.

Yella and I would much rather climb into an airplane to congratulate you in person. Good lord, it will have to stay in our thoughts. *When are you coming to visit?* We miss you terribly! I embrace you, dearest — greet you from the bottom of my heart — stay healthy and keep that wondrously fresh and lively spirit that you share with others.

A LOVING HUG AND KISS!

Your old
Mary

∽

April 22, 1966 (II)

Darling Hanya!

Today the mail brought a stream of letters to us in the seclusion of our little bungalow in Lagonissi. Among them was one from you in Tokyo.[1]

That just about put me to shame, and so I would like — despite heat exhaustion and indigestion — to send you my thanks and many, many sincere greetings and wishes.

Our vacation time is at an end. It went so quickly that one hardly noticed it. Lagonissi is totally a bungalow town, erected on the steep cliffs of a peninsula on the Greek coast (Athens-Piraeus-Cape Sounion), overlooked by *one* hotel. Thanks to the loving help of my Greek friend, our little bungalow became an ideal residence. The landscape is hot as summer — while it is very cold at night — and we are ecstatic that we can warm our little hut so nicely.

Hebby Binswanger visited us over Easter, and because he got along so well with the Greek friend, we spent wonderful days here. And again you have a monstrous work before you! How much I wish for you that you may be crowned with success! That it will be prima because of *you* I do not doubt for a moment!

Hesschen greets you a thousand times — she has already gone to
bed. Also my greetings come to you, dearest. A loving embrace
from

your

Mary

1. Holm and the Broadway producer Arnold Saint-Subber went to Japan to
research and cast a planned musical, *Softly,* based on the play *Teahouse of the
August Moon*. It never went into production.

∾

Mary Wigman, 1 Berlin 33 (Grunewald) Taubertstrasse 4

undated (II)
[December 1966 per contents]

Dearest Hanya!

Time has flown by so quickly. It seems like yesterday that we
were all together, and so happy![1] And actually a whole month has
gone by. Thoughtlessly, I almost tripped over this huge amount of
mail, but now half of it has been overcome.

Then the so-called worst came for me, the physical breakdown.
But I took it on gladly. The only one who was upset about it was
my doctor. Yesterday I heard him tell Hesschen, "You may never
again allow her to celebrate at a large party, if you want to keep her
around a little longer. She was just about done for — and it is
difficult to make things a little better for her."

So now I am much more worried about Hesschen, who also
totters from exhaustion and from time to time groans, "It's a dog's
life." To that we always say how wonderful everything was and how
we enjoyed it.

I thank you again from the bottom of my heart, beloved Hanya,
for coming. It made me so happy! Thank you again for your
splendid gift, and all the others for their 81 dollars. It will be put
away for the spring trip that's coming up — because I won't be able
to survive the everyday rubbish until summer.

You will be no less shocked than I when you hear that Helmut
Kuhnert has been diagnosed with cancer. Yella was very brave, and
knew enough to take on his fear of the future. We all hope that
after the very thorough operation *nothing* is left behind.

Hopefully you arrived back in New York well, without fog, etc.

Beloved, I embrace you in my thoughts, and send the most wonderful greetings for Christmas, together with innumerable good wishes for 1967. Hesschen toils in the kitchen — and roars her good wishes for you over to me.

A kiss — and very much love from

your

Mary

1. Holm came to Germany to celebrate Wigman's eightieth birthday. Gret Palucca; Wigman's sister, Elisabeth; Berthe Trümpy; Harald Kreutzberg; Yvonne Georgi; Jan Veen; Jacqueline Robinson; Jerome Andrews; and many others were among the celebrants. Wigman's career and the birthday gathering were well covered in the American dance press. Holm, in a tribute in the November issue of *Dance News,* expressed her love and deep respect for Wigman: "Mary Wigman is one of the giants of our age, who has left a deeper mark on the art of the dance than can be fathomed at this time." Holm also wrote, "She is the carrier of THE SECRET, the indivisible, the unexplainable, the immaterial, the no-beginning and the no-end" (1966:10).

∽

Mary Wigman, Berlin 33-Grunewald, Taubertstrasse 4

February 26, 1967 (II)

Sweetheart Hanya!

Another year has passed — on March third you celebrate your birthday. Over there where you are no one asks how old you are. But in the end a person is one year older, AND IN THE LONG RUN one starts to notice it. May you be spared for many more years from the *difficult* advances of age.

How much I wish again this year to be able to knock on your door with an arm full of spring flowers and congratulate you personally. Maybe your true Elsa will do it for me!

Yella and I had determined to celebrate your birthday on Taubertstrasse. But she has to go into the clinic for treatment of the lower half of her body. And I have to go into the dentist's chair. You could say there's always less of me — and also say: this will pass.

Today was the first in many days without a storm. And one can sense the coming spring. What trust nature must have in the cosmos! Suddenly the snowdrops pop up in the front yard, the crocuses

Hanya Holm and Mary Wigman at Wigman's eightieth birthday celebration,
Berlin, November 13, 1966. (Headwaiter for the reception at the Akademie der
Künste stands in the background.) Photograph by Klaus Lehnartz. Courtesy
Jerome Robbins Dance Division, The New York Public Library for the
Performing Arts, Astor, Lenox and Tilden Foundations.

shoot out of the earth as if hatched. The forsythia is starting to bloom — and the first green shimmers in the bushes.

I have a difficult time behind me! My heart is acting up like never before — and I am getting over a bacterial problem which attacked my stomach and intestines. Both Hesschen and I were hit, and — in the best German — we puked and shit like no cow ever did.

Mid-March — good lord: vacation on the island of Tenerife — our beloved Mediterranean coast is still too cold at this time of year.

And now, Hanyuschka, I embrace you in my thoughts with all my love and congratulate you on your birthday. Many, many loving greetings to your children and grandchildren!

A birthday *kiss*

from

Mary

∾

Mary Wigman, Berlin 33-Grunewald, Taubertstrasse 4

Pentecost Sunday, 1967 (II)

My dear Hanya!

I have wanted to write for a long time. But it wouldn't have been a good idea because I did not want to just complain. When a person is in an awful mood day in, day out, it is better to remain silent than to let the misery come through in writing.

Even before the trip to Tenerife I did not feel especially well, but I had expected real rest from the vacation. I was bestowed instead with a genuine cardiac infarction and was glad just to make it home. It required every last ounce of my strength.

The process of recuperation now begins, very slowly. This is when a person's age and the loss of the powers of regeneration are felt.

Nevertheless, I can't complain! You know what happened to Jan Veen! It is unbelievable that for 10 weeks now a heart is beating, while the rest of the person is gone. The doctors say he *doesn't suffer*. If only we could be sure! It affected me deeply. I cannot help but think about how happy he was with us in November — and how many plans he had.

Today is Pentecost Sunday, and a real *holiday:* sun and warmth. As early as it is people are already streaming into the Grunewald with bag and baggage. Our balcony has recovered its summery decoration of flowers and invites a person to take a seat. Still, I won't be able to stand it here for much longer. The noise from the street and planes grows every year!

A visitor from Finland. Do you remember Martha Broyer? She was in Dresden in 1923–4. Now she has become a somewhat tottery old lady, and I don't know exactly what I'm supposed to do with her. Today we had her over for lunch. It was excruciating. On top of it all she is staying for 4 weeks and sits in the school every day from 9 to 1, watching.

The dissolution of my school is in progress. It is a difficult process, from the mere fact alone that I am dependent upon the assistance of the Senate, and the Senate's mills grind slowly, just like God's.

Hesschen, who is just coming back from a walk in the Grunewald, sends her heartfelt greetings. Wallmann was supposed to be here. One of her Berlin stagings is being taken back into the repertory tomorrow, so she was expected at the rehearsals, but neither the Opera nor the Kuhnerts, nor I — no one — knows if she will show up.

In the USA Pentecost Sunday is almost never celebrated, so I assume that this Sunday is no different for you from any other. How I hope and wish that you are well, darling Hanya. Only when the so-called "physical domain" begins to falter does one know what *health* means.

My God, how your 3 grandchildren will have grown and changed! But of course they bring you great joy. How is it going for our dear "Elsa?" Give her an especially warm greeting for me!

Will you be back in Colorado this summer? I can't imagine that the work for a new "musical" takes place in New York in the *summer*. That's got to be next to murderous.

Beloved Hanya, I greet you affectionately and embrace you. I think of you with devotion and am

ever your old
Mary

❧

Mary Wigman, Berlin 33-Grunewald, Taubertstrasse 4

November 5, 1967 (II)

Dearest Hanya!

I was absolutely not in the mood to write, or you would have heard from me a long time ago. The dissolution of my school brought such a flood of necessary correspondence with it that in the end I was fed up with writing of any kind.

Beautiful and long vacation in our beloved Ascona, on Monte Verita! Very well rested, but some bad luck: for 10 days as good as motionless on or in the bed. An infection set in to a tiny injury on one toe, and as a complication a horribly painful erysipelas [strep infection of the skin] that was there immediately took over the other foot. It seems to be fading now, but it is a tedious process and I will have to have a great deal of patience. I am trying very hard not to let my head hang and not to do anything foolish.

And you have returned to "show business!"[1] How nice that you can still manage it physically. I hope it is a fascinating project for you! My "retirement" has not really sunk in yet. That is probably because for the first time in my life I have to pay "taxes," which will be taken from my retirement money. Tant pis.

Last year you were here, and we were all so happy together. For me that was a wonderful celebration. If it were to take place this year, Jan Veen would not be there. He was a very good friend, and I miss him.

Hanya, dearest, I greet you and embrace you. All good thoughts surround you and my most affectionate wishes are with you.

HUG AND KISS

from your
Mary

Hesschen also greets you from the heart!

1. Holm became involved in an effort to convert John Steinbeck's novel *East of Eden* into a musical called *Here's Where I Belong*. *Dance Magazine* reported on her rehearsals (Estrada 1968:50–53).

∾

November 22, 1967 (II)

Dearest Hanya!

With all this birthday mail, this cannot be a long letter. But I do not want to knock on your door with a printed thank-you card. I rejoiced from the heart at your thoughts and thank you deeply for your good wishes.

The thirteenth was a holiday for me — an oasis among difficult times, so to say. The aggravating wound on my feet was fading away, and I could get around in slippers. But a few days later my teeth started acting up. And now that the troublemaker has been removed, the very last veterans will have to be babied in the next few days. I am a coward, I'm afraid, because I cannot take any more pain at the moment. Now I just hope that this new year will bring me a chance to actually enjoy my "retirement!" There will always be plenty to do.

Yella called earlier and said that the work for the new show has begun. Hopefully the delayed start of rehearsal will not bring a huge amount of work with it! We will all cross our fingers for good luck.

Stay healthy, dear. I thank you and send you many thousands of greetings from

your
Mary

∾

Mary Wigman, Berlin 33-Grunewald, Taubertstrasse 4

January 4, 1968 (II)

Dearest Hanya!

How much I would have liked to send you my wishes for the New Year on time! But it just couldn't be; we were blessed with so many visitors that the two of us nearly lost our heads.

Now the great rush is over, my room has regained its usual look, and I can finally sit down at my desk, which had been a Christmas altar the whole time.

I admit that I am actually writing in bed. Midnight has long since passed, but I cannot sleep. A few hours ago I learned that

Dore Hoyer is dead. We were here with her on December 23 and very happy, with Palucca, who was able to be in West Berlin for Christmas. Dore left for Frankfurt that night to celebrate with her best friend, and wanted to be back January 10. This evening she was found dead in her bed. Suicide, naturally. She had always played with the idea. But none of us thought she would go through with it. I am still very shaken, and I am besieged with many questions for which I just don't have answers.[1]

Darling, I hope things are going well for you, and hope more than anything that your work on the musical doesn't do you in and that you may still enjoy yourself. Were you able to have a nice Christmas celebration with your children and grandchildren?

And now let me send you my sincere wishes for 1968. Most important is the wish for "health" because I know from experience how very difficult it is to keep the "SPIRIT" up when the body denies you. May 1968 be a good, healthy and happy year for you.

I embrace you with love in my thoughts and am from the heart

your
Mary

1. Hoyer had ingested poison on New Year's Eve. She was fifty-six, the age at which Wigman had given her final performance. Hoyer's last performance, on December 18, 1967, just two weeks before her death, had drawn a disappointingly small audience, and she realized that the German public was not interested in the intense, mystical style of dancing that she had inherited from Wigman and developed in her own way. She confessed to her diary, "The work of my life has become worthless in this world" (Müller, Peter, and Schuldt 1992:70).

∽

February 2, 1968 (II)

Dearest Hanya!

How lovely that you wrote, so I know how things are going for you and how things look over there. I can imagine the debates, conflict and arguments when you decided not to do the show.[1] A person puts more into such things than working time! Will this mean great financial loss for you?

I almost have to laugh when I think of my life now! Everything plays out on such a small stage. But it doesn't bother me like it does Kreutzberg, who has it so hard in life without publicity! I find just the opposite to be wonderful and could stand a little more quiet, to thoroughly enjoy myself. Although that, of course, requires good health, which is not always forthcoming.

At the moment, for example, the dentist is trying to give me a new mouth with which I can speak clearly and bite. Hesschen is anxiously awaiting the moment when she can switch from making broth to "NORMAL" cooking.

Imagine, Yella has been in the hospital for 5 days. Second bladder operation. Understandably she is in poor spirits, won't let me visit her, and curses God and the world. The bladder problem had become unbearable. What is one to do when soaking wet from the waist down, day and night, changing a diaper every hour? We can only hope things are better after this second attempt!

All week long I have been so upset by Dore Hoyer's death that I have not been able to get around to anything. It was horrible what was in the letters that came to me and that I had to answer.

Live for today, Hanuschka! Take care, and stay as prima as you are. We love you very much! In my thoughts you are embraced by .

your old, true
Mary

[Snapshot of Wigman and Palucca enclosed, dated January 1968]

1. Holm withdrew from *Here's Where I Belong* before its opening, and Tony Mordente took over the choreography. The show opened and closed on the same day.

ᖆ

February 28, 1968 (II)

The third of March nears, and that is the day of our dear Hanya's birthday. We won't include the number of years here, since they shouldn't be mentioned over there. But we old Europeans still hold the day sacred — and this year's birthday is a special date that holds great meaning for us here.[1]

We greet you with love, embrace you with the deepest wishes for your continued happiness.

The book that is being shipped to you directly by my bookseller — and hopefully arrives on time — is one of my favorites — and perhaps you will enjoy paging through and looking at the pictures, which are beautiful for the most part.

HAPPY BIRTHDAY
DEAR HANYA!
HAPPY BIRTHDAY TO YOU

Hesschen includes her wishes with mine!

1. Holm never made anything of her birthdays, but for her seventy-fifth, Klaus and Heidi organized a surprise party, inviting old friends who delighted Holm with their unexpected presence.

∽

September 29, 1968 (II)
Ascona

Dear Hanya!

Once again, the summer has quickly passed. It almost seems as if there *was* no summer! Two weeks with old friend Hebby in the mountains, without seeing a single peak. Only rain, thick fog and dampness. And now 6 weeks in Ascona where there was only supposed to be sun and warmth. Instead, we can count the sunny days on our fingers. Here, too: storms, pouring rain and the damned humidity which does not at all suit the old resort.

But it was wonderful here in a little house where we lived like 2 nuns in a private cloister. Very still and tucked away. But the "world" still came to us. And that was lovely. The Sorells visited us a few times. And do you remember Carletto Thieben?[1] One day we discovered a note on the door: "If Mary Wigman lives here, please call Casa Pabrizia. I'm looking all over Europe for M.W." Well, he came — lives in Mexico — and we spent a few wonderful hours together.

It is very sad that Bibi is suffering terribly from arteriosclerosis, which has affected her spirits greatly. She spends almost all her time in bed, impatient. And she is constantly surrounded by 7 cats — she has lost all sense of time and calls at night as well as during the day. She is like an old, spoiled child, who should only be treated as such. I feel so sorry for her adopted son, who tries so hard to make things easy for her. She believes she is very sick, and insists on going to a clinic. No one will accept her, though, as she is 100% physically fit.

We will be picked up by car here in a few days — off to Zurich. A doctor's care there and then to Munich. Back in Berlin on the 15th.

But you, dearest! Did you have a good summer? And are you really working on a great "MUSICAL?"[2] Can you manage it physically?

Oh, two old friends are thinking of you lovingly and send you their fondest greetings and wishes:

Mary and Hesschen

1. Carlo Thieben, an Italian who was principal dancer with both the Berlin Opera and La Scala, toured Europe and South America between 1929 and 1934 with programs of solos and duets in a wide range of subject, period, and music.

2. Holm was invited to choreograph *Ambassador*, a musical based on the Henry James novel *The Ambassadors*, but producers changed their plans and engaged another choreographer. The show never made it to Broadway (Widney 1999).

෴

December 10, 1968 (II)

Dear Hanya!

"Midnight draws near — and Babylon lies still in the silence."[1] The *old* Babylon, of course — but New York, the Babylon of the 20th century, will not be silent yet.

I thank you so much for your dear birthday letter. It was so good to hear from you and to know that things are going well for you. Unfortunately, I can't say that about myself. I was very ill. Lungs and heart — the worst is over now. But I just can't seem to get my strength back. For that I am just too old.

Anyway — I can't complain. I am surrounded by love, and everything is going well for me.

In the gardens of the Grunewald the Christmas trees are burning in the darkness. *Advent* and Christmas are around the corner. I hope you are celebrating the holiday in your circle of children and grandchildren.

All my fondest wishes will be with you and lead you into the New Year.

How lovely a reunion in *1969* would be.

LOVE, DARLING.
Always your old
Mary

1. Wigman quotes *Belsazar* by Heinrich Heine.

❧

December 13, 1968 (II)

Dear Hanya!

A pale winter sun is peering through the fog, and pushes away the awful gloom of this time of the year. The barometer of my spirits immediately rises a few steps more, like the frog on his stalk.

I am overwhelmed by your wonderful Christmas gift. May I even accept it, when I can never reciprocate? But it is lovely. Now I can look at my very large medical bill in peace. I have been very ill all week, and this time it is taking a while to recover. Lungs and heart both attacked by an infection. And such an old body has no more reserves! But the doctor promises he will get me back on my feet, and I'm doing my best to cooperate.

Thank you, dearest! And I wish you and yours a beautiful Christmas and a Happy New Year. If only we could see each other again!

Much love and a heartfelt embrace.

Your grateful
Mary

❧

February 27, 1969 (II)

On March 3 our dear Hanya has her birthday. So our thoughts come to her in special love and bring the most sincere wishes for the new year of life. May it stand under a *good* sign, so that you can enjoy it and feel joyful and happy.

Every year I have wished to be able to join personally in the birthday chorus! And this year I wish it more than usual because the span of life that lies before me grows shorter with every year, and one never knows "WHEN AND FOR WHOM THE BELL TOLLS." Since last November I have been nothing but ill, and that was not pleasant. Now everything seems much better and we are looking forward to Spring.

Right now, though, we are being graced by deep winter, and the white snowflakes keep falling gently from the gray sky. It is freezing, and our Grunewald side-street has become a skating rink. For me: strictly forbidden to go out!

Hanyuschka, darling, please come to visit us again in Berlin; we
miss you deeply.

HAPPY BIRTHDAY, DEAR HANYA, HAPPY BIRTHDAY TO YOU.

All my love and affection, from your

Mary
with her Hesschen

෨

1970 (II)

Darling Hanya!

Your birthday is around the corner, and my thoughts and
wishes are with you in love. From the heart I hope that the 3rd of
March will be a lovely and festive day for you, and that you are
well enough physically to be able to enjoy the hours of this day
completely.

If the Kuhnerts were in Berlin we would celebrate your birthday
together and empty a bottle of "Veuve Cliquot" — a gift from
Margherita Wallmann — to your health. But they are traveling
and will not be here until Yella's birthday. So I will have to toast
you by myself.

Except for a very few exceptions, I have not been able to leave
our apartment since November and I have started to feel like a
house plant. Winter was and is still terrible. Snow and such icy
streets that a person's life is risked with every step. Every time
you look from our window, though, it is a magical "winter fairy
tale!" There is no sun and the endless gray is like a burden. But
we have managed very well, despite the bad weather and storms
we had to get through. And today, in the year 1970 I can once
again congratulate you on your birthday, and embrace you in
devoted love.

Your ancient cognac,
Mary

[A snapshot is taped to page two of the letter.]

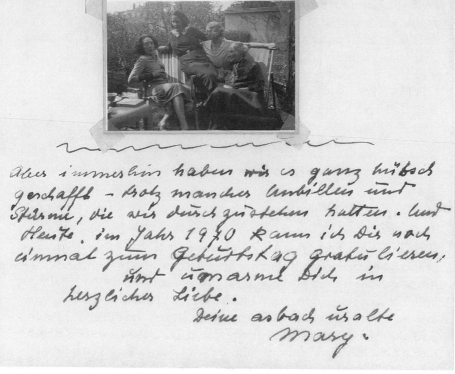

Second page of a 1970 letter from Mary Wigman to Hanya Holm. In the snapshot labeled "long, long ago," Holm sits second from right with (from the left) Mary Wigman, her sister Elisabeth, and the Wigmans' mother. Wigman's closing can be read as a pun comparing herself to well-aged brandy. Courtesy Jerome Robbins Dance Division, The New York Public Library for the Performing Arts, Astor, Lenox and Tilden Foundations.

undated (II)
[Postmarked December 31, 1971]

Darling Hanya — the chaos on my desk is unimaginable. The birthday mail is in the thousands. The secretarial help sent to me by the Akademie der Künste made the chaos even worse though, so I do not even know if I have thanked you for your wonderful birthday gift or not. You made me very happy with it. The terrible doctor and hospital bills of the last year and a half have stripped me bare, but now the little ship is afloat, for a while, at least! I thank you from the bottom of my heart!

It is good to know that you are not *alone* in your house.[1] Too bad that you cannot fly to us over the Atlantic as a white sea gull.

THANKS — in Love

    THANKS — with affectionate greetings

       THANKS — and a thank-you kiss

Your

Mary

1. Holm had acquired a dog. Rex was her beloved house companion for eight years.

This is the last letter that Wigman wrote to Holm. Later her former student Shirlee Dodge received a brief note in which Wigman admitted to weakness, pain, and blindness (Wigman 1973). Wigman's almost illegible script runs downward off the page. Wigman died on September 19, 1973. Holm flew to Germany to attend the funeral. Dancers and the dance press worldwide mourned her passing and celebrated her achievements. A lengthy obituary in the *New York Times* on September 20 dwelt on the lasting influence in the United States of her three tours.

Holm's concert choreography had been absent from New York since 1949, but between 1975 and 1985 she choreographed four dances, which the Don Redlich Dance Company toured and presented at the Joyce Theater in New York City in 1985. One dance, *Jocose,* had another life in 1994 in the repertory of Mikhail Baryshnikov's White Oak Project. Thus from Wigman's radical experiments in the 1910s to Holm's last choreography in the 1980s, the careers of two intimately connected dance artists spanned the eight central decades of the twentieth century.

Holm taught at the Juilliard School and the Nikolais/Louis Dance Theatre Lab until 1986. Then a series of small strokes and advancing blindness confined her to her house. She died on November 3, 1992, at the age of ninety-nine.

APPENDIXES

REFERENCES

INDEX

Appendix 1

◆

SUMMARIES OF LETTERS FROM
JOHANN GEORG BENKERT TO HANYA HOLM

Holm saved twenty-nine letters and cards written by Hanns Benkert from June 9, 1928, to May 11, 1931, plus drafts of three letters that she wrote to Benkert, four telegrams the two exchanged, and two notes from Frau Renger, Benkert's housekeeper. They give the flavor of Holm's relationship with Benkert, date the beginning of his infatuation with Wigman, and provide evidence that Holm was eager for the New York assignment and that Benkert supported her aspirations.

Benkert wrote to Holm again in 1947 and early 1948. His letters are valuable documents of Germany's condition after the war. They also show that Benkert was concerned for Wigman's well-being. From his reports it is clear that in Wigman's letters to Holm, Wigman was not being completely forthcoming about the hazards of her professional situation in Soviet-dominated East Germany

Benkert's letters to Holm are in the Jerome Robbins Dance Division, The New York Public Library for the Performing Arts.

On June 9, 1928, Benkert was in Essen at a professional meeting. He wrote of his delight at a telephone call from Holm and reported that he had left the evening's banquet early in order to write to her. Seemingly startled at his own enthusiasm, he wrote that he did not want to analyze the feelings that were overwhelming him, declaring that reason should have nothing to do with experiencing such feelings. He imagined her in front of him and compared their love to different flames—his a blazing conflagration, hers a quiet glow.

Later in the summer, while Holm was in Ommen, Holland, choreographing and directing Euripides' *Bacchae,* she and Benkert exchanged
letters almost daily. He reported on his work, his friends, and visitors
and described his plans for a trip that they would take together
through Austria and the Balkans in his new automobile. He often
wrote philosophically about topics such as freedom and the role of
ego and frequently declared his love—sometimes rather stiffly and
sometimes passionately. In an introspective letter of July 22 he wrote
about fidelity and virtue, again rejecting analysis, and declaring the
right of the young to live without restraints. On July 24 he lamented
her absence of fourteen days and claimed that he could not be patient
while waiting for the only thing he cared about. On July 30 he con-
gratulated Holm on the progress of her work and ended tenderly with
a thousand kisses.

Letters to Holland continued through the first week of August.
The motor trip that Holm and Benkert then made is well documented
by snapshots he took of scenery along the route. Holm is in the center of many photos, always smartly dressed, pretty, and obviously
happy. Her son, Klaus, was with the lovers but rarely appears in the
photographs. Clearly, Holm was the center of Benkert's attention and
his delight. The snapshots are among the personal photographs in the
Hanya Holm Collection in the Dance Division.

Holm introduced Benkert to Wigman in late 1929 and he soon
became infatuated with her. On February 14, 1930, he wrote Holm a
short note from Würzburg, where his father had been stricken with
a serious illness, and he closed his letter with greetings to both Holm
and Wigman. By May he acknowledged that he was suffering, not
only because of his terminally ill father but about the state of affairs
between him and the two women. He questioned how he, an intelligent human being, could become a slave to self-interest and sexual
drive. Although he recognized that ghosts of ambiguity and injustice
were haunting him, he acknowledged that Wigman had become everything to him. Remembering all that Holm had meant to him for the
past two years, he was so anguished that he felt himself breaking
apart. He asked Holm and Wigman, who were in Munich preparing
Totenmal for the Third Dancers' Congress, to solve the dilemma that
the three of them were in; he was shattered.

Telegrams passed between Holm and Benkert, she asking for a
meeting, he resisting. In a draft of her own letter Holm chastised him

for his refusal to meet and for the chaos that he was visiting upon himself. In a long tortured letter of May 27 Benkert professed that he was not certain of Wigman's feelings toward him but that nonetheless he had to leave Holm.

Early in July 1930 Benkert wrote a consoling letter, explaining that he had been uncontrollably drawn to Wigman, that he had not sought adventure; some things are beyond human understanding, he professed. On August 21 he wrote of his relief upon learning that Holm would not break off further work with Wigman.

Holm's collection of letters from Benkert contain two more drafts of letters that she wrote, asking that they remain friends: "It is not necessary that we prowl furtively around each other like panthers, cringing and dodging each other." The disharmony between them frightened and disturbed her.

In the last of Benkert's letters from this period, he assured Holm that although she had not had word from Wigman, he was certain that New York would turn out according to her wishes. He reminded her that Wigman was dancing every other night and had to travel long distances between performances. He had heard from Hanns Hasting, Wigman's accompanist, and was sure that everything was on track.

After the war Benkert wrote long letters to Holm in which he described the German social fabric. His observations are damning. He wrote that at a time when people needed to rally together and help each other, they were instead engaging in denunciations, hatred, and persecutions, making the daily struggle for food and heating material ever more difficult. He blamed the "insane creature" who had started the war, leaving death and destruction in his wake. While denouncing the evils of the Third Reich, he also acknowledged his own error in believing that war could change the world and that disaster would cleanse and purify humanity. Benkert reminded Holm of the days when they were happy together and did not see the inevitable.

Benkert's past as a Nazi official plagued him. Without being specific, he referred to "snake-like accusations" that were threatening to choke him. Unable to gain clearance to return to an executive position, he was working nine and a half hours a day at a bone-wrenching job in a locksmith shop. He suffered bruised hands and rasping lungs from the hot air of a dirty, run-down shop, from which he hurried home to tend a garden that supplied his family with food. He described the cramped basement in which he lived with his wife and her mother; items that they would appreciate receiving from Holm were cleaning agents, toothbrushes, and toothpaste. Parcels for his family and for Wigman began to arrive in April 1947, and Benkert thanked Holm often for the joy that they brought. His wife, Anneliese, also wrote letters thanking Holm.

From the British sector of Berlin, where he lived, Benkert observed with disgust the political and social restructuring of East Berlin under communism, telling Holm that the communist system was a dictatorship not of the people but of a tiny, unscrupulous clique. He saw not ideals of community, brotherhood, and peace but slogans and emptiness that were hiding methods of bondage. Quoting many authors whom he had read, he questioned whether humanity could ever rise above blind obedience and insectlike organization. He even questioned the possibilities of making a better world. He was sure, he wrote, that both capitalism and the governmental capitalism of the communist system were disasters for humanity.

Despite his work and responsibilities, Benkert read avidly and was aware of intellectual currents in Europe. He recommended books to Holm and suggested reading for Klaus. Obviously trying to come to terms with large existential issues raised by the war, and believing that the learning of the past centuries had led to materialism and the present collapse, he was seeking, he explained, a metaphysical synthesis of technology, natural science, and philosophy.

Benkert reported what he knew of people Holm knew. About Wigman, he wrote that she was in such a state of exhaustion that he feared for her life: "Thanks to your care she does not go hungry, but the pain she suffers because of circumstances beyond her control might be worse than hunger." He had managed to see a program that Wigman had organized with her students, and he opined that his former lover had attained a level of artistry that he found almost uncanny. He pronounced her a truly noble woman.

Benkert disclosed that the school that Wigman had been able to rebuild in Leipzig was on the verge of being taken over by the East German government, not by force but with the expectation that Wigman would turn it over to demonstrate appreciation for the regime. He had tried to advise her about emigration but conceded that Wigman had always been indecisive. Although he wondered whether a new beginning somewhere else might be beyond her strength, he suggested that Holm invite Wigman to the United States.

Benkert suffered two episodes of heart failure in late 1947, and after doctors' examinations he was excused from manual labor. With relief that he could again use his brain instead of his muscle, he reported on his successes with industrial reorganization, at the same time lamenting the primitive nature of the technical infrastructure with which Germany had to cope. With his reprieve from manual labor his outlook brightened somewhat. While continuing his criticism of the power struggles and greed that he saw all around him, he expressed amazement at the ingenuity with which ordinary people were improvising an existence. A heart attack killed him six weeks after his letter of April 25, 1948.

Appendix 2

❧

Louise Kloepper taught the 1932 summer session at the New York Wigman School while Holm was in Germany and then stayed on as Holm's assistant. Of the several letters and cards that Wigman wrote to her former student, the two that follow show that Kloepper may have been more conscientious in reporting about the school than was Holm. A letter from Holm to Kloepper is undated but most likely was written in late summer 1934 when Holm was in Germany after teaching at Mills College and then directing a demonstration of German dance in the last week of the Bennington Summer School of Dance.

❧

August 23, 1932
Dobbiaco, Italy

My dear Louise!

Your school report just arrived, and with it your lovely letter from July that lay in vain in Innsbruck for a long while, until it finally reached me in my vacation idyll.

I would like to thank you sincerely for both. The official report pleases me, not only because it shows that there is interest on the part of the students, and not only because your own contribution and your love for the work are revealed between the lines; it also pleases me because it shows that you have a clear vision of organizational matters.

I am happy that you find the work satisfying and would like to give you, in effect, my approval for your continued employment at the NY school in autumn. You will best understand why I cannot make a *binding* promise if I explain the school's financial and organizational situation, which has not been completely resolved as yet. The final decision must be dependent upon how much promise the school shows at the beginning of October, when Hanya will be there, and we can only then really determine if the amount of work is substantial enough to keep two people occupied, and also profitable enough to pay both.

Can you wait that long? I hope so!

Hanya wants to leave at the beginning or middle of September, in order to be there early enough to get everything necessary in order, like a new, better-suited and less expensive studio, flyers, publicity, etc.

So I hope that the situation will clear up of itself.

Who has the responsibility for all the office (secretarial) work? Mr. Pallister [attorney]?

And now I send you my sincerest greetings and wishes, dear Louise, and am always

> your
> Mary W.

◆

Mary Wigman • Dresden-Neustadt • Bautznerstrasse 107

October 29, 1933

My dear Louise,

I just wrote a few lines to Hanya, but I also want to quickly send you a greeting and thank you for writing me in such detail.

Naturally I was horribly shocked at the news about the operation and everything that goes with it, but because I received a letter from Margaret Gage that held relatively good news, I could set my mind at rest.

First of all it is good that Hanya will be free of her discomfort and will be healthy, and I also think that you yourself are a splendid person and that you will bring the school through these weeks just fine. Hopefully you rested a little this summer and are no longer as pale and thin as in the beginning here in Dresden!

Everyone here sends Hanya loving greetings! We wish we could all visit her in turn!

We are working under full steam here. In a few days I am going "on Tournée." It is almost unbelievable that I am not going back to the US. Now: Berlin, Hamburg, Göttingen, Erfurt and many other German cities are on the schedule. THE BIG EXCITEMENT OF THE OCEAN TRIP, THE LANDING AT NEW YORK IS SOMEHOW LACKING!

DARLING, thank you that you wrote so soon!

We are working on some fine things this week: amateur show (tiptop!) with an introductory speech by me. Early today a special demonstration for the Theater — Gretl worked this out, also tiptop, and I spoke. In any case there is much initiative down the line. Greetings to the students! And to you an affectionate kiss from

your,
Mary

❧

[from Hanya Holm]

undated
[context implies August 1934]

Dearest Louise,

For rapidity I will write in German again. Please discuss this letter and prospectus with Marjory [Forschmer, the school secretary]. First, I find the design of the prospectus good. The pictures of Mary on the first and last page could be the same. My picture and her picture must be chosen. With the same mail glossy copies that [Charlotte] Rudolf made are being sent. I will bring more of these. She couldn't finish them. The text is half in English, half in German on purpose. I have not translated it because if everything is not quite right it might not be clear. Perhaps Nikolai might be able to help, in case you don't understand? It is really very difficult to make the translation understandable so that it doesn't sound German. Please do not print until I arrive, but you can translate and set up the prospectus for printing. As far as I am concerned it can be printed on September 19 or 20, then we can mail them all before the end of September. It is very important

how the print is laid out. The most important part must be clearly
arranged and big, the remaining text can be smaller. The prices are
separated into amateur and professional. Amateurs get a 10%
discount with more than 3 hours a week, otherwise 50 cents per
hour. Professional students have that discount already in the total
fee. The practice hour that I am going to introduce, after the
Dresden example, is not compulsory and will be included at $1.25.
The price for BEGINNERS of $45 is for the professional students
only. I hope that we will get a new beginners' class together. The
amateur classes are separated into health and dance classes, health
are for the good old fat ladies who don't want to dance but merely
move. Under the dance classes fall all classes called beginner until
now. When something in the text does not seem good to you, I
mean when it is poor when translated, then I am very open to
counterproposals.

   What Marjory writes about the price the lady in Baltimore wants
to pay is not enough, I think. The other one in Philly pays $75, in
Baltimore only $40. That is not adequate.

   About Steinway Hall, I am disgusted that you simply rented it
again without letting me agree to it. Marjory knows only too well
the disadvantages of the place.

   No ventilation and because of the street noise the windows can
not be opened. Because of this, many people did not come. Then the
awful acoustics so that one cannot understand the spoken word at
the end of the studio. Last, not least, the high rent and the cost of
alterations. When Mary learns about this she will go through the
roof. No one has written me anything about price, etc. I am utterly
furious that mismanagement to this extent is going on. If Mr.
Pallister agrees to everything then I have to take the responsibility.
I have no desire to work *for the rent only,* and on top of it to have a
noisy shack. I hope that there will not be any more stupidity like
putting in an expensive wooden floor, etc. There is not a penny that
can be spent without purpose.

   Maybe my agitation is unnecessary, but what I understand of the
situation makes me feel very uneasy. We must not have such an
expensive studio. We can only afford to be moderate.

   Were you to think that there is enough money, this would be an
error, and Mary will want to have it paid back to the last penny. So
please, no grandeur that I will have to pay for with my blood.

It does not make sense to write much more as we can soon talk about these things.

Many cordial regards and good-bye until September 18.

Your
Hanya

P.S. [written on the side of first page]
Under the pictures there must be the name of the photographer.

Appendix 3

❧

Pola Nirenska, a prewar student of Mary Wigman's and a member of the group that Wigman brought to the United States on her third tour, formed an especially close relationship with her mentor. The two exchanged letters before the war and corresponded regularly after the war ended. In five 1951 letters to Nirenska, Wigman wrote of her difficulties in obtaining a visa to visit the United States with more emotion than she displayed in her letters to Hanya Holm. Nirenska had arrived in the United States recently, so Wigman wrote in English to help her former student with the language. Writing with playful familiarity, she was not as careful with English grammar as she was in her correspondence with others in the United States. Occasionally, she lapsed into German phrases, which are shown by small capital letters.

❧

January 4, 1951

Pola, Darling,

You did keep me waiting for a letter. But — yesterday — I got one at last. And I hasten to thank you for it.

The new year is already 4 days old, so it isn't the moment anymore to send the traditional New Year's greetings. Though of course, and independent from a fixed date, mine are these for you, a whole big bunch of wishes for your personal welfare, for your work, success.

I do not know how or whether my planned visit to the States (for the New London summer session) will come to reality. I was asked privately, but the official invitation did not come yet. Maybe it does during the next weeks.

It will be a hard job to get the visa and the permission to enter the states, as there seem to be new and special restrictions for that, and, as I heard, most of the invited artists landed in Ellis Island instead of N.Y. and this idea does not just appeal to me. Of course I would love to come! It would interest me so much to see, to know, about dancing there. I have not the slightest idea whether they would like *my* teaching. I know perfectly well that spiritual as it is, it is very simple, too. Maybe *too* simple for a sophisticated mentality. And *very* European after all!

Your letter with all that self-complaint, darling, is very sweet. I imagine so well that your life has become a hard struggle. To adapt yourself at the one side and to stay what you are at the other one and in the end, to combine the two sides, necessary to live and to dance.

Of course it would take pages and pages of paper to tell you about the happenings of a whole year. It has been a specially hard one for me. With 4 months of serious illness — hardly any rest or vacation during the summer — a crisis in the school coming back from Switzerland in September. Marianne Vogelsang, my chief teacher left all of a sudden to open a school of her own in the Russian section of Berlin, taking quite a number of pupils with her. Hard months followed, the lack of money being more than bearable. I hope, by now, I am over it.

Sick in bed just now: an operation — they took part of the teeth, upper row, away. I know it had to be done, as a bad inflammation was spreading out more and more. And the worst is over by now. It does not hurt so badly anymore than it did a few days ago.

I hope you can read what I wrote. But it was a job to decipher *your* handwriting, [illegible] you and I *did*! So you try to read mine!

Darling, there is so much love for you, always!

I wish I could talk to you instead of writing. Maybe we can again — in summer.

A hug, a kiss from

Mary

∽

February 18, 1951

Dearest Pola,

TWO LETTERS FROM YOU TO WHICH YOU HAVE NOT YET had an answer. But I console myself with the thought that you will understand why one sometimes cannot write. With me the reason is almost always lack of time.

Also: Darling, thanks for the letters. I have been working on the "Visa" since weeks, and it will not be my fault if the U.S. Consulate refuses to give me the Visa. I hope they don't! But you never can tell anything in advance. Not knowing much about politics, and the situation in the U.S., it is difficult for me to understand the reason of the limits and restrictions (in connection with visas and permits to enter). For the protection of the country, against communism? One of the paragraphs says, that you have to have lived in Western Berlin for at least *3* years. Well, I have not. In April it will be *2* years that I have lived here. The reason for this does, of course, interest no one.

I have never been a member of the Nazi party and you know that the Nazis did not like my work and that I did not give up my Dresden school just for fun. The fact that I was a member of the "Reichstheaterkammer" seems suddenly to be a political sin. But every German artist had to join this organization, if he did not or could not, he was forbidden to work at all. I wonder about Rosalia Chladek, who got that scholarship last summer. She *must* have been in the Theaterkammer too. But maybe last year the restrictions were not as tight as they are now! — Well, we'll wait and see. — But truly, it is a heavy load to be a German, what I am, what I can't help, and would not even like to change.

Well, Darling, *if* I can come, and you will be there too, it would be wonderful. I have not the slightest idea about help or not being helped there. But if it means a *help to you* and your coming, then you shall have *to help me*. At any rate, we will enjoy life, work, won't we? You know that I am asked to do some choreography. Group dance of course. There again I do not know what sort of idea, THEME, motive, I ought to choose.

Don't know about musician either. Should I take a piece of music like Bartok or anyone else — or have it composed there and *with* the dance in creation? First I thought of bringing a musician with me (Aleida Moutijn) but with the visa *so* difficult for *me* already, I do not believe I could obtain a second one, for a musician who is not invited personally. Then, of course, *that* would cost so much that the total sum offered by Connecticut to me, would not be enough. But *what* musician, I do not know.

I am glad the Philadelphia performance went well! I did not know Hanya wrote an article about me. Is it for the book you tell me about?

Hanya must be in London now, but I did not hear from her at all.

I have to stop, the letter must not be too heavy — cost too much otherwise.

Love, Pola CHILD, greetings, wishes,

your,
Mary

ᖙ

March 17, 1951

I SIMPLY COULDN'T WRITE, POLA, BECAUSE I PROBABLY WOULD HAVE SPOKEN NONSENSE. WHAT DEPRESSES ME, MAKES ME DESPAIR, AND INFURIATES ME WAS THE INTERVIEW CONCERNING THE US VISA.

It seems they refused to give it believing me to be or to have been — I don't know what! A communist, an agent? Ridiculous. And I probably behaved stupidly. Ought to have laughed right out! But couldn't! It was not even what they asked and told me, but the way it was done. I felt like [I was] sitting in a nazi office and not in a vice consulate's office of the freest democracy, God's own country, called the U.S. No use telling all the details — at any rate I can't do anything anymore about it — and it is up to Connecticut to try, if they can and still want me to come.

I made a poem about that visit, a sarcastic one and since then I feel much better. I was so mad about this matter that I decided to fly to Hamburg to see Dore Hoyer's theatrical work at the State Opera there. And am glad I did. Her group work though, is not as strong as her solo dances are. I saw her dance (afterward in Berlin) a solo composition cycle she calls "Der Grosse Gesang." She was wonderful, there is no one, in Germany at least, whom you could compare with her.

The Hamburg days were exhausting, as I met so many people, most of them I had not seen since '42, when I danced there for the last time. During the intermission: dancers from all over the country, pupils from the earliest Dresden times, who had studied together with Hanya. And before the curtain rose for the second part of the program, a man's voice in the silence, saying that this performance was an especially festive one, as M.W. was sitting in the audience, and then asking the audience to get up and honor M.W. by this. There I was, sitting alone, feeling shy, and the applause went on for minutes, until I could get up and say my thanks. And I remembered my first appearance in this city — the first one, after many defeats, when a whole audience got on its feet and applauding, called my name. The first real and great success of the modern dance. That must have been in 1919 — 32 years — my god what a time, and what a long time!

Darling — I do not know if I can come — that depends how that damned visa business is going to turn out. And I have to wait until I hear from Connecticut. But you know how glad, and happy, I would feel to know you would be there!

Maybe it would be better if you don't tell anybody about this visa story, let them first work on it. Too much publicity would not do any good!

School here ok — the students preparing for their examination and I too. [illegible] that I always feel I have to pass them, too, and therefore preparing myself very thoroughly.

Hesschen sends her love! This afternoon we went to town together: the whole city crowded with people and "EASTER EGGS." Very chic coats and costumes too in the windows — but I had to look away, as the so carefully saved money for a new spring outfit went into the plane fare to Hamburg. Darling — happy Easter.

And my love to you.

And please don't get upset about what I told you about the visa. You needn't and it would not be worth it. Hug and kiss

from

Mary

≈

April 25, 1951

Pola, darling, I thank you for the Hanya essay. I read it
all by myself and I was happy about it. Of course I will
not show it to anybody.

Besides, there is hardly anyone who knows enough English to
understand the meaning. My God, when I read things like that, I
just feel awful thinking that I am supposed to give a lecture at
Connecticut. My English *is* primitive, I *know* that! But if I write
down what I want to say and have it translated, it does not seem to
be my own language anymore. What do *you* think I should do
about it?

Confidently told, I am not at all sure that I really can come.
Nothing happened with the visa. I got to know that there is
someone in Frankfurt working on it. But never a word came from
him since weeks. The uncertainty gets on your nerves. There are
some very fine things I could have done over here during the
summer. I can't give a summer course in Berlin because — if I *get*
the visa — I shall have to leave at once. So if I can't come over my
whole summer will be just rotten!

And it would be terrible as well to disappoint the Connecticut
people! Let's still hope.

I saw "The Consul" (opera) in Hamburg, just after I went
through my experience at the U.S. Consulate here! Not even now
do I know whether I really liked the *work* but it was staged so
marvelously well that I was fascinated from the first to the last
moment.

I do hope you feel better, poor thing! And the dancing? Have
you worked on new dances? A job? You don't write much about
these things, darling. So I am not quite up to the whole picture.

My dear Hesschen is crazy with our little garden, planting,
watering with enthusiasm. And it *is* lovely beyond words to see it
all growing and blossoming once again. Personally I am not in a
too good condition just now: overworked. Examination at the
school and at the Volksbildungsamt of Western Berlin. Uff! But my
students *did* well, outstanding even. So I can tell myself: one step
forward again! But always these terrible finances.

You never get as far as to *swim*, always the same struggle to keep your head above the water.

Well, dearest, I have to stop. Once more thank you for the letter and article. All my love, my good, warm, hearty wishes to you.

A hug and a kiss from
Mary

Hanya was here for a short visit. We had a wonderful time together. There were two other women, too, who studied with her in Dresden and were members of my group for 5 years.

∼

June 19, 1951

POLA BABY,

You'll probably know by now that I cannot come, at least not this summer. I got a cable from Connecticut telling me so. And at the same time Marion Yahr, whom you probably remember from the Zurich courses, staying for a short visit, went to see the Consul *here* — as I had not been notified yet, to ask for the real reason of the whole business. She was told that there were still things to be cleared up. So I shall try to see the man myself, maybe he finally tells me what objections they have.

The nervous strain of all that waiting, that uncertainty, and the distinct feeling that you were never believed and always mistrusted, has been next to unbearable and at the moment I feel so tired, that I cannot even be furious or personally disappointed — it is only on account of the Connecticut people that I worry. They have been so very, very nice from the beginning. And now this!

I was offered such an interesting work to do here in Berlin, to stage a work written for orchestra, chorus and dance by a modern German composer, Boris Blacher. But I did not and could not accept it on account of my given promise to Connecticut. Now it is too late for the staging here!

Maybe, I can still go to Switzerland but even that I don't know. And it is probably too late for that too. The thing is I must earn some extra money in August, as with the school having the summer vacation, there is no income that month. And I being responsible for all and everything have to suffer most, that is financially. But I'll get over that, too!

Maybe they'll all believe me to be or have been a terrible communist now! The idea is ridiculous! I hope *you* don't believe it, Darling. What *I know* is, that by no means, you can make anyone understand about your private and professional life and what it really was during those years of terror and hardship — who has not gone through the same things.

Perhaps now I can find out what there really is which prevents me from coming.

And you, Pola dear? I did not hear from you since a while! Do write again!

My love, always and untouchable.

A hug, a kiss
from
Mary

References

Abbell, Nahami. 1996. Telephone interview with the author, October 21.

Alter, Judith B. 1991. *Dance-Based Dance Theory: From Borrowed Models to Dance-Based Experience*. New York: Peter Lang.

Anderson, Jack. 1987. *The American Dance Festival*. Durham, N.C.: Duke University Press.

———. 1997. *Art without Boundaries*. Iowa City: University of Iowa Press, 1997.

Arnest, Barbara M. 1965. "In Celebration of Her 25th at the Colorado College, Hanya Holm Gets a Dance Festival." *Colorado College Magazine*, Fall, pp. 5–11.

Bender, Jane. 1943. "Hanya Holm and Group." *Dance Observer*, February, pp. 20–21.

Benkert, Hanns. 1947. Letter to Hanya Holm, September 4, Jerome Robbins Dance Division, The New York Public Library for the Performing Arts [hereafter JRDD].

Brooks, Lynn Matluck. 1979. "Making Connections with Mary Wigman: A Talk with Helmut Fricke-Gottschild about His Choreography and Research." *Dance Dialogue*, Fall, pp. 14–20.

The Contribution of Hanya Holm to American Modern Dance: A Dialogue Between Holm and Valerie Bettis. [videorecording] 1981. Produced by Daniel Labeille. Prepared in conjunction with the Festival of the Early Years of American Modern Dance, 1900–1930s, hosted by the State University of New York at Purchase, April 9–12. JRDD.

Crichton, Ronald. 1957. "Babilée's Dance Marathon." *The Dancing Times*, December, p. 125.

David, Simone. 1997. "Dance a Link to Life Itself." *Ballett International/Tanz Aktuell*, February, p. 56.

Denby, Edwin. 1986. *Edwin Denby: Dance Writings*. Edited by Robert Cornfield and William MacKay. New York: Knopf.

Dodge, Shirlee. 1951. "Mary Wigman, Summer, 1950." *Dance Observer*, March, pp. 36–37.

————. 1995. Telephone interview with the author, October 22.

Dougherty, John. 1961. "Masami Kuni at Los Angeles' New Dance Theatre." *Dance Magazine,* August, pp. 15–16.

Dudley, Jane. 1996. Telephone interview with the author, March 1.

Estrada, Ric. 1968. "American as Apple Strudel." *Dance Magazine,* February, pp. 50–53.

The Evolution of Wigman's Dance [videorecording] 1986. Produced and directed by Dr. Robert Beck at Aaron Davis Hall, City College, New York, February 17. Panel discussion, moderated by George Jackson, held as part of Mary Wigman Centennial Day and the Society of Dance History Scholars Conference. JRDD.

Gage, Margaret. 1979. "Reminiscences of Mary Wigman." Interview by Betty White. Audiotape and typed transcription. JRDD.

Gentry, Eve. 1992. "The 'Original' Hanya Holm Company." *Choreography and Dance,* Vol. 2, part 2, pp. 9–39.

Gitelman, Claudia. 2000. "Finding a Place for Hanya Holm." *Dance Chronicle,* Vol. 23, no. 1, pp. 49–71.

Gottschild, Hellmut. 1996. Telephone interview with the author, September 6.

Graff, Ellen. 1997. *Stepping Left: Dance and Politics in New York City, 1928–1942.* Durham, N.C.: Duke University Press, 1997.

Hamm, Christine. 1995. "Paul Reck: A Life in Theater." *Concord Monitor,* February 13, pp. 3–4.

Holm, Hanya. 1935. "The German Dance in the American Scene." In Virginia Stewart and Merle Armitage, eds., *Modern Dance,* pp. 79–86. Reprint. New York: Dance Horizons, 1970.

————. 1938. "Trend Grew Upon Me." *Magazine of Art,* Vol. 31, no. 3, March, p. 137.

————. 1956. "Who Is Mary Wigman." *Dance Magazine,* November, pp. 22–26.

————. 1966. "Mary Wigman Celebrates Eighty Years This Month." *Dance News,* November, p. 10.

Holm, Heidi. 1997. Interview with the author, Wilkes Barre, Pa., March 16.

Holm, Klaus. 1994. Interview with the author through Heidi Holm, Wilkes Barre, Pa., May 29. [Paralyzed by a stroke, Klaus was able to communicate with the help of his wife.]

Houloose, Jean. 1996. Telephone interview with the author, April 10.

Howe, Dianne. 1996. *Individuality and Expression: The Aesthetics of the New German Dance, 1908–1936.* New York: Peter Lang.

Jeschke, Claudia. 1997. "Marianne Vogelsang: Ausdruckstanz-Choreographer in the German Democratic Republic." *Society of Dance History Scholars (U.S.). Conference (20th: Barnard College) Proceedings.* New York, June 19–22.

Jeschke, Claudia, and Gabi Vettermann. 2000. "Between Institutions and Aesthetics: Choreographing Germanness?" In Andrée Grau and Stephanie Jordan, eds., *Europe Dancing: Perspective on Theatre Dance and Cultural Identity,* pp. 55–78. London: Routledge.

Kerr, Harrison. 1938. "Reproduced Music for Dance." *Magazine of Art,* Vol. 31, no. 3, March, pp. 143, 184.

Kim, Mimi. 1995. Interview with the author, Oakland, Calif., June 8.

Klein, Wolfgang. 1996. Letter to the author, November 11.

Kloepper, Louise. 1976. "Interview with Louise Kloepper." Conducted by Mary Brennan. Audiotape and typed transcription, JRDD.

————. 1996a. Telephone interview with the author, April 12.

————. 1996b. Interview with the author, Madison, Wisc., June 18.

Koegler, Horst. 1974. "In the Shadow of the Swastika: Dance in Germany, 1927–1936." *Dance Perspectives* 57, Spring.

————. 2001. "Dancing on Political Minefields" (book review). *Dance Chronicle*, Vol. 24, no. 2, pp. 231–36.

Kostock, Oliver. 1955. "Hanya Holm's Fifteenth Summer at Colorado College." *Dance Observer*, November, p. 131.

Kriegsman, Sali Ann. 1981. *Modern Dance in America: The Bennington Years.* Boston: G. K. Hall.

Kriehn, Ruth. Undated. Personal journal. Special Collections, Golda Meir Library, University of Wisconsin–Milwaukee.

LaMothe, Birgit. 1996. Telephone interview with the author, April 10.

Lauterer, Arch. 1938. "Design for the Dance." *Magazine of Art*, Vol. 31, no. 3, March, pp. 138, 142–143.

Limón, José. 1957. Report to Friends. Boxed in "Julliard Materials—Photographs and Duplicates." José Limón Archive, José Limón Dance Foundation, New York.

Lloyd, Margaret. 1937. *Christian Science Monitor*, May 4.

McIlhenney, Pamela, and Edmund McIlhenny. 2000. *Dodge Days: Dance and Other Adventures of Shirlee Dodge*. Avery Island, La.: Pamela McIlhenny.

Manning, Susan A. 1993. *Ecstasy and the Demon: Feminism and Nationalism in the Dances of Mary Wigman*. Berkeley: University of California Press.

Martin, John. 1946. *The Dance: The Story of the Dance Told in Pictures and Text.* New York: Tudor.

Mueller, Catherine. 1996. Telephone interview with the author, April 13. [Paralyzed by a stroke, Mueller was able to communicate with the help of her husband.]

Müller, Hedwig. 1983. "At the Start of a New Era." *Ballett International/Tanz Aktuell*, December, pp. 4–12.

————. 1986. *Mary Wigman: Leben und Werk der grossen Tänzerin* (Mary Wigman: Life and work of a great dancer). Berlin: Quadriga.

————. 1987. "Wigman and National Socialism," translated by Susan Manning. *Ballet Review*, Vol. 15, no.1, Spring, pp. 65–73.

Müller Hedwig, Frank-Manuel Peter, and Garnet Schuldt. 1992. *Dore Hoyer: Tänzerin*. Köln: Deutsches Tanzarchiv Köln and Berlin: Edition Hentrich.

Ocko, Edna. 1935. "Anti-Fascism" (Letter to editor). *Dance Observer*, November, p. 93.

————. 1996. Telephone interview with the author, April 13.

Partsch-Bergsohn, Isa. 1994. *Modern Dance in Germany and the United States: Crosscurrents and Influences.* Chur, Switzerland: Harwood Academic.

Preston-Dunlop, Valerie, and Susanne Lahusen, eds. 1990. *Schriftanz: A View of German Dance in the Weimar Republic*. London: Dance Books.

Robinson, Harlow. 1994. *The Last Impresario: The Life, Times, and Legacy of Sol Hurok*. New York: Viking.

Robinson, Jacqueline. 1997. "Mary Wigman, a Magician." *Dance Chronicle,* Vol. 20, no. 1, pp. 23–47.

Sabine, Robert. 1947. "Old Works for New: The Return of Harald Kreutzberg." *Dance Observer,* December, p.113.

Schönberg, Bessie. 1996. Interview with the author, Bronxville, N.Y., February 8.

Sears, Vera. 2002. Interview with the author, Denver, Colo., May 21.

Shearer, Sybil. 1993. "My Hanya Holm." *Ballet Review,* Vol. 21, no. 4, pp. 4–7.

Sieben, Irene. 1997. "Memories of Manja Chmièl." *Ballett International/Tanz Actuell,* February, p. 57.

Siegel, Marcia B. 1981. "A Conversation with Hanya Holm." *Ballet Review,* Vol. 9, no. 1, pp. 5–30.

———. 1993. Moderator, "Hanya Holm: From Concert to Broadway Stage." *Journal for Stage Directors and Choreographers,* Vol. 7, no. 1, pp. 41–49.

Sorell, Walter. 1957. "Hanya Holm: A Vital Force: From Convent to Wigman to My Fair Lady." *Dance Magazine,* January, pp. 22–27, 86–89.

———. 1969. *Hanya Holm: The Biography of an Artist*. Middeltown, Conn.: Wesleyan University Press.

———. 1996. Letter to the author, July 5.

Stein, Becky. 1996. Telephone interview with the author, March 2.

Steinbeck, Dietrich. 2001. "Tatjana Gsvosky on Her 100th Birthday." *Ballett International/Tanz Aktuell,* March, p. 19.

Stöckemann, Patricia. 1989. "Flugkraft in goldene Ferne ... Bühnentanz in Hamburg seit 1900." Catalogue of the exhibition (concept Nils Jockel) by Nils Jockel and Patricia Stöckmann, Museum für Kunst und Gewerbe, Hamburg in Zusammenbeit mit dem Zentrum für Theaterforschung der Universität Hamburg.

Tejani M.D., Nergish. 1996. Interview with the author, Ossining, N.Y., August 24.

Thiele, Til. 1996. Telephone interview with the author, September 7.

Thimey, Erika. 1995. Telephone interview with the author, May 15.

———. 2000. "The Lessons of Mary Wigman." *Dance Magazine,* April, pp. 58–59.

Thomas, Emma Lewis. 1996. Letter to the author, August 14.

Tobias, Tobi. 1981. "A Conversation with May O'Donnell." *Ballet Review,* Vol. 9, no. 1, pp. 64–96.

Todd, Arthur. 1952. "My Darlin' Aida with Choreography by Hanya Holm." *Dance Observer,* December, p. 153.

Underwood, Sharry Traver. 1986. "Ballet Ballads." *Dance Chronicle,* Vol. 9, no. 3, pp. 279–327.

Waechter, Cora. 1945. Transcript of Rundfunk radio broadcast about Mary Wigman. Collection of Ruth L. Kriehn, Special Collections, Golda Meir Library, University of Wisconsin–Milwaukee.

Weiss, Inga. 2002. Telephone interview with the author, July 28.

Widney, Bud. 1999. Telephone interview with the author, May 19.

Wigman, Mary. 1929. "Weibliche Tanzkunst" (The Art of Female Dancing). *Blätter der Staatsoper und der städtischen Oper Berlin,* Vol. 10, no. 6.

————. 1949. Letter to Katharine Wolf, February 28, JRDD.

————. 1950a. Letter to Martha Hill, February 8, Miscellaneous Manuscripts, JRDD.

————. 1950b. Letter to Hedwig Burger-Deck, October 6, private collection.

————. 1950c. Letter to Katharine Wolf, November 19, JRDD.

————. 1951a. Letter to Pola Nirenska, February 18, JRDD.

————. 1951b. Letter to Martha Reuther, April 9, private collection.

————. 1954. Letters to Margaret Gage, June 29, May 30, June 11, JRDD.

————. 1956. "My Teacher Laban." *Dance Magazine,* November, pp. 27, 71–72.

————. 1966. *Mary Wigman: The Language of Dance.* Translated by Walter Sorell. Middletown, Conn.: Wesleyan University Press.

————. 1973. Letter to Shirlee Dodge, July 17, JRDD

————. 1975. *The Mary Wigman Book.* Edited and translated by Walter Sorell. Middletown, Conn.: Wesleyan University Press.

————. 1982 *Arbeitshefte. Positionen zur Vergangenheit und Gegenwart des modernen Tanzes* (Notebooks. Positions on the Past and Present of Modern Dance). *Schriftenreihe des Präsidiums der Adademie der Künste der DDR,* Nr. 36, Berlin.

————. 1987. Mary Wigman's *Skizzenbuch Choreographisches 1930–1961: München, Leipzig, Mannheim, Berlin* (Choreography Sketchbook). Edited by Dietrich Steinrich. München: Edition Hentrich.

————. Undated a. "Meisterklasse" (Master Class). Manuscript, Mary Wigman-Archiv der Stiftung Archiv der Akademie der Künste, Berlin.

————. Undated b. "Richtlinien zur tänzerischen Berufsausbildung." (Guidelines for Professional Dance Training). Manuscript, Mary-Wigman-Archiv der Stiftung Archiv der Akademie der Künste, Berlin.

————. Undated c. Letter to Pola Nirenska, JRDD. [From its contents, it is certain that this letter was written shortly before 3 March, 1958.]

Wirth, Nicholas. 1935. "Mary Wigman—Fascist." *New Theatre Monthly,* August, p. 5.

Woodbury, Joan J. 1956. "Christmas with Mary Wigman, Berlin Germany 1955." *Dance Observer,* March, pp. 39, 40.

Index